# Experiences of Immigrant Professors

A book like no other that informs and prepares potential immigrant professors for a challenging experience.

*—Professor Comfort M. Ateh, Providence College*

Educational institutions all over the world attract the services of foreign-born scholars. In addition to the culture shock that immigrants experience in unfamiliar countries, these scholars often undergo "pedagogical shock." Through autobiographical accounts of foreign-born professors from Africa, Asia, Europe, and the United States, this volume examines the experiences of foreign-born professors around the world to provide insight on the curricular, school-systemic, and sociological differences and challenges that are encountered and how to help resolve them. It will help administrators, institutions, and immigration and comparative education scholars understand the cross-cultural challenges and coping strategies that define the private and professional lives of foreign-born professors across the globe.

**Charles B. Hutchison** is Associate Professor of Education at the University of North Carolina at Charlotte, USA.

# Routledge Research in Higher Education

**Sustaining Mobile Learning**
Theory, research and practice
*Edited by Wan Ng and Terry Cumming*

**The Experiences of Black and Minority Ethnic Academics**
A comparative study of the unequal academy
*Kalwant Bhopal*

**Higher Education Access and Choice for Latino Students**
Critical Findings and Theoretical Perspectives
*Edited By Patricia A. Pérez, Ph.D. and Miguel Ceja, Ph.D.*

**Globally Networked Teaching in the Humanities**
Theories and Practices
*Edited by Alexandra Schultheis Moore and Sunka Simon*

**Reconsidering English Studies in Indian Higher Education**
*Suman Gupta, Richard Allen, Subarno Chattarji and Supriya Chaudhuri*

**University Access and Success**
Capabilities, diversity and social justice
*Merridy Wilson-Strydom*

**Academic Building in Net-based Higher Education**
Moving beyond learning
*Edited by Trine Fossland, Helle Mathiasen and Mariann Solberg*

**From Vocational to Professional Education**
Educating for social welfare
*Jens-Christian Smeby and Molly Sutphen*

**Understanding HIV and STI Prevention for College Students**
*Edited by Leo Wilton, Robert T. Palmer, and Dina C. Maramba*

**Activity Theory, Authentic Learning and Emerging Technologies**
Towards a transformative higher education pedagogy
*Edited by Vivienne Bozalek, Dick Ng'ambi, Denise Wood, Jan Herrington,
Joanne Hardman and Alan Amory*

**Refocusing the Self in Higher Education**
A Phenomenological Perspective
*Glen L. Sherman*

**Academic Governance**
Disciplines and Policy
*Jenny M. Lewis*

**Developing Creativities in Higher Music Education**
International perspectives and practices
*Edited by Pamela Burnard*

**Integrative Learning**
International research and practice
*Edited by Daniel Blackshields, James Cronin, Bettie Higgs, Shane Kilcommins,
Marian McCarthy and Anthony Ryan*

**Experiences of Immigrant Professors**
Cross-Cultural Differences, Challenges, and Lessons for Success
*Edited by Charles B. Hutchison*

# Experiences of Immigrant Professors

Cross-Cultural Differences, Challenges, and Lessons for Success

Edited by Charles B. Hutchison

NEW YORK AND LONDON

First published 2016
by Routledge
711 Third Avenue, New York, NY 10017

and by Routledge
2 Park Square, Milton Park, Abingdon, Oxon OX14 4RN

*Routledge is an imprint of the Taylor & Francis Group, an informa business*

© 2016 Taylor & Francis

The right of the editor to be identified as the author of the editorial material, and of the authors for their individual chapters, has been asserted in accordance with sections 77 and 78 of the Copyright, Designs and Patents Act 1988.

All rights reserved. No part of this book may be reprinted or reproduced or utilised in any form or by any electronic, mechanical, or other means, now known or hereafter invented, including photocopying and recording, or in any information storage or retrieval system, without permission in writing from the publishers.

Trademark notice: Product or corporate names may be trademarks or registered trademarks, and are used only for identification and explanation without intent to infringe.

*Library of Congress Cataloging-in-Publication Data*
CIP data has been applied for.

ISBN: 978-1-138-80696-2 (hbk)
ISBN: 978-1-315-75134-4 (ebk)

Typeset in Sabon
by Apex CoVantage, LLC

Printed and bound in the United States of America by Publishers Graphics, LLC on sustainably sourced paper.

**I dedicate this book to all migrants of the world.**

**To all migrants of the world, an ode:**
You, who kissed distant lands
And left less to the imagination;
You, the irony of being:
While strangers in new lands
Impoverished for want of the familiar
You could not afford, but to march forward
And so became soldiers of the intrepid.
As strangers in new lands
You were pressed, stretched, and tempered more
And by such treatments
You became refined
Like fine gold:
You become more.

# Contents

Acknowledgments       xiii

1 The Private and Professional Lives of Foreign-Born
Professors: From Abstractions to the Practical       1
CHARLES B. HUTCHISON

2 Foreign-Born Professors and Their Quests for a Social and
Psychological Home: Integrating Social, Cultural, and
Professional Dimensions of Life       22
AMY CARATTINI

3 A Portrait of the Life and Work of Expatriate
Educators in Cambodia       35
ALEXANDER JUN, REBECCA HONG, CURTIS CLINE, AND FAITH FITT

4 The "Unusual" Professors: The Experiences and
Impact of Foreign Professors in Post-Franco Spain       50
ALICE GAIL BIER, XAVIER COLLER, AND LOUIS LEMKOW

5 Conversations on Ethnicity, Adaptation, and Belonging:
Autoethnography at the Base of the Ivory Tower       62
MARCIA D. NICHOLS, AMINUL HUQ, BIJAYA ARYAL, AND XAVIER PRAT-RESINA

6 Voices From Behind the Scenes: How Foreign-Born English
Teachers Find Their Place in the French Education System       76
CLAIRE GRIFFIN

7 Challenges and Self-Efficacy of Female East Asian–Born
Faculty in American Universities       88
HYEYOUNG BANG

x  *Contents*

8  The True Meaning of Integrity: Reflections
   on a Professional Life in Japan                                    100
   ROBIN SAKAMOTO

9  Moroccan Imams and the "Girl Professor": Positionality
   and *Epistemai* in a Classroom-Based Cross-Cultural
   Exchange of Knowledge                                              110
   EMILIE ROY

10 Not so Fast: Navigating the Complexities of Teaching in
   an American University as a Foreign-Born Teacher Educator          122
   EUCABETH ODHIAMBO

11 My Professional Teaching Experience in the United States,
   1977–2014: The Case of an African-Born Immigrant                   133
   PETER F. B. NAYENGA

12 Negotiating the Trilogy of Blackness, "Africanness," and
   "Accentness": A "Native-Alien" Professor's Tale                    144
   OBED MFUM-MENSAH

13 From Essential and Central to Constructivist Trenches:
   Navigating the Transnational Contexts of the Instructional
   Practice of a Foreign-Born Professor                               155
   FONKEM ACHANKENG

14 Unpacking the Invisible Knapsack of African-Born
   Professor's Identity in the U.S. Academe                           166
   MICHAEL TAKAFOR NDEMANU

15 Not an Easy Road: Journey of a Jamaican Academic                   177
   LEONIE J. BROOKS

16 "Almost American": The Challenges of a Canadian
   Professor Working in the United States                             188
   SCOTT KISSAU

17 Drained Brains: Canadian Professors in the United States           202
   DAVE EATON

18 Identity Construction of a Second-Language Educator                213
   TANITA SAENKHUM

*Contents* xi

19 My American Academia: At Home and Abroad 223
MOHANALAKSHMI RAJAKUMAR

20 Musings of a Foreign-Born Philosopher in the
American Academy: *Come è duro calle / lo scendere
e 'l salir per l'altrui scale* 234
LUCIO ANGELO PRIVITELLO

21 The Unified Voices of Immigrant Professors and Their
Cross-Cultural Teaching Lives: Lessons Learned 246
CHARLES B. HUTCHISON

*List of Contributors* 265
*Index* 267

# Acknowledgments

I wish to acknowledge Routledge's Christina Chronister, Trevor Gori, Lauren Verity, Merritt Duncan, and Stacy Noto for their guidance in the publication process. I also wish to acknowledge Dr. Kwabena Akurang-Parry for his encouragement to write such a book and his help in disseminating the Call for Chapters.

# 1 The Private and Professional Lives of Foreign-Born Professors
## From Abstractions to the Practical

*Charles B. Hutchison*

### VOICES OF IMMIGRANT PROFESSORS

I had long admired the word integrity and had envisioned myself becoming a person of integrity in my professional life. Imagine my surprise, therefore, when I found that the Japanese translation of integrity was "foolish diligence". . . . The realization that the language skills I had possessed all my life were no longer available to me to express my worldview may have very well been the catalyst that forced me to leave the Honeymoon Stage and embrace the challenges of culture shock.

—Robin Sakamoto

I have been as much of a shock to them as they have been to me over the past year of working together. Through a careful negotiation of our differences and commonalities, we nevertheless have created, in cooperation, a positive learning environment where the expertise of all parties was recognized and where fruitful exchanges were made possible.

—Emilie Roy

A fellow immigrant colleague once remarked that even after teaching for sixteen years, he still was nervous before going to teach his classes. In my early years, I also felt this same challenge. . . . My issue was not that I did not have a mastery of the subject matter in my field, but rather, I was initially disheartened to read some students' evaluations making remarks such as, "I do not understand his accent" . . . Through the complexity of methods of approaches . . . I have attained . . . a successful professional record.

—Peter Nayenga

Most of the [immigrant professor] colleagues I have mentioned in this [my] chapter seem to. . . experience varying stress levels, emotional discomfort, depression, anxiety, anger, and distress. . . . I often feel so tired after classes that I cannot do anything else the rest of

2  *Charles B. Hutchison*

the day. I either have to sleep or watch a movie to relax my nerves. One of my colleagues . . . informed me that she had to drink alcohol whenever she had to teach. Many FEA faculty reported that they have cried, screamed, and drank to release their stress. They have had second thoughts about teaching in America and have dreamt about returning to their home countries.

—Hyeyoung Bang

In addition to being a young, white man who speaks fluent English, I was very familiar with both the United States and American culture . . . I quickly developed a close circle of friends, and had an active social life. To many onlookers, my transition to life and work as a postsecondary instructor in the United States must have appeared seamless. Unfortunately, appearances can be deceiving . . . I have encountered numerous, unexpected difficulties along the way. While these obstacles did not derail my career trajectory, they were at the very least annoying, occasionally harmful, and often could have been avoided.

—Scott Kissau

## FIRST PRINCIPLES: THE POSSIBLE HUMAN AND HUMAN MIGRATION

One should live if only to satisfy one's curiosity.

—African proverb

United Nations Population Division (UNPD) and International Labour Organization (ILO) statistics, cited in this chapter, confirm that life refuses to be confined to one region and to be defined along contrived categories. That is why even in the harshest of places on earth—and now, possibly on comet 67P—organic molecules have been "sniffed." From time immemorial, in harmony with life itself, migrations have defined human existence, and the elemental human has refused to obey the concept of artificial borders. Genetics-based studies such as the Human Genome and the Genographic Projects indicate that humans are wondrously opportunistic and restless beings. At the existential level, humans, as with other forms of life, have spread across the world and yielded their very bodies to variations, including differentiated body shapes, complexions, and even aspects of their physiology, to take advantage of new habitations, some of which are very precarious. One is compelled to wonder, why go to such extremes, when milder forms of existential struggle would suffice? Why contort your very psychology and your body, experience harshness, and shift the very center of definable comfort to such extremes? Wouldn't staying put among kinfolk qualify for a life well spent? At the philosophical level, such are the questions that define the immigrant professor (IP). The reader is invited to

## The Private and Professional Lives of Foreign-Born Professors    3

engage his or her mental spectacles and travel with me as we explore why the IPs in this book would make profound sacrifices to live in foreign lands.

For the existential human, the African proverb bears a compelling reason humans want to know: it proffers that people should live if only to satisfy their curiosities. In other words, to know is worth a living, and it is worth living, just to know. Curiously, the pursuit of knowledge appears to be surreptitiously engineered into humans. François Jacob, in his book *The Possible and the Actual* (University of Washington Press, 1982), pondered why, in the human body, reproduction is a function that needs to be performed by an organ of which an individual carries only one half and is therefore compelled to spend vast amounts of time and energy to find the other half. The compelling power of sexual reproduction makes silent, unwitting-but-willing prisoners of humanity who, through sexual attraction, succumb to its force akin to the way we obey the law of gravity. Beyond the aforementioned existential questions, mortal beings have been imprisoned to the jaws of perennial questions including "Who are we?" "Why are we here?" and "Are there other beings besides us?" In the ancient past, such questions must have included "What is on the other side?" and "Who are the rain god, the fertility god, and the god of harvest?" Although the answers to such perennial questions are beyond the jurisdiction of this book, we are certain of one thing: humans are prisoners of curiosity.

As if by design and akin to the force that compels humans through the trickery of half-complete reproductive organs, we always face the seemingly unknowable and the infinite; we are therefore unsuspectingly compelled to pursue the outer limits of knowledge and experience the possible, even if we have to pay a dear price. In fact, our very ancestry indicates that we are willing to experience the possible by pushing the limits of our very bodies—literally, by placing ourselves in situations where natural selection compel our bodies' evolution over multiple generations (cf. Genographic Project and human migrations across the world). Here again, IPs become defined as they pursue knowledge or seek new opportunities, often at high personal and emotional cost—but nothing stops them because this quest is indelibly inscribed within them.

Through human interactions fueled by human curiosity and commerce, societies have deemed it propitious to assemble pantheons of the nobles—the wise ones, no matter whence they come—to shed light on, not only the reality of the external world but also the internal world—human thought itself—so as to extend civilization and the possible human (cf. Bronowski, 1973).

The possible human is born through knowledge intersections. Humans try to make meaning of their surroundings; therefore, there is a direct relationship between human realities (and thus, knowledge) and their natural surroundings, because people's surroundings stimulate what they can even begin to think about. This concept, engendered by Sapir-Whorf hypothesis, helps to buttress the relationship between language and thought (cf. Vygotsky, 1962). As global travels evolved into global conquests and

## 4 Charles B. Hutchison

colonization, sociolinguists would assert that human languages—and therefore human thought processes themselves—had become subordinates to human migrations and human learning.

In effect, one may conjecture that the immigrant teacher is an important agent in the transformation of human civilizations and the formulation of the possible human. If one follows the thread of the human of the Brazilian rain forest to the human of the Brazilian capital as an example, the near-invisible aspect of this thread that connects them is that, through knowledge intersections, one has emerged into the information age, but the other has not. The existential point here is not that one form of the existential human is better than the other; the only point is that one has become far removed from the other because of knowledge intersections: One uses the computer, is connected to the other side of the globe via a cell phone, and can experience a physical, time–space compression by flying on an airplane, whereas the other is restricted to mental time–space compression, but not the physical. In other words, through knowledge intersections, humans have been able to unburden themselves as they can now answer—and de-perennialize—ancient, perennial questions such as, "What is on the other side?" and "Who are the rain god, the fertility god, and the god of harvest?" For the feats of migrant teachers who ferry new information across new terrains and help to extend the possible human, one may sing the encomiums of ancient writers: "How beautiful on the mountains are the feet of the herald" (Isaiah 52:7).

### Immigrant Professors, Knowledge Intersections, and the Advancement of Human Civilization

In traversing this book, readers will become convinced that, true to their ancient predecessors, IPs (together with other categories of immigrants) have helped advance human civilization from ancient times through the birth of the information age. As the statistics in this chapter—in harmony with the research on "brain drain"—indicate, even in the advanced economies of the world, there are significant numbers of IPs in strategic, vital areas of knowledge production, especially in the science, technology, engineering, and mathematics (STEM) disciplines. The narratives in this book also present insights into the specific processes by which different streams of knowledge intersect and combine to create new kinds of knowledge because migration compels such new forms of knowledge. As Lucio Privitello notes in his chapter contribution in this book,

> My foreign education allows for a way to live with a text, and not forget about its nuance, its seductive creative engagement, its foreignness. This is possible because I can feel the text in its cultural atmosphere.

As a student who was taught by immigrant professors, Coller (now a professor himself) noted that "being exposed to these "unusual" [i.e., immigrant] professors would be a life-changing experience" for him. He continued that

*The Private and Professional Lives of Foreign-Born Professors*   5

> for young students at the time [in 1980s Spain], these unusual professors were practically the functional equivalent of what the Internet is today. [They] provided windows through which students could learn from international comparisons and, above all, from ideas developed in other countries. I had my first contact with new sociological theories (for example, socio-biology) in those classes. I was exposed as well to explanations that were not commonly used in Spanish classrooms because they had yet to be integrated into Spanish sociological thought. . . . As a result, we can generate better explanations of social phenomena and get closer to the giants whose shoulders we climb to see better.

When students' minds are extended such that they can understand the new information in its intended sense but are also granted the capacity to extrapolate the information into unintended trajectories, it creates expansive learning, broadens their worldviews, and fosters insights. That is human progress.

IPs further advance human civilization because human curiosity, by its very nature, compels others to want to know the *other*. For this reason, IPs help to reduce the incidence of xenophobic and hegemonic tendencies among those who otherwise would have been relegated to unfounded racial and ethnic mindsets. Research indicates that cross-cultural contact can ultimately result in empathy and better cross-cultural relations (Pettigrew, 1997; Stephan & Finlay, 1999). Besides, when people are ignorant of other cultures, they are likely to maintain their native knowledge, including societal prejudices and stereotypes; however, when they are provided with information that either negates or disconfirms their societal prejudices and stereotypes, the same will be reduced (Crocker, Hanna, & Weber, 1983). Could one love Chinese food but hate the Chinese? Could one love basketball and not admire those who dominate the sports? In a male-dominated, traditionalist society, how could one genuinely maintain misogynist views or consider females as his inferior when he has experienced the intellectual acumen of a female professor? Furthermore, to the points mentioned earlier, IPs, by the nature of their professions, are at the very top of academic and professional ladders—honorable positions by any measure—be they male or female, white or colored, religious or irreligious, straight or gay. For this reason, they shine for all the groups they inadvertently represent and are likely to change people's perspectives wherever they migrate.

In conclusion, IPs, just by their cultural and very embodiment (via gender, personal values, sexuality, religious orientation, etc.) help break down several cross-cultural barriers, thus fostering human rights across the world. In so being and doing, they foster human progress.

## MIGRATION THEORY AND TRENDS, BY THE NUMBERS

UNPD (2009) estimated that in 2010, about 214 million migrants, accounting for 3% of the world's population, would cross international borders

## 6 Charles B. Hutchison

throughout the world. About half of them were expected to be women who were often accompanied by children or spouses. In harmony with UNPD figures, ILO estimated that in the same year (2010), economically active migrants would be approximately 105.4 million and that these migrants and their family members accompanying them would account for about 90% of total international migrants. This report noted that although international migration can be a positive experience for many migrant workers, many experience

- poor working and living conditions, including low wages;
- unsafe working environments and a virtual absence of social protection;
- denial of freedom of association and workers' rights, discrimination, and xenophobia; and
- distressing migrant integration policies.

The ILO (2010) report further noted that "despite a demonstrated demand for workers, numerous immigration barriers persist in destination countries" (p. 2).

The trends in global migration are near intuitive because they follow basic concepts of migration theory, which state that migration trends follow "push" and "pull" factors: Whereas push factors constitute unfavorable conditions within the country or area in which one lives and therefore push the local inhabitants out, pull factors are favorable conditions that attract others into the area (Lee, 1966). According to Lee's conception, push factors may include inadequate jobs and life opportunities, uncomfortable physical conditions, and political and religious fear and persecutions—and their opposites are true for pull factors. For this reason, differences in such conditions determine the direction of global migrations, to the extent allowed by international laws, distance, and physical barriers.

As a reflection of migration theory, a World Bank study (Ratha & Shaw, 2007) reported that in 2005,

- two of every five global migrants (approximately 78 million out of 191 million migrants) were residing in a developing country.
- most of these migrants were likely to have come from other developing countries.
- by estimate, approximately 80% of South–South migration took place between countries with contiguous borders.
- most migrations appear to have occurred between countries with relatively small differences in income.
- partly because many South–South migrants lack adequate travel documents, they were restricted to overland migration.
- ethnic, family, and religious ties link communities across borders, particularly in Africa (where colonial boundaries straddled tribal groups), but also in other parts of the world.

The World Bank study also noted that in general, whereas proximity can be important in shaping South–North migration, large income differences encourage migration over greater distances. Furthermore, several developed countries, although top destinations for migrants, are themselves exporters of citizens to other highly skilled, developed nations, and this trend falls on a continuum across different developing countries in the world. For example, Canada sends large numbers of skilled workers to the United States, as does Germany. Similarly, Malaysia sends workers to Singapore, and Bangladesh and Pakistan send workers to India.

In terms of content discipline areas, in the United States for example, the 2004 National Study of Postsecondary Faculty (NSOPF: 04) indicated that in 4-year institutions, 8% of the faculty were noncitizens, and that 16% of natural sciences faculty and 17% of engineering faculty were noncitizens, compared with 4% to 10% of faculty in other program areas (Cataldi, Fahimi, & Zimbler, 2005). This accords with brain drain numbers, where highly skilled workers—especially in technical or STEM areas—leave their home countries for better lives, partly because industrialized economies are not able to produce adequate brain power to serve their technical industries. For this reason, industrialized economies clamor for specialized visas to import foreign skills (cf. the immigration policies and debates in the United States, the United Kingdom, Canada, Australia, and, to a lesser extent, China). In many industries, the related job functions requiring skills in local shortage are often exported if the skilled workers cannot be imported. In the academia, however, it is still traditional to import the skills in person, partly for its cultural value.

Beyond the push and pull factors of migration, once in the host country, migrants are likely to have different experiences—and they appear to anticipate some of the potential challenges. There is therefore what appears to be a self-selecting principle directing migrant flow: People follow the path of least resistance in subtle ways. For example, Oliver-Smith and de Sherbinin's (2014) studies noted that gender, age, class, and ethnicity are key markers of vulnerability during migration. These findings are in agreement with Ratha and Shaw's (2007) studies, noted earlier, which indicated that people tend to migrate by following ethnic, family, and religious ties. Oliver-Smith and de Sherbinin further noted that the resettlement process involves complex interactions of many cultural, social, environmental, economic, institutional, and political factors in ways that are not predictable. For this reason, resettlement processes are not amenable to rational planning. This is why all migrants should understand several factors—especially cultural variables—if possible, reduce their transitional shocks.

## TEACHING AS A CULTURAL ACTIVITY

Teaching is a cultural activity (Stigler and Hiebert, 1999), and culture, as a worldview, influences how people receive and generate knowledge (Kearney,

8    *Charles B. Hutchison*

1984). People's cultural backgrounds and worldviews (or cultural paradigms) influence how they view the world and, consequently, how they learn (Cobern, 1991; Shumba, 1999). Spector and Lederman (1990, p. 23) suggested that some of the parameters specified by a socio-cultural frameworks or paradigms may include

a. how the world works;
b. what questions should, or can be asked;
c. procedures for answering questions (i.e. research method);
d. what constitutes acceptable hypotheses; and
e. what constitutes acceptable answers.

Although a professor is, *ceteris paribus*, the master of knowledge, the IP naturally becomes transformed into the student because knowledge is brewed in the crucible of cultural traditions or paradigms, but the professor is not fully familiar with the host culture. Thus explains why IPs, no matter where they come from, experience culture and pedagogical shock. In fact, culture and pedagogical shocks are inescapable experiences, and anyone who plans long-term stay outside his or her culture must expect to face and manage them as comfortably as possible, or be rudely shocked by the reality of the experience.

## Cultural Differences and Multiple Realities

> I have also learned to laugh at myself often and to try and view how my actions must look to someone from Japan. I had the unique opportunity to return to that remote village twenty years later and meet with many of my former colleagues. To hear their stories of when I first arrived in Japan from their perspective made me see things from a completely and often unflattering view. While I know in my own mind what I am trying to accomplish, to others it might seem to be just plain crazy.
>
> —Robin Sakamoto (emphasis added)

As argued earlier, once in the host country, migrants are likely to become differentiated, partly because of who they are, how they act, and how they respond to others. The results of such Hegelian dialectical processes are likely to define whom they become (through identity transformation processes; Hutchison, Quach, & Wiggan, 2006) and to determine how successful they become in the host country. This is a very slippery zone for them to navigate because it is laden with invisible phenomenological twists, turns, and surprises, but those who understand and embrace such processes are more likely to become successful in their host countries.

Cultural differences and different worldviews can create multiple realities (Ogawa, 1989) and can therefore split a single reality into differentiated

*The Private and Professional Lives of Foreign-Born Professors*   9

realities for immigrants. Nisbett, in his book *Geography of Thought* (2003), emphasizes that there are significant differences between Eastern and Western approaches to thought, partly because of the respective influences of Confucian and Aristotelian philosophies. Consequently, over millennia, these two societies have developed vastly different metaphysical and sociocultural practices, especially their views of the self and what they may focus on during sociocultural interactions. Of particular interest is Nisbett's assertion that such differences have created vast differences in the reasoning patterns of Easterners and Westerners, such that Asians and Westerners explain and interpret events differently because they literally see and perceive different things—partly because they are unwittingly acculturated to hone in on different aspects of things. Nisbett's claims, however, are arguable because there are studies that have found no significant differences in the learning approach of Asians and Westerners. For example, the research of Egege and Kutieleh (2008) indicate that differences within cultural groups may be as significant as those between groups.

The idea that differences in cultural traditions can generate different perceptual worlds, however, is evident in society. To illustrate this point, consider the election of President Barack Obama, the first Black American president. Initially as a candidate, he nearly lost the election "primaries" to Hillary Clinton, his opponent; however, he quickly capitalized his position as a younger candidate and connected with America's youth, using technology, which has its own micro-culture. He then capitalized on his biracial status and its related dual cultural capital to appeal to different racial demographics because he appeared to understand the multiple realities in existence for different demographic groups.

In an article titled "Blacks, Whites Hear Obama Differently," Nia-Malika Henderson (2009) noted that candidate Obama's "language, mannerisms and symbols resonate deeply with his Black supporters, even as the references largely sail over the heads of white audiences" (para. 8). Yet, when necessary, Obama, with the cultural capital of the Harvard graduate and a strong command of Standard American English, was able to capture his White audiences and voters to handily win his first election and to become reelected against historical odds (in a recession). Candidate Obama knew that there were code words that can elicit specific emotional responses from different segments of the population, along the axes of race and ethnicity, religion, gender, sexuality, and socioeconomic status. What he knew was that, similar to Nisbett's (2003) Eastern and Western societal evolutions, multiple realities born from historical asymmetries between Blacks and Whites in the United States have differentiated the consciousness of the two racial groups. It is therefore possible to make assertions that would be affirmed by one group but be disaffirmed by the other. The two racial groups are therefore galvanized by different social codes.

IPs should benefit from insights about the dynamics by which their own cultures may interface with the local culture.

10   *Charles B. Hutchison*

## Multiple Realities and Phenomenological Orientations

> Whatever is, is.
>
> —Anonymous

The elemental power of the concept of multiple realities intersects with phenomenology because it speaks to the oft-hidden nature of human processes—processes that create outcomes (or emotional products), which then sink into one's subconscious or unconscious repositories. These emotional products, however, later arise to influence one's social interactions and create new realities. Maurice Merleau-Ponty (1946/2013) noted that

> phenomenology is the study of essences, and according to it, all problems amount to finding definitions of essences: the essence of perception or the essence of consciousness, for example. But phenomenology is also a philosophy that puts essences into existence, and does not expect to arrive at the understanding of man and the world from any starting point other than that of their "facticity." (p. vii)

Phenomenology defines IPs' world because of its vast connections and influence on the humanities. Because of its fundamental nature, Heidegger (1927/1996) linked it to existentialism and redefined it along a new axis: existential phenomenology, being the investigation of the ontological essences of humanity. Given that ontology deals with the nature of being itself—a metaphysical issue—it is interesting to reflect on Husserl's (1907/2010) conceptualization of human consciousness itself, because, to him, objective truth can only be captured when one is conscious of a phenomenon. To Husserl, perception is reality because what is *experienced by people* is more reliable for predicting human interactions than is external reality itself. For the IP who may not be aware of what phenomenological signals he or she has sent into the environment to elicit new realities, can he or she be aware of whatever is or is not? Consequently, how can he or she be sure of any knowledge that is reliable and actionable? How then can he or she begin to certify social realities—and thus pedagogical and collegial relationships?

Another philosophical area of interest to the IP is axiology (concerned with the study of human values), which defines ethics and aesthetics. Granted the heavy dependence of culture on axiological assumptions, predicting why character traits valued in one cultural, and therefore pedagogical milieu, would be different from another is easy. More important are the results of the interfacing of these different character traits. This is where the twin sister of phenomenology, symbolic interactionism, comes to the rescue. In human interactions, perception is easily mistaken for reality, and reality is easily mistaken for the truth. For this reason, misperceived cross-cultural actions and cues are likely to be reacted to, as if they were one's own cultural truths. In this process, an innocent, well-meaning act of kindness can be mistaken

# The Private and Professional Lives of Foreign-Born Professors

for an insult and responded to accordingly, creating a confused, complex imaginary for both parties. No wonder, Thomas and Johnson (2004) noted IPs' lamentation of the lack of collegiality between themselves and their U.S. colleagues. As a related point, Collins (2008) noted that foreign-born faculty members felt isolated and lonely. Perhaps, these observations should not come as a surprise, and may help explain why the phenomenon of culture shock is ubiquitous across the world.

## Creating and Functioning in the "Third Space"

> The salât-ritual moment was a rich point in my classroom: it required me to delve into my students' understanding of salât in order to attempt a reconciliation with my own understanding of ritual based in the academic tradition of religious studies. When the two epistemai collided during this discussion, the only way to bridge the gap was for me to understand my students' position and their difficulties with the new material I was presenting. Only after doing so was I able to re-explain the concept of ritual in religious studies effectively. I needed first to learn from my students' perspective in order to teach them a new one in a way that was acceptable to them.
>
> —Emilie Roy, *Canadian in Morocco*

With an andragogical or teaching predisposition to a cultural world that now does not exist—partly because the IP is now in a new land where the history, philosophy, teaching, and learning are all different—a new andragogy is compelled and necessarily invoked. The IP's personalized, hybridized andragogy is defined by the elements of pedagogical content knowledge (PCK), including knowledge of the content matter, knowledge of the students, and knowledge of the new instructional environment (Cochran, DeRuiter, & King, 1993). If one argued within the limits of PCK alone, one can envision how that the IP has a vast, fertile landscape that needs to be explored, understood, and implemented to become successful in the new teaching landscape.

The IP is necessarily an explorer, and once in the host country, he or she is circumstantially compelled to create new realities for him or herself in several spaces, including the classroom, department meetings, and in the community. Hutchison and Bailey (2006) argued that in the classroom, international teachers reside in a *pedagogical imaginary*, which is a novel pedagogical space defined by two polar concepts: *insularity* (the pure state) and *hybridity* (the mixed state). Young's (2003) concept of insularity proposes that school curricula have social and political origins that have epistemological and pedagogic significance. Consequently, in the context of cross-cultural teaching, IPs are likely to pay a pedagogic penalty if they do not acknowledge the existence of such knowledge boundaries. The notion of *hybridity*, however, insinuates the existence of the *pure*, which has been combined with

## 12   Charles B. Hutchison

the *other* to create the *new*. Brandsen, Ribeiro, van Hout, and Putters (2005) noted that internal conflicts arise because of mixing pure brands to generate the new. Such internal conflicts are evident when one views IPs' lifeworlds through the filters of third space theory: By combining their native and host countries' educational practices, IPs create and simultaneously experience a new, hybridized reality. This new reality is forcibly precipitated on them as they attempt to make sense and create new, oft-imperfect meanings of a different life environment. This new, hybridized reality is explicable via third space theory, which asserts that whenever an individual enters a different context to which they need to adapt, they are compelled to create a new (third) space that is different from one's original (first) knowledge world and the new (second) knowledge world (Bhabha, 1994).

In the context of teaching, Moje et al. (2004) assert that the third space is a hypothetical space created when a person combines the knowledge and experience gained from his or her most dominant space (e.g., family, peers, or community influences) with the knowledge gained from an institutionalized space (e.g., school and work influences). Because IPs may have moved from a traditionalist to a nontraditionalist classroom, for example, they will find their new third-space classrooms to be laden with tension because they will experience their new classroom environments as imagined realities created as a solution to perceived challenges. In essence, because people cannot solely reside in their first or the second spaces, they will find themselves having to constantly negotiate a new reality by merging disparate forms of knowledge (Moje et al., 2004) to create hybridized, or third, spaces.

It is safe to assert that the third or hybridized space is synonymous with the anthropological notion of liminality, which, true to its Latin root, means "threshold" and insinuates the "between and betwixt." Liminality is a peripheral space where all things are new. It connotes the state of unpredictability and the compulsion to learn to establish new, more predictable schemata and a *terra firma*—a solid ground—to tread on. It is to this world that IPs are baptized and ushered, with no other choices left except to return home. Yet, with their own unique forms of cosmic invocation, they throw themselves to fate (because time and the future embrace all) and become the products of phenomenological processes addressed thus far.

## Immigrant Professors and Identity Development

> I thought to myself that the scream of the newborn has something of a question in it. It was a signal sent out by the newcomer to see if he had arrived at the right place. The sound most similar to a newborn's scream is the sound of children, which is why children in my village are required to cry out in confirmation of the newborn's arrival. This confirmation satisfies something in the psyche of the newborn, who is now ready to surrender to being present in this world. I have often wondered, what would happen to the newborn if there were no

## The Private and Professional Lives of Foreign-Born Professors    13

answer? Can infants recover from the damage done to their souls as a result of a message at birth that they are on their own?

—**Malidoma Some (1998, *p. 93*)**

There exist professions in which the saying "We are the tools of our trade" holds true, and teaching is one of them. To this end, the very personhood of the instructor—including his or her mannerisms, dispositions, knowledge base, communication ability, and even outlook on life—becomes something akin to one simple tool that stands in front of an assembly of students—as the professor. It is partly for this reason that other people's reactions to our *selves*, as professors, is taken very personally, with identity-transforming consequences. This complexity of responses—that is, professors' responses to both their students and other people in their life intersections—comprise the recipe for one's identity. Claire Griffin noted the following in her chapter:

> *One of the signs is this supposedly British teacher's French accent. . . .* She appears to be overtaken by her jeering students who take advantage of their teacher's obvious comprehension difficulties when it comes to fleeting French quips and fast interaction. *Arthur, who embodies the typical bad boy, tries her patience when he says, "Excuse me? Tamaget au baconnet?" which is complete gibberish. We could interpret this nonsensical question as an attempt to reverse the habitual pedagogical roles whereby language learners are often reduced to frustrated individuals who fail to comprehend what people are saying. Instead of the learners themselves being excluded as a result of the learning,* the teacher finds herself in the uncomfortable, marginal position of the fool. (Houssaye, 1988, 2000, emphasis added)

What becomes of the teacher who appears incompetent because of language improficiency? What becomes of the guest whose cultural act of graciousness is misperceived? What happens to the person whose smile is not reciprocated? Malidoma Some's opening quote raises a serious, fundamental question that resides at the core of the human experience—that of acceptance and fitting in. Anthropologically, biologically, and sociologically speaking, the human proclivity to fit in and to be accepted is part of the very idea of evolutionary success: good fit within one's physical environment so as not to be exposed to predators, and good fit within the social group so as not to be ostracized to the societal periphery and vulnerability. No matter how academically competent IPs may be, they will find themselves seeking to become a good fit within their host environments—both in the academic environments and in the broader social environments. This quest for acceptance is likely to precipitate a shift in one's psychological landscape, creating a new identity.

One's identity is something that is intangible and that therefore defies definition. It is an existential state of being—an experience that is the collective product of one's multiple senses at play. Because of the variability of

## 14   Charles B. Hutchison

human experiences, identity is so fluid that it can only be the daughter of the humanities. Differentiated perceptions based on differentiated experiences, interfacing with differentiated environmental factors, are apt to precipitate a wide range of human experiences that then define a person. Perhaps, it is for such reasons that Nietzsche (1961, p. 56) suggested that people's identities lie on two axes: the "plastic self" and the "expressive self." Whereas the plastic self is more elastic and flexible, the expressive self is more concerned with the maintenance of one's integrity in light of external forces. In the normal environment, therefore, the interplay of these two selves ultimately create one's identity.

As has been variously hinted in this chapter and is further addressed across this book (especially in the chapter contribution of Nichols, Huq, Aryal, and Prat-Resina), the identity formation process is dialogical. It is a process whereby a person, during his or her interactions (with new people, sights, smells, emotions, and other compounding factors) within the new environment, constantly negotiates new points of dynamic, identity equilibrium. Akin to third space theory, identity formation involves the reconciliation between one's native (or first) identity and the second identity imposed on him or her in the new environment. The intermixture of these conflicting identities result in a third identity (cf. third space), in which "the original position is lessened and mitigated" (Hermans & Gieser, 2012, p. 15) but a hybrid identity is created. Among other factors in this process, IPs will discover what may be termed *identity expansion*, as the Ghanaian (which the author is) becomes simply African, the Peruvian becomes South American, and the Lithuanian becomes Eastern European—simply because it is easier for locals to remember broader regions people come from, as opposed to specific, unfamiliar countries. In addition, broader but contrasting identifications become more significant. For example, the lone Christian in an Islamic country is more likely to be identified as such and vice versa (this is indicated in several chapters across this book, especially in Emile Roy's and Nichols, Huq, Aryal, and Prat-Resina's chapters).

Finally, IPs will find the process of identity development in a new environment to be comparable to adolescents' process of psychosocial development. As they struggle in their current environments to emerge into productive, successful adults, they are likely to encounter challenges to their current selves. Adolescents may struggle with their *self-concepts* (defining who they are), often along the following issues: (a) who they currently *really* are (and therefore how they actually behave and function), (b) who they think they are (and therefore how they are not behaving or functioning), (c) who others think they are (possibly based on stereotypes, and also how they behave and function), (d) who others think they think they are, (e) who they want to become, and (f) who they think others want them to become, among other issues (Rice & Dolgin, 2005). The cumulative effect of these *estimates* of themselves generate a final product: a self-estimation or *self-esteem* (Rice & Dolgin, 2005), which then influences one's life success in the new environment.

*The Private and Professional Lives of Foreign-Born Professors* 15

In the contributing chapters, it is evident that the self-esteems of several of the contributing IPs were challenged (or, better put, compromised) for several reasons (as discussed thus far and with further discussions in the subsequent sections). The result is that these professors—who have legitimately earned their doctoral degrees and have been hired through rigorous, academic search processes—were forced to second-guess themselves and wonder if they are really *fit* for the job, in what Leonie Brooks identified as the "impostor syndrome." If such processes are not identified and resolved, they can create a complexity of self-fulfilling prophecies of vicious cycles. No wonder, therefore, Obed Mfum-Mensah noted that several IPs he personally knew had not been successful in staying in one institution. Arguably, such IPs, unaware of their larger circumstances, have become sentenced to a perpetual search for idealized immigrant spaces that do not exist in real life.

## The Intersections of Race, Class, Gender, and Other Factors

The term *immigrant* is a complex concept because it is complicated by several sociocultural categories such as race, gender, class, religion, particular geographical derivations, power dynamics, and other marginality issues. Across this book, readers will discover narratives that align with the literature of different social categories, which are discussed. Furthermore, readers will realize that such narratives form a part of the identities of the IPs in question. In this section, for lack of space, these issues are summarily illustrated but with pointers as to where the fuller, related treatment of the issues are presented in the book (with fuller treatment of the literature).

*Gender issues.* Across this book, female professors were more likely to experience negative gender stereotypes than their male counterparts. First, they are more likely to be sexualized (Hune, 2011), especially when young and match certain categories. Second, they are more likely to face peculiar challenges that may be manifested as personal confrontation with students who find it difficult to take instructions from someone who is not only female (and therefore a "minority" of sorts), but compounding this factor, an immigrant (and therefore a "guest" in their home country). (As guests, both male and female IPs are held to perceptively unexpected standards; after all, aren't guests supposed to be nice and gentle to their hosts?) For example, the narrative of Hyeyoung Bang (from South Korea) and Mohanalakshmi Rajakumar (born in India) illustrate that female Asian professors were likely to experience discrimination, sexual harassment, and physical and verbal offenses in the United States. In Morocco and outside her local gender role, Emile Roy (from Canada but teaching in a male-dominated society) initially faced resistance from his male students who viewed her as the "girl professor," with the related connotations implied, until she proved herself as fitting for her professorial position.

*Language and ethnicity issues.* Accents may be viewed as good or bad or even as criminal. For example, Dixon, Mahoney, and Cocks (2002) described the negative consequences of accent prejudice in the United Kingdom,

## 16 Charles B. Hutchison

whereby people with certain accents are more likely to be viewed as guilty in the legal context. Although no one is fully immune from linguistic and ethnic challenges, migrants from previously colonized countries are more likely to experience racial and linguistic discrimination than those from European or industrialized nations. For example, David Eaton of Canada noted that "although my accent served to differentiate me from my students, it has not been a major concern. Americans seem to view Canadians as cute, but rustic cousins, and in the classroom it is more a source of amusement than anything else." To the contrary, Eucabeth Odhiambo (a female Kenyan) noted the following:

> Within weeks of starting classes, I observed a strange atmosphere in my classroom—I couldn't explain it. My students seemed standoffish; I felt unable to reach them. . . . Then I learned that students had been visiting the department head's office complaining that they could not understand my accent. . . . Students wrote in my evaluation that my accent was too thick to understand, and questioned why the department employed people who could not speak English.

Accent perception falls on a continuum. In many parts of the world (especially in the Commonwealth countries), the British accent is stereotyped in the media as intellectually superior, partly because of British historical influences on the education of her past colonies, including the United States. People who speak with "lesser accents" are therefore more likely to be misperceived as less intelligent. Accent perception is also complicated by the psychology of wealth, whereby the accents of nations that are recipients of aid are likely to view the accent of the benefactor as superior to the local English accent.

*Stereotypes and related factors.* Rakow and Bermudez (1993) asserted that cultural perspectives can influence the way people are viewed. They believed that teachers carry a variety of cultural stereotypes based on their native cultures and that such stereotypes influence how they view their own students. The reverse, however, is also true: Instructors who speak with an accent are more likely to be challenged (Braine, 1999), but it must be noted that the issue of accent is rather complex because it is often a proxy to other prejudices. When students are uncertain about their own feelings towards immigrants, such certainty is often a *je ne sais quoi*—in this case, a combination of societal prejudice, innocent ignorance, and personal discomfort. Because such people do not know exactly how to interact with the necessary Other—their IP—one natural avenue left for them is to report them to people they are familiar with, or to lambast them in their course evaluations as ultimately incompetent, with no justifications. Ultimately, even if prejudice and stereotyping are viewed as a part of natural human sociology, professors with accents are more likely to be avoided, even if they are effective and enjoyable (Alberts, 2008).

*The Private and Professional Lives of Foreign-Born Professors* 17

The complexity of sociocultural intersectionalities of race, class, gender, and religion, among others, is evident in the experiences of Leonie Brooks (a Black woman from Jamaica) who recalled "an incident early in my teaching career when a White female student consistently addressed me as 'Ms. Brooks' while addressing my White male colleague who taught her in another class as 'Dr. X.'" Such experiences are not easily categorized, but form a part of the continuum of what Leone Brooks identified as micro-aggressions on IPs of color.

In summary, several sociocultural factors can converge to confound IPs, thus leaving them with the question, How would you approach teaching and learning, in light of how others perceive and treat you?


## MARCHING TOWARD SUCCESS

*Self-agency of IPs.* Although IPs may be viewed as prisoners of sociological processes that yield predictable products or life outcomes, they are not passive in their existence because they exhibit some degree of self-agency. The day-to-day perfunctory activities of IPs fit the sociological notion that, as willful or inadvertent actors within our environments, humans (a) act on and change our natural environments and thereby construct and reconstruct them through our collective social actions and (b) perceive the natural environment in a way that is dependent on the prevailing sociocultural framework (Hobson, 1993). There is therefore a cyclical process whereby human actors actively change their environments or circumstances through their actions and then rechange the results of their actions into ever-new products. Humans are, therefore, the creators and the products of their own actions. For this reason, IPs are not always at the mercy of sociological processes.

Thus comes the good news: Notwithstanding the notion that IPs are "prisoners" of sociological processes that yield certain predictable products, the good news is that, since predictable social processes are often subject to human agency and interventions, IPs can actively engineer such processes to control their own destinies (or life outcomes or products). For example, in this book, all the IP authors who have lived to tell their stories have managed to do so by learning concepts that naturally lead to success. For example, Nayenga, Kissau, and Sakamoto not only survived but later also became their departments' chairs. At the time of writing, all the contributors were successful at their jobs, with Leonie Brooks becoming promoted to a full professor, despite her earlier challenges, and the rest attaining tenure, where applicable.

*Attitudes for success.* As may be expected from the chapter thus far, success becomes achievable through the adoption of certain attitudes. For example, as much as one must maintain a modicum of native identity (and authenticity), the contributors insinuated the fact that there are certain life

## 18 *Charles B. Hutchison*

outlooks or personal dispositions that contributed to their survival—in what Claire Griffin, in her chapter, call "stories to live by." This observation is in harmony with Traweek's (1992), who noted that within the academic community, cross-cultural transitions should be negotiated with great care and subtlety. He observed that humor, selected conformity, power, and politics commonly define such transitions. For this reason IPs should learn subscribe to what may be viewed as *universal lingua franca* (the elemental language of all humans, such as smiles, humor, and respect) when working with colleagues and other people within the social environment, and *pedagogical lingua franca* (such as respect, storytelling, good planning, and reasonable assessment system) when working with students in the classroom environment.

*Acculturation pathways and success.* Acculturation to a new environment may happen in varying degrees and speed into the mainstream culture. Rice and Dolgin (2005) observe that individuals acculturate to the culture of the majority group in four ways, ranging from assimilation, integration, marginality, and separation. In the context of IPs *assimilation* may involve the loss of one's native values and characteristics and the embracement of new ones that identify them with the host culture. As is evident in the narratives of this book, this is a rarity for IPs who arrive in their host culture as adults because their cultural and aesthetic values would have been well established in their native countries before emigration. This phenomenon is reflected in the literature of language learning, where those who arrive very early in life can fully assimilate into the language world and acquire the fluency of *native* speakers; those who arrive somewhere in their teen years function as *second-language* speakers; and those who arrive late in life function as *foreign-language* speakers (Roberge, 2005). *Integration* for IPs would involve their identification with their own cultural groups but the need to take on adequate characteristics of the host cultures to become proficient in their work and social lives. Immigrant professors will learn that, at a minimum, some level of integration is necessary to function well in the classroom; otherwise, it is virtually impossible to achieve the tenets of pedagogical content knowledge. In fact, constant learning of the local culture is necessary, because, having arrived in the host country late in life, it is impossible to catch up on the local knowledge base that was missed as a result of being born elsewhere. This is why the IP, beyond professional development expectations, should expect to live as a student for the rest of his or her life, just to catch up on the social knowledge that supports pedagogy. One form of integration is *biculturalism*, whereby IPs may function well in both their native and host cultures. Rice and Dolgin note, however, that *marginalization* can occur in acculturation, and for IPs, this may translate as the loss of one's own culture and no involvement with the host culture. In the extreme situation of *separation*, IPs may there is little or no interaction with the majority group. Given that the work of the professor necessarily involves collegial and student interactions, the last two acculturation modes (separation and isolation) are likely to yield unsuccessful IPs. In reality, therefore, most IPs will find themselves functioning in the integration mode at best and marginalization mode at worst.

## CONCLUSION

The term *migrant* is a triplet word that has two sisters: *emigrant* and *immigrant*. It is noteworthy that the same person who left home is the one who arrived elsewhere. If home is operationally definable as the place where one knows intimately, then the foreign location is the place where one has significant learning to do so as to function seamlessly. For the international pedagogue in the foreign classroom, we can invoke the third space theory and assert that this foreign classroom is a space where "participants teach each other and learn from each other, and is marked by dialogue which builds [new] relationships" (Cook, 2005, p. 86). To become successful, the IP becomes his or her students' student and needs to become acculturated to the host environment. The scope and depth of cultural knowledge to be learned to become successful as an IP should therefore forewarn the IP: be willing to be changed (at least, to some degree) or be rudely changed.

One fact remains clear: People are oblivious to their cultural positions (which are often the very positions that IPs may confront, partly because IPs carry with them their own unconscious cultural positions). This is exactly the reason why IPs should not easily take offense at others' cross-cultural blindness, because in any human exchange, especially in the classroom, instructors generally *impose* their cultural wills on their fellow discussants and conversationalists and hope to be accepted—and that includes the IP.

## REFERENCES

Alberts, H. C. (2008). The challenges and opportunities of foreign-born instructors in the classroom. *Journal of Geography in Higher Education, 32*(2), 189–203.

Bhabha, H. K. (1994). *The location of culture*. London: Routledge.

Braine, G. (1999). *Non-native educators in English-language teaching*. Mawah, NJ: Lawrence Erlbaum Associates.

Brandsen, T., Ribeiro, T. D., van Hout, E., & Putters, K. (2005, March, 2005). *Hybridity: A distinct reality (You cannot fly on one wing only)*. Paper submitted to the Third Sector Study Group Conference of the European Group of Public Administration, Bern.

Bronowski, J. (1973). *The ascent of man*. Boston/Toronto: Little, Brown and Company.

Cataldi, E. F., Bradburn, E. M., Fahimi, M., & Zimbler L. (2005). *2004 National study of postsecondary faculty* (NSOPF:04). Washington: National Center for Educational Statistics Report. Retrieved November 28, 2014, from http://nces.ed.gov/pubs2006/2006176.pdf

Cobern, W. W. (1991). Worldview theory and conceptual change in science education. *Science Education, 80*(5), 579–610.

## 20  Charles B. Hutchison

Cochran, K. F., DeRuiter, J. A., & King, R. A. (1993). Pedagogical content knowing: An integrative model for teacher preparation. *Journal of Teacher Education*, 44(4), 263–272.

Collins, J. M. (2008). Coming to America: Challenges for faculty coming to United States' universities. *Journal of Geography in Higher Education*, 32(2), 179–188.

Cook, M. (2005). 'A place of their own': Creating a classroom 'third space' to support a continuum of text construction between home and school. *Literacy*, 36(2), 85–90.

Crocker, J., Hanna, D. B., & Weber, R. (1983). Person memory and causal attributions. *Journal of Personality and Social Psychology*, 44, 55–66.

Dixon, J. A., Mahoney, B., & Cocks, R. (2002). Accents of guilt? Effects of regional accent, race, and crime type on attributions of guilt. *Journal of Language and Social Psychology* 21(2), 162–168.

Egege, S., & Kutieleh, S. (2008). Dimming down difference. In L. Dunn & M. Wallace (Eds.), *Teaching in Transnational Higher Education* (pp. 67–76). New York: Routledge.

Heidegger, M. (1996). *Being and time* (J. Stambaugh, Trans.). New York: SUNY Press. (Originally published in 1927)

Henderson, N.-M. (2009, March 3). Blacks, whites hear Obama differently. *Politico*. Retrieved March 11, 2009, from http://www.politico.com/news/stories/0309/19538.html

Hermans, H. J. M., & Gieser, T. (2012). Introductory chapter: History, main tenets and core concepts of dialogical self theory. In H. J. M. Hermans & T. Gieser (Eds.), *Handbook of dialogical self theory* (pp. 1–28). Cambridge: Cambridge University Press.

Hobson, D. (1993). In search of a rationale for multicultural science education. *Science Education*, 77(6): 685–711.

Houssaye, J. (1988). *Le triangle pédagogique*. 3e éd. Berne: Peter Lang.

Hune, S. (2011). Asian American women faculty and the contested space of the classroom: Navigating student resistance and (re)claiming authority and their rightful place. *Diversity in Higher Education*, 9, 307–335.

Hutchison, C. B., & Bailey, L. (2006). Cross-cultural perceptions of assessment of international teachers in U.S. high schools. *Cultural Studies in Science Education*, 1(4), 657–680.

Hutchison, C. B., Quach, L., & Wiggan, G. (2006). The interface of global migrations, ESL teaching and learning, and academic cosmopolitan identity development. *Forum on Public Policy Online*, Fall 2006 Edition. Retrieved from http://www.forumonpublicpolicy.com/archive06/hutchison.pdf

Husserl, E. G. A. (2010). *The idea of phenomenology* (L. Hardy, Trans.). The Netherlands: Kluwer Academic Publishers. (Original work published 1907)

International Labor Organization. (2010). *International labour migration: A rights-based approach*. Geneva: International Labor Organization. Retrieved November 26, 2014, from http://www.ilo.org/wcmsp5/groups/public/—-ed_protect/—-protrav/—-migrant/documents/publication/wcms_208594.pdf.

Jacob, F. (1982). *The possible and the actual* (The Jessie and John Danz lectures). Seattle, WA: University of Washington Press.

Kearney, M. (1984). *World view*. Novalto, CA: Chandler & Sharp.

Lee, E. S. (1966). A theory of migration. *Demography*, 3(1), 47–57.

Merleau-Ponty, M. (2013). *Phenomenology of perception* (Colin Smith, Trans.). New York: Taylor & Francis. (Original work published 1946)

Moje, E. B., Ciechanowski, K. M., Kramer, K., Ellis, L., Carrillo, R., & Collazo, T. (2004). Working toward third space in content area literacy: An examination of everyday funds of knowledge and discourse. *Reading Research Quarterly*, 39(1), 38–70.

Nietsche, F. (1961). *Thus spoke Zarathustra* (R. J. Hollingdale, Trans.). London: Penguin Books.

Nisbett, R. E. (2003). *The geography of thought: How Asians and Westerners think differently and why*. New York: Free Press.

Ogawa, M. (1989). Beyond the tacit framework of "science" and "science education" among science educators. *International Journal of Science Education, 11*, 247–250.

Oliver-Smith, A., & de Sherbinin, A. (2014). Resettlement in the twenty-first century. *Forced Migration Review, 45*, 23–25.

Pettigrew, Tomas F. (1997). Generalized intergroup contact effects on prejudice. *Personality and Social Psychology Bulletin, 23*(2), 173–185.

Rakow, S. J., & Bermudez, A. B. (1993). Science is "ciencia": Meeting the needs of Hispanic American students. *Science Education, 77*(6), 669–687.

Ratha, D., & Shaw, W. (2007). *South–South migration and remittances* (Working Paper No. 102). Washington, DC: World Bank. Retrieved November 26, 2014, from http://siteresources.worldbank.org/INTPROSPECTS/Resources/334934-1110315015165/SouthSouthMigrationandRemittances.pdf

Rice, F. P., & Dolgin, K. G. (2005). The *adolescent: Development, relationships, and culture* (11th ed.). Boston: Allyn & Bacon.

Roberge, M. (2005). *Who are Generation 1.5 Students?* Southern New Hampshire University, Manchester, NH. Conference. Retrieved October 1, 2006, from http://www.nnetesol.org/conference/RobergePP.pdf

Shumba, O. (1999). Relationship between secondary science teachers' orientation to traditional culture and beliefs concerning science instructional ideology. *Journal of Research in Science Teaching, 36*(3), 333–355.

Some, M. P. (1998). *The healing wisdom of Africa: Finding life purpose through nature, ritual, and community*. New York: Penguin Putnam.

Spector, B. S., & Lederman, N. G. (1990). Science and technology as human enterprises. In B. Spector & M. Betkouski (Eds.), *Science teaching in a changing society* (pp. 1–26). Dubuque, IA: Kendall/Hint Publishing Company.

Stephan, W.G., & Finlay, K. A. (1999). The role of empathy in improving intergroup relations. *Journal of Social Issues, 55*, 729–744.

Stigler, J. W. & Hiebert, J. (1999). *The teaching gap: Best ideas from the world's teachers for improving education in the classroom*. New York: The Free Press.

Thomas, J. M., & Johnson, B. J. (2004). Perspectives of international faculty members: Their experiences and stories. *Education & Society, 22*(3), 47–64.

Traweek, S. (1992). Border crossings: Narrative strategies in science studies among physicists in Tsukuba Science City, Japan. In A. Pickering (Ed.), *Science as practice and culture* (pp. 429–465). Chicago: University of Chicago Press.

United Nations Population Division. (2009). *Trends in International Migrant Stock: The 2008 revision*. New York: Author.

Vygotsky, L. (1962). *Thought and language*. Cambridge, MA: MIT Press.

Young, M. (2003). Curriculum studies and the problem of knowledge: Updating the enlightenment?' *Policy Futures in Education, 1*, 553–564.

# 2 Foreign-Born Professors and Their Quests for a Social and Psychological Home

## Integrating Social, Cultural, and Professional Dimensions of Life

*Amy Carattini*

### INTRODUCTION

Most immigrants come to the United States in pursuit of a "better life" (International Organization for Migration, 2013, p. 1). However, this new reality entails unforeseen challenges based on where the foreign-born professors grow up, when they migrate, and whom they meet along the way. As one foreign-born professor illustrates,

> I grew up in a sheltered, small town, brought up by professional parents. . . . So for me to say I was looking for a 'better life' is a little facetious. But, I was looking for a different kind of life, a different social structure than I had. (Arjun, Interview, 2013, p. 7)[1]

One can argue that the nuances between a "better life" and a "different social structure" circumscribe the incorporation experience of many foreign-born professors who are adapting to the United States within the context of the global environment. They are not only acculturating and evolving as professionals in a new country, but they are also testing their frameworks for esteem and self-actualization, and for home and family life, all while experiencing "different social structures."

### Life Course Approach: An Anthropological Perspective

During 2012 and 2013, I interviewed 48 professors at a major research university. I used the life history method, which is both a chronological account of the events making up a person's life and an intimate story used to construct an identity against the backdrop of the human condition (Freidenberg & Thakur, 2009; Jackson & Russell, 2010).

The findings from this research indicate that they tend to think of moving as a strategy to enhance their career productivity. Additionally, many remain in the United States for longer stays than originally anticipated, some choosing to reside permanently or indefinitely. Career opportunities,

*Foreign-Born Professors and Their Quests for a Social* 23

promotions, marriages, family, friends, and other life events often alter their choices—much the same for all people. In fact, the decision to stay long-term often evolves over time.

Because anthropologists are invested in how cultural and social behaviors are maintained and transformed in the context of new surroundings (Foner, 2003), they tend to examine micro-level data such as the individual, the household, or the small group (Brettell & Hollifield, 2013). The result is an in-depth look at the relational and structural elements that define immigrant realities. From an anthropological perspective, therefore, the guiding question for my research is, "What variables influence domains of connection for foreign-born faculty?"

## Incorporation Responses

One way to approach this understanding is to describe the temporal and relational aspects of professors' migration(s) and, in so doing, examine the challenges they faced in navigating a new society, as well as the coping mechanisms they used to adjust to their new circumstances. The variables included in this process are noted in Table 2.1.

In the next sections, these variables will be explored to investigate what domains and relationships are used to produce "culture" for this group (Levitt, 2011). Based on my analysis, foreign-born professors adapt to their new circumstances first through the lens of their profession, but in so doing, they experience other factors that have an impact on them and their incorporation responses. Two different responses are described to illustrate this point.

## Between and Betwixt

Nicolas, an assistant professor from South America, was born in the late 1960s in a capital city, which had more than 1.5 million people (Nicolas Interview, 2013, p. 2). His family has a history of international migration, with his mother's family originating in Spain and his father's in Italy (Nicolas Interview, 2013, p. 1). Nicolas grew up in the aftermath of an urban

*Table 2.1* Variables Used by Foreign-Born Professors to Enact Within Cultural, Social, and Professional Frameworks

| Historical | Socio-Spatial |
| --- | --- |
| Year of Birth | Family History with Migration |
| Year of Arrival | Locality of Formative Years |
| Arrival Age | International Moves Before Arrival |
| Years in the U.S. at Time of Interview | Local/Regional Settlements in the U.S. |

## 24 Amy Carattini

guerrilla movement. In 1968, the armed forces closed the civilian government and established a civilian-military regime:

> The '70s were politically turbulent times, so [my country] went through some guerilla fighting issues and then there was military war. . . . So '72 was the time I entered school, and my parents decided that it was considerably safer to send me and my sister to private school. (Nicolas Interview, 2013, p. 2)

In 1984, civilian rule returned. The first administration implemented economic reforms and consolidated democracy. These events structured the career opportunities available for Nicolas, who was considering a profession in engineering:

> The prospects for engineering were to be employed probably in a state industry . . . a lot of the companies are owned by the state. . . . So being an engineer you have a risk . . . that you end up being an administrator. . . . That wasn't tremendously appealing intellectually. (Nicolas Interview, 2013, p. 4)

In fact, the impetus for coming to the United States was presented as a "fortuitous" opportunity that came as Nicolas became increasingly interested in physics and astronomy:

> Somebody knew somebody and this person was working in the U.S . . . at the Center for Astrophysics and . . . he was coming to visit. . . . So I did a project with Emilio, and Emilio convinced two of us for applying to U.S. schools . . . and I was accepted in one of them. (Nicolas Interview, 2013, p. 4)

### Challenge: To Stay or Return

When Nicolas came to the United States in 1993, he was a young adult in his mid-20s, seeking professional experience as well as leaving the limited structure for career advancement in his country of origin. He arrived during the Clinton administration, which was an era of economic expansion and the "dot-com bubble." Funding opportunities in the sciences were good. He entered as a PhD student in Boston, Massachusetts, and since then, he has also lived several years in California, as a postdoc and research associate before accepting the position he currently holds at his current university. While Nicolas has considered at times returning to South America, he has decided to stay because of the professional development and intellectual curiosity that continues to stimulate his work:

> Well, I mean . . . if I wanted to be a good researcher in astronomy, grad school wasn't enough; I had to do a postdoc. . . . I could always have

gone back, taken the final exams . . . in engineering . . . but I would have probably considered that a defeat of some sort. (Nicolas Interview, 2013, p. 6)

### Challenge: Integrating Culture of Origin With Host Culture

At the time of our interview, Nicolas had been in the United States for 20 years, had become a citizen, and had a wife and three children who were born in the United States. Yet, he still was not sure if he would remain permanently in the United States—unsure if he had found a place of cultural comfort. He travels each year to his home country for the holidays:

> We try to go, every year, for Christmas. Particularly since we have children, it was important for them to see their grandparents and to see the extended family. And we wanted the children to be comfortable culturally and with the language back home. (Nicolas Interview, 2013, pp. 9–10)

While Nicolas feels comfortable interacting in both countries, he expresses that something is always missing, thus creating a sense of indeterminacy:

> No place feels like home, because there are elements of home in each one of them. . . . It doesn't mean that I don't feel comfortable here or there. It just means that when I am here, I miss something that's there. When I am there, I miss something that is from here. (Nicolas Interview, 2013, p. 10)

### Challenge: Inhabiting Social Structures

Part of Nicolas's loss stems from a difference in expectation between work and social interactions. Nicolas finds that social interactions in the United States are more formal and limited:

> Here, it's very impolite not to call somebody to say essentially whatever your plans are . . . distances are larger—so it's a little bit of chore to get people in a car and then meet somewhere at some place just to be there and then come back. (Nicolas Interview, 2013, p. 11)

Nicolas misses the shorter distances and longer, more informal interactions that mark his time in his capital city. He also speaks of other structural elements that affect this positioning:

> I am completely a non-religious person and my wife is not particularly religious either. So we are not part of a church group or anything like that. I don't know if you have noticed, but many social interactions in the U.S. happen in that type of environment. (Nicolas Interview, 2013, p. 11)

## 26   Amy Carattini

By contrast, at work, he finds that his career trajectory and colleague interaction is very satisfying:

> I mean, what I do is astronomy. . . . And so, I enjoy talking to my colleagues about the X, Y or Z of some arcane topic in physics or astronomy or even engineering sometimes. So that's the intellectual simulation that we all need. It's at least what makes life interesting for me. (Nicolas Interview, 2013, p. 11)

He does acknowledge that having children has added another dimension to his life and that life would be "easier" and more integrated from his perspective "if we [my wife and I] had extended family here, or if we had already friends by the time we had children" (Nicolas Interview, 2013, p. 11).

### *Incorporation Response: Betwixt and Between Places*

Regarding political aspects of incorporation, defined here as one's decision to naturalize, Nicolas considers himself a triple citizen: of Spain, of the United States, his current location, and of his country of birth. As a result, he tends to see himself in terms of an "international identity":

> Would I have become a citizen of the U.S. or of Spain if that wasn't convenient? And, would I have become a citizen of [my home country], had I had any voice in that particular question?. . . . I tend to see . . . nationality [as] . . . something that is more practical than anything else. (Nicolas Interview, 2013, p. 12)

A third variable of interest is Nicolas's places of settlement within the United States, all of which have been East and West Coast city living, which have different cultures in and of themselves. It is worth remembering that Nicolas came to the United States as a young adult seeking professional experience and recognition for his work as a serious researcher. He also entered the United States during a time of economic prosperity and strong support for the sciences. Since his time of arrival, he has attained esteem and recognition in his field and recently was promoted. Yet, he still misses his extended family and the social structure of his country of origin. More particularly, he misses the capital city he grew up in, which makes distance less of an obstacle between people. Nicolas feels that the people in the city where he grew up are more culturally attuned to the relational aspects of being rather than the austere time constraints he has sometimes experienced in the context of U.S. society. Additionally, he has no extended family living nearby to ease the demands of parenthood and to create a more balanced social life. He acknowledges that, in the future, he will have more time for exploring social interactions, as his children grow and become independent.

For Nicolas, all of these factors noted earlier create both satisfaction and longing. He recognizes that his children will most likely feel connected to

*Foreign-Born Professors and Their Quests for a Social* 27

American society, having been born here, and that he, too, has opportunities for career development and advancement in his field. Yet, he has a desire to inhabit the "comfort" of familiar relationships that he has yet to wholly experience in the United States. As a result, he situates himself between and betwixt two locations. While acknowledging that his long-term intention is to stay, he does not dismiss the notion of moving entirely. He is in a perpetual state of liminality:

> An attractive job in South America would be attractive. So I don't know . . . I am open. I think what we [my family and I] have works, so I don't have a problem with it. It could be better but . . . On the other hand, there is no reason for not moving somewhere else if I think it would be a better place or it would have a long-term value. (Nicolas Interview, 2013, p. 13)

While Nicolas grew and adapted, as a young man, to a professional culture within the context of the United States, he has not experienced the same growth and flexibility in his personal interactions. Those habits and expectations were developed in the context of an urban environment within his country of origin. Although he has continued to inhabit cities, he has yet to find the culture of one that is optimal for him. Consequently, his professional and cultural comfort zones are in different locations, making him feel simultaneously attached and detached as he moves between these locations. The reality is that he could live almost anywhere that supports his professional well-being.

## Permanently En Route

Elyse, a professor from Europe, was born in the mid-1950s in London. However, from the age three, her family moved to several places within her home country, eventually settling in the suburbs of the capital city where she attended school and went to university:

> Because of my father's work, we moved every two or three years to various places . . . until we settled next to [the capital city] in the suburbs when I was ten. I spent the years I was in middle school and high school there. Then I moved to [the capital city] for my university. (Elyse Interview, 2013, p. 1)

Both Elyse's mother and father were pioneers of a sort, coming from established families within their respective countries of origin: "They both are really rooted [both families]. . . . [My mother] was the one who really didn't want to stay there and moved . . . to explore something different" (Elyse Interview, 2013, p. 2).

Although Elyse lived in several places during her early, formative years, she expresses that the capital city is her "home." She arrived in its suburbs

28    *Amy Carattini*

at the age of 10, in the mid-1960s, amid the burgeoning politics of national independence. She speaks of an environment that sought to expand educational access to everyone:

> The nice thing about the . . . system, for me, is that it is the same education, the same program, the same assessment, in the public system, wherever you are in [the country], so basically, there was no major change in terms of content or way of teaching [in all my moves], whether I was here or there. (Elyse Interview, 2013, pp. 2–3)

However, by 1968, the country was experiencing social unrest, culminating in students revolting against government policies and creating a national strike. In this political milieu, Elyse visited the United States for the first time on a family vacation and found that she was interested in the social and cultural structure and wanted to learn more:

> I knew that I would go back [to my country of origin], so I [went back and] finished all my college studies. I went through the whole scope of the . . . system. I decided then it would be time for me to pursue my studies in an American university, but at a graduate level. (Elyse Interview, 2013, p. 3)

When Elyse came to the United States in 1980, she was a young adult in her mid-20s, seeking new experiences and testing whether they would give her the framework she sought. Reagan had just been elected president and addressed a divided political system with "pragmatic conservatism" (Brownlee & Graham, 2003). In this context, the U.S. public was focused on fiscal, social, and national security issues and expected the government's role to focus on fostering liberty and protecting national interests. Elyse describes her admiration of individual expression that she experienced in the United States:

> The [United States] is also a much more democratic society, for the better and the worse, in the sense that everybody has a voice, or tries to. . . . You don't always have to go through your representative. . . . Here, you have a lot of power given to communities, to organizations. (Elyse Interview, 2013, p. 5)

She also observed this social liberty in the context of the media environment:

> I also liked the fact that the media reflected society in a much more accurate way. I am not saying positive . . . [but] there was this idea that somehow the media had to respond to all groups within society, whereas in [my home country] . . . routine was a big concern . . . [at least] in the beginning of the '80's. (Elyse Interview, 2013, p. 5)

Initially, Elyse attended film school in California, and during this time she found structural aspects of U.S. society that resonated with her: "I really liked what I found here . . . the society and the professional training and the university system" (Elyse Interview, 2013, p. 4). Additionally, she describes the process of self-realization that occurred when a fellow student committed suicide—someone who she thought was the most talented of everyone there:

> They [artists] have a special way of looking at the world. . . . Most of us didn't have this. We were just happy kids working there with a comfortable life. . . . So, it doesn't mean that it is the end of the world. It just means that, well, there are other things we can do. (Elyse Interview, 2013, p. 7)

### Challenge: To Stay or Return

As Elyse realized that being an artist was not her long-term vocation, she started to appreciate some of the possibilities that she perceived the United States had to offer, such as a less hierarchal professional structure and the ability to more easily reinvent herself later in life.

Since then, Elyse has spent most of her life living between two countries, with long-term stays in Boston, Massachusetts, and San Francisco, California, through studies abroad and work-related opportunities. She has also reinvented herself as a professor:

> Every time . . . I went back [to my home country], I found something to do here [in the United States]. And after a while, my contract would end, so I would go back to [to my home country]. Then, I decided to become a professor and I was not happy with the situation in [my home country], so I started applying for a position here [in the United States]. (Elyse Interview, 2013, p. 4)

In 2001, Elyse decided to live more permanently in the United States and to pursue a tenure-track position at a university. At the time of our interview, Elyse had been residing in the United States for 12 years and was currently in the process of applying for citizenship. Although she travels to her home country at least twice a year, she has also decided to permanently reside in the United States: "I finally got my green card some time ago, and I intend to renew it and go through the application for citizenship process. I am here for good" (Elyse Interview, 2013, p. 10).

### Challenge: Integrating Culture of Origin With Host Culture

Elyse has found a social and cultural framework that gives her a sense of continuity. Rather than express loss or longing in her interactions with her family in her capital city of origin or with her life at the university in the United States, Elyse expresses a complementary view of both environments—describing how they add to her life, yielding both the instinctive comfort of her youth and the learned comfort of her adult choices. Two factors perhaps account for this ease or comfort: First, she lived between both environments for 20 years before deciding to move to the United States permanently, thus giving her the opportunity to evaluate the strengths and weaknesses of both places. Second, she did not have family encumbrances, thus allowing for independence of movement without the added complexity of immediate family concerns. As she noted in her 2013 interview, "I was not married. I did not have any children. I can imagine, for women, it becomes a bit more difficult. You have to drag the whole family" (p. 4). For Elyse, the United States offers her the professional environment that continually renews her inner search for fulfillment, while her home country offers "the language, the routine, [and] years and years of daily life there" (Elyse Interview, 2013, p. 9)—her mental or psychological sense of home.

### Challenge: Inhabiting Social Structures
For Elyse, however, the longer she remains in the United States, the more she realizes that some of her comfort level has diminished, especially with the terrorist attacks of September 2001 and other catastrophes: "I know that it is a huge change since 2001 and the situation related to 9/11, and subsequently, what happened" (Elyse Interview, 2013, p. 4). Furthermore, she sees that the social structure of the United States is shifting and that the democratic ideal that she has come to expect is changing:

> I must say that also, unfortunately, I see that things have changed . . . over the past twenty years. . . . For instance, I would say power of big organizations [such as] banks seem to me much bigger now. There is less balance between the little people and some powerful groups. (Elyse Interview, 2013, p. 6)

### Incorporation Response: Continuity Among Places
As regarding political aspects of incorporation, Elyse does not view herself as international or a hybrid; rather, she views herself as intrinsically part of the capital city she grew up in, while having learned to navigate and inhabit another social structure: "It doesn't make you a global person that can go anywhere. . . . On the contrary, you become more aware of the differences, not the commonalities" (Elyse Interview, 2013, p. 13). Elyse first came to the United States as a young adult but then decided to stay in the United States at a later stage in her adult life. Initially, she sought to discover new social structures and to test their relevance for her life—which she has now decided to fully inhabit and embrace, but not at the exclusion of one over the other.

All of the previously mentioned factors together create a sense of inner liberty. Elyse recognizes that she can travel back and forth between the two locations that together give her a sense of wholeness and continuity. As a result, she situates herself as permanently en route between two locations—two homes. While signaling that her long-term intention is to stay in the United States, she also acknowledged that she will continue to live part-time in her city of origin. Elyse grew and adapted to this fluid reality over a lifetime, and consequently, she is now securely fixed in both places.

## LESSONS LEARNED

Several lessons can be gleaned from the narratives of foreign-born professors' in this chapter. For the benefit of a newly arrived foreign-born professor, however, the narratives of this chapter can be summarized into two main ideas: experience life in and outside the university campus and consciously construct a lifestyle that best fits your life.

### Lesson 1: Experience Life In and Outside the University Campus

Foreign-born professors generally made a distinction between home and work life in their narratives, describing their work lives as the motivating factor for movement. Kamil, for example, says the following about his place of residence: "I would have been equally happy in Minnesota or California or anyplace even though I may have a preference. . . . But this is absolutely secondary" (Kamil Interview, 2013, p. 11). And Jan finds that the distinction between these two realms of life is attached to different levels of satisfaction:

> So there's a clear distinction between the work environment here, academically . . . another thing is the place where you can live, where you lead your life and where you interact with neighbors and friends. (Interview, 2012, p. 26)

Overall, professors indicated that part of getting connected to U.S. society was about living in an international area, where they could either socialize with other people from their countries of origin or with others living abroad like themselves. Professors also described living with other types of diversity, including social class, religious, and political. They describe how these differences often help them to establish a connection to their home lives as they become engaged in understanding this diversity and finding their place among the variations.

Both Nicolas and Elyse are immigrants in the sense that they have naturalized or are in the process of doing so, yet their intentions to do so have evolved over time. This distinction is important to examine more closely how they and others who follow similar paths make this decision, commit

## 32   Amy Carattini

to this decision, and gain a level of comfort in doing so. One important lesson learned that participants communicated over and over again was their ability to identify which social structures worked for them and which did not. More important, this type of evaluation is not just relegated to life in the United States but to life in all the various regions and locales they have lived over their life courses. Participants who could evaluate and articulate their satisfaction and their distress with different social frameworks, such as living independently versus more collectively or with different aesthetic sensibilities or with varying degrees of hierarchy, were often better equipped to construct a lifestyle that made sense in the context of United States as they actively sought the best of all their experiences—resulting in a lifestyle that made them feel comfortable.

Additionally, many had lived in more than one region of the United States—arriving at their current university after learning about the different realities that circumscribe different campuses, as well as how different colleges and universities are ranked within the culture of U.S. academia. This learning process helped them to evaluate the diverse range of experiences possible within U.S. academic life.

## Lesson 2: Consciously Construct a Lifestyle That Best Fits Your Life

Often staying in the United States was not about finding a home but about finding what some participants referred to as "my place." The United States was not described so much as a political entity but rather as a place where many layers of individual experience operate at an optimal level, spiritually, intellectually, physically, and emotionally: "I love my country; I love my city, and I love my people. But I live here, and this is my place" (Dani Interview, 2013, p. 7). Amit elaborates further:

> For the first 10 years after I started the career here, the idea was, yes, I will pack up and leave. It was in 1979/'80 that I took my sabbatical, went to . . . [my country of origin] for four, five months with the explicit purpose of trying to assess where I could fit or what I could do. And what I found was that I can help . . . [my country of origin] much better by building a good strong group here than going back there. (Interview, 2013, p. 16)

Amit found that his faculty position in the United States, in particular at his university location, was the place where he could accomplish his goals and be the kind of person he wanted to be.

Ultimately, choosing to stay in the United States is about a variety of factors, often connected to finding one's place—where one can function in the best possible way. In fact, foreign-born professors' choices often have less to do with a specific country and more to do with work opportunities.

## Foreign-Born Professors and Their Quests for a Social    33

Although many professors express that their social interactions and emotional lives are tied to other countries, they find that their faculty positions in the United States allow them to construct a lifestyle that gives them a sense of satisfaction.

Nicolas and Elyse, for example, are not fixed in one location. They have the ability to live creatively between several places. Nicolas continually travels between several locations, his country of birth being one location among the many, and in his narrative, he constructs himself as an international. For Nicolas, cultural production is about finding an expressive alchemy that combines his past enculturation experiences with his present appreciation of new and diverse social frameworks. Although he acknowledges that his life in the United States "works," he also admits that he would be interested in moving should the right opportunity present itself. By contrast, Elyse does not describe herself as a global person but rather as someone who has learned two very specific contexts. For Elyse, cultural production is about finding and defining her social field—one that spans two locations and that operates comfortably with her daily lifestyle.

## CONCLUSION

The possibilities for cultural production discussed in this chapter indicate that there are many ways of constructing interpersonal realities while inhabiting and contributing to new social structures and that these pathways are not mutually exclusive. Perhaps immigrant professors are not so different from other immigrants who also carry aspects of their past and integrate those into their new social, cultural, and professional lives as immigrants. However, immigrant professors often have access to resources that can facilitate their lifestyle preferences, making their stories unique in how they accomplish their goals and in how they evaluate their success.

## ACKNOWLEDGMENTS

Amy Carattini (acaratti@umd.edu) recently finished her PhD in sociocultural anthropology at the University of Maryland. She is interested in professional migration and comparing immigrant experiences. She would like to thank the editor of this book, Charles Hutchison, for his guidance in writing this chapter, as well as acknowledge Darryl Carattini, Judith Freidenberg, and Ken Maniha for their thoughtful review of drafts.

## NOTE

1. Pseudonyms were created for each interviewee to protect identities.

## REFERENCES

Amit Interview. (2013). Transcript. Interviewer Amy Carattini. Jan. 14.

Arjun Interview (2013). Transcript. Interviewer Amy Carattini. Feb. 1.

Brettell, C., & Hollifield, J. (2013/2000). Introduction. In C. Brettell & J. Hollifield (Eds.), *Migration theory: Talking across disciplines* (pp. 1–30). New York: Routledge.

Brownlee, W. E., & Graham, H. D. (Eds.). (2003). *The Reagan presidency: Pragmatic conservatism and its legacies.* Lawrence: University Press of Kansas.

Elyse Interview. (2013). Transcript. Interviewer Amy Carattini. Jan. 25.

Dani Interview. (2013). Transcript. Interviewer Amy Carattini. Jan. 16.

Foner, Nancy. (2003). *Americana arrivals: Anthropology engages the new immigration.* Santa Fe, NM: School of American Research. (Introduction section.)

Freidenberg, J., & Thakur, G. (2009). Immigrant life histories as a heritage resource for civic engagement. *Practicing Anthropology,* 31(3), 30–35.

International Organization for Migration. (2013). *World migration report.* Geneva, Switzerland: International Organization for Migration.

Jackson, P., & Russell, P. (2010). Life history interviewing. In D. DeLyser, S. Herbert, S. Aitken, S. Crang, & L. McDowell (Eds.), *The sage handbook of qualitative geography* (pp.172–92). London: Sage.

Jan Interview. (2012). Transcript. Interviewer Amy Carattini. Dec. 19.

Kamil Interview. (2013). Transcript. Interviewer Amy Carattini. Jan. 14.

Levitt, Peggy. (2011). *A transnational gaze. Migraciones Internacionales,* 6(1): 9–44.

Nicolas Interview. (2013). Transcript. Interviewer Amy Carattini. Jan. 16.

# 3 A Portrait of the Life and Work of Expatriate Educators in Cambodia

*Alexander Jun, Rebecca Hong, Curtis Cline, and Faith Fitt*

## A PORTRAIT OF THE LIFE AND WORK OF EXPATRIATE EDUCATORS IN ASIA

Knowledge production lies at the heart of the mission of universities, and several Asian nations have become notable expressions of this reality. However, the perception that Asia is an emerging powerhouse of knowledge production should be tempered by the understanding that the region is quite diverse. The successes of more advanced and wealthier Asian nations should not detract attention from the challenges faced by other nations in the region. Although less developed countries can learn from metropolitan academic systems (Altbach, 2004), they ultimately have to forge their own paths to address national needs and priorities and to make their own contributions to global knowledge production.

One consequence of national movements toward globalization has been an increase in North American citizens recruited for faculty positions in Asian universities. In this study, we sought to explore some of the impacts of globalization on higher education by understanding and documenting the experiences of North Americans who taught in various disciplines with English as the primary medium of instruction on college campuses in the Kingdom of Cambodia, one developing Asian nation. We contextualize our study in the landscape of current research in the following pages.

## EXPATRIATE EDUCATORS: A REVIEW OF THE LITERATURE

This section discusses research related to professors teaching abroad, which has produced clusters of themes, among which are culturally diverse expectations of instructors' roles and performances, unexpected teacher–student interactions, supportive or unfriendly work settings, the relative efficacy of instructional strategies, challenges to utilizing technology, and challenges to evaluating student performance.

## Expectations of Instructors

Perceptions of teachers vary culturally across degrees of social distance and across expectations of rights and obligations (Bodycott & Walker, 2000; George, 1995; Walker, Bridges, & Chan, 1996). Where instructors' understandings of the social roles of teachers and students differ significantly from their students' understandings, personal stress and professional inadequacy may result (Crabtree & Sapp, 2004). Additionally, instructors who work in non-Western educational contexts may bring expectations of workload and range of duties that may not be compatible with local requirements (Crabtree & Sapp, 2004; Shin, Morgeson, & Campion, 2007). In several studies, immigrant instructors reported difficulties in acquiring detailed contracts; sudden and unannounced changes to contracts; classes assigned that were outside their areas of expertise; unusual expectations for services beyond teaching (including coaching athletics, chairing committees or departments, leading band, guest lecturing in other departments, representing the university at social functions, etc.); discrepancies in salary; unwieldy class sizes; and insufficient time for research (Bodycott & Walker, 2000; Burton & Robinson, 1999; Garson, 2005; George, 1995; Getty, 2011; Herman & Bailey, 1991). Most studies conclude that patience, flexibility, and readiness to adapt greatly reduce international professors' frustration with job ambiguity.

## Teacher–Student Interactions

Although research has demonstrated the importance of the frequency and quality of faculty–student interactions (cf. Kuh & Hu, 2001), studies show that transnational teacher-student interactions are often different from what international professors anticipate. Crabtree and Sapp (2004) found that cultural asynchrony between U.S. faculty and Brazilian students created teacher–student interactions (as well as student-student interactions) that the international professor found surprising and often unwelcome. Degrees of formality, hierarchy, and proximity can be located on intersecting continua. The Brazilian students in the study expected a less formal interaction, more equal social roles, and more emotional and physical contact with one another and with the instructor than the instructor expected (Crabtree & Sapp, 2004). In other parts of the world, instructors sometimes find themselves located nearer the other extreme of the continuum, expecting less formality, more equality, and more degrees of closeness than their students expect (Bodycott & Walker, 2000).

## Foreign Work Environment

In addition to unexpected patterns of personal interaction, professors may find international work situations to be difficult in other ways. Bodycott and Walker (2000) found that indirect communication styles in a university department in Hong Kong created a work environment that was confusing for Western faculty. They also found that some of the international professors' habits and actions fostered resentment among national colleagues. Getty (2011) found that communication with national colleagues was difficult, with the result that a work environment in China was not perceived as supportive. As a positive contrast, work environments that are easier to navigate than those at home are a pleasant surprise to some international professors. George (1995) noted the experience of one instructor, working in Malaysia, who found that cooperation and generosity within the department created a work context that was less stressful than the competitive atmosphere present at her U.S. institution. Overall, research studies typically conclude that, although foreign work environments are often difficult to navigate at first, international professors who are flexible can adjust and learn to appreciate the distinctiveness of their host cultures.

## Pedagogical Differences

Pedagogical differences across cultures can also produce stress for international professors. Pedagogical methods proven to be effective for fostering learning in U.S. settings are often bound by cultural barriers when transplanted overseas (Crabtree & Sapp, 2004; Fowler, 2005). Some international instructors are reluctant to abandon the creative and active learning strategies that served them well in U.S. contexts to adopt methods founded on transactional theories of education. In several studies, international professors were found to conduct their work amid the tension between accommodating the cultural learning styles of students in host countries and imposing instructional strategies empirically supported by Western-based research—ones that local students may have found uncomfortable and even offensive (Crabtree & Sapp, 2004; Fowler, 2005; George, 1995).

## Technology Limitations

Previous studies also report logistical challenges to utilizing technology and cultural challenges to evaluating student performance. Students' personal access to technology and the availability of classroom technology vary widely. International professors found themselves constantly adapting and readapting to the changing accessibility of resources (Garson, 2005). Testing and assessment also presented challenges because expatriate instructors encountered unconventional institutional policies and ethnically diverse student and faculty behaviors (Garson, 2005; George, 1995; Getty, 2011).

The literature related to the experiences of international teachers is rich with descriptions of the challenges and opportunities of living and working in international higher education. Less evident in the literature are descriptions of the types and effects of teacher preparation, which the current study partially sought to fill.

38 *Alexander Jun, et al.*

## DESIGN AND METHODOLOGY

Previous studies produced rich descriptions of cross-cultural work environments in some countries. The current study employed a similar, qualitative approach to investigate the living and working experiences of international instructors situated in globalizing higher education in Cambodia.

To capture a fuller picture of the life and work of these international instructors, we employed various qualitative methodologies, including grounded theory techniques, phenomenology, and ethnographic case study approaches. We relied on multiple sources of evidence, including observations, individual interviews with faculty, and document analysis, and employed careful data analysis techniques to derive meaning from the data.

### Site Selection

We purposefully selected a developing nation in which higher education is changing rapidly because of global influences. To understand the challenges and opportunities surrounding globalization through the experiences of international instructors, we selected two campuses in Phnom Penh, the political and cultural capital of Cambodia. Cambodia College (CC), a public university in Cambodia, embraced globalization by creating an "English only" undergraduate Department of International Affairs. Cambodia Institute of South East Asia (CISA) engages globalization through their hallmark, English-based International Major. Both CC and CISA have a history of competitive admissions, adopt western teaching practices in their curricula, employ faculty with advanced degrees, and are positioned at the heart of change within Cambodia's higher education system.

### Participant Selection

Eight North American instructors participated in this study. The instructors were full-time educators who taught undergraduate and graduate courses primarily in English. All the instructors received training in cross-cultural adjustment and pedagogy before arriving in Cambodia; several had received formal training in teaching, and some had prior international experience. Longevity of employment in Cambodia ranged from 6 months to 3 years. Male and female instructors participated in this study. All participants were citizens of the United States and fulfilled their teaching responsibilities voluntarily on behalf of one nongovernmental organization (NGO).

### Data Collection

We conducted two in-depth, semi-structured interviews with each international professor. Each interview lasted between 50 and 80 minutes. We audio-recorded and later transcribed the interviews to ensure accuracy during data analysis. To help triangulate and validate the data, we conducted observations both on and off the university campuses and especially noted the ways in which the international professors interacted with students and other faculty. We also conducted document analysis to understand the institutions and the environment in which the international professors were employed.

## Data Analysis

Data analysis occurred through ongoing and continuous reflections and analytic questions posed throughout the study. We modeled a constant-comparison method of analysis, integrating new data as they were collected and allowing each set to shape, clarify, and comment on the others. We approached the interview data using open coding and separated the data into parts, examining and comparing different data sources. We employed interrater reliability techniques to ensure accuracy as categories emerged. We also explored and examined rival explanations from the findings, juxtaposing our findings with findings from the relevant literature.

## FINDINGS

Three broad themes emerged from the data that reflected the complexities, tensions, challenges, and benefits of living and working in international higher education: (a) the presence and effects of various degrees of cross-cultural and professional preparation, (b) different elements and evidences of cross-cultural adjustment, and (c) tensions, challenges, and coping mechanisms related to cultural difference.

## Cross-Cultural and Professional Preparation

The data indicated that the international professors had engaged in varying degrees and types of formal and informal preparation for cultural and professional adjustment before moving to Cambodia. Some instructors received formal teacher education, while others had no formal preparation to teach. Types of preparation included orientation provided by the sponsoring NGO, various individual efforts made by the instructors, and the instructors' previous international experience.

### Orientation for Cultural and Professional Adjustment

Several faculty members received what they considered to be extensive, intentional preparation from the NGO. For example, one of the international professors, a 20-something teacher named Katya, who had no formal teaching experience before arriving at her university, indicated that the NGO provided "a month-long intensive training program where they teach us about

40  *Alexander Jun, et al.*

how to be English teachers overseas and specific cultures [*sic*]. Before that, they sent reading materials to us in the States and we had to read." Ted, a middle-aged instructor who also had no previous teaching experience, explained that the international professors received "teaching methodology training . . . to recognize that people have different learning styles." Ted further explained that leaders of the orientation program helped the new teachers adjust to their new culture and encouraged them to employ interactive pedagogies in their classrooms. The orientation leaders urged the new teachers to "try to get [students] to maximize the time they spend in actually speaking English, you know, not just sitting there quietly trying to take notes, [but] . . . trying to get students involved in the teaching."

The teachers also employed different strategies for developing cultural awareness. For example, second-year teacher Rick read teaching manuals that provided "some practical stuff on what it's like to be a teacher in Asia." Maggie, who had 4 years of teaching experience in another Asian country, described her strategy:

> *Killing Fields, Living Fields*—I had read that a few years before. I read a short history of Cambodia, but I didn't know anything about what these people live like today. Or why they do the things they do. I talked to some friends who live there.

Gemma, who had the most teaching experience and was pursuing a master's degree in teaching at the time of our interviews, supplemented her preparation for cognitive and emotional adjustment to Cambodia by purchasing a movie called the *Rice People*:

> It was by Rithy Panh . . . It's all in Khmer with English subtitles. And it shows like basically one calendar year of a Khmer village, and so you see the whole rice harvest throughout the year planting, protecting it from infestations from crabs, protecting it from crows, from birds, transplanting it, putting the water, they would pedal and these little coconuts would bring water, it was so cool.

Other than the 1 month of orientation provided by the NGO, the international professors were on their own to supplement their preparation for work and life abroad.

### International Travel as Cultural Adjustment
Several of the faculty believed that previous international experiences helped prepare them for cultural adjustment in Cambodia. Katya had traveled overseas and experienced several different cultures before arriving in Cambodia. Maggie had also traveled internationally and worked with the sponsoring NGO in another Asian country for over eight years. Maggie indicated that a previous visit to Cambodia helped her adjust to the culture.

## A Portrait of the Life and Work of Expatriate Educators 41

She explained: "I had a glimpse of it [Cambodia]. And I'll be honest, of all the places that I've traveled in the world, there were two places [that] when I left, they didn't actually leave me, and Cambodia was one of them."

Some faculty felt more deeply and formally prepared than others. The degrees of preparation varied from no formal preparation to advanced formal preparation.

### Absence of Formal Preparation to Teach

Some of the international professors had no prior formal preparation to teach. Ted's undergraduate degree did not include any pedagogical education. His previous career was in political media. However, Ted indicated that his Teaching English as a Foreign Language (TEFL) credentialing provided by the NGO qualified him as a teacher at his host institution. John, a novice instructor whose undergraduate degree was in engineering, explained:

> I don't have a teaching background. I still have a lot of room to grow—like I said, I feel a lot differently about being in the classroom than I did six months ago, [but] then a couple of years from now, I'll feel a lot differently than I do now.

Maggie, who had been teaching at the university for more than 2 years, commented that she did not receive any training until 6 months after she arrived. However, she actively learned on the job: "I would say I've been teaching for six months [and] I've been learning [how to teach] for a year and a half."

### Advanced Formal Preparation to Teach

Some international professors, like Gemma, received or were currently earning advanced academic degrees in teaching. Gemma commented that she "was the only one on the team with a master's; my team leader didn't have a master's." (The team leader, Carson, was an expatriate administrator whose primary role was to serve as the ombudsman between the international faculty and the host institution's administrative leaders.) Katya's education included a bachelor's in a romance language and advanced course credit units toward a master's degree in elementary education. Although Katya taught at the university level, she believed that "elementary education really fits in the population of [university] students," in terms of broad pedagogical concepts.

Maggie did not have previous education in teaching; however, she explained that her ongoing graduate education benefited her adjustment to teaching in the Cambodian university system:

> I'm working on a master's, and the master's is in TESOL. I'm taking classes on cross-cultural classroom learning, and the lights just come on, you know. . . . Honestly, that's what I would say; this degree has really been a key to all of it . . . those master's classes have been [a] huge help.

## 42　Alexander Jun, et al.

## Elements and Evidence of Cultural Adjustment

Adjusting to life and work in a foreign culture was often difficult for the international professors, and the pathway to feeling at home was different for each individual. The data revealed different strategies and helpful components of the instructors' own cross-cultural adjustments.

### Independence and Routines

John indicated that personal independence helped him feel at home in his new environment. He said,

> I can pretty much get around town. . . . I know enough to at least like, you know, go to the market and whatever, get my bike fixed and those types of things that whatever you need to do around town, you know, I'm able to do that, and so that is one part like feeling at home.

Katya offered a similar perspective of the importance of personal independence, stating,

> When we first arrived here, you can't do anything, I didn't know how to do anything; everyone has to help you go to the market to buy food, things like just contacting your landlord to fix my house, knowing how to get places, how to get a took-took driver, just basically what you used to do in your normal life.

Katharine summarized the perspectives offered by her colleagues by indicating that she felt at home by "knowing how to do things; . . . human nature is just to build routines."

### Language Acquisition

The faculty members also cited language acquisition as a means of feeling more at home in the host culture. Maggie admitted that challenges with learning Khmer, the national language of Cambodia, affected her adjustment to Cambodian culture:

> I struggle with the language, so I definitely stick out that way and feel like a foreigner in that sense. Not understanding why things happen the way, like I don't always grasp the mindset and the logic or lack thereof, at least where I can tell, and that makes me feel outside of the culture.

Conversely, Katya indicated that she considered herself fairly well adjusted to the Cambodian culture after 2 years, and attributed part of her adjustment to previous language study and learning Khmer. Katya believed that her previous "experience studying a foreign language extensively before . . . helped me when I came here to another language. So I think when I learn[ed] the language faster, I adjusted a lot faster."

Learning the local language may assist with adjusting to the culture; however, the experience may not be easy. Ted shared that he had been in the country for almost 8 months, had taken language lessons 3 times a week but was frustrated because he did not feel like he was learning as much as he should. Ted heard other expatriate coworkers conversing with host nationals and speaking in complete sentences, which caused him to wonder, "Oh man, why can't I do that? I just have a hard time trying to remember words, and so it's been a frustrating experience."

### Relationships

Adjustment to life in Cambodia developed as the international instructors developed relationships. Katya felt more at home when she felt "that I have friendships." She explained that relationships provided a significant resource for cultural adjustment:

> [My] teammates helped me a lot; they're always there when I had questions, even if that was a stupid question. It was helpful to have Americans there, Americans and a Canadian friend that had experience in Cambodia, and I wasn't afraid to ask them. They understood what it's like to be new in a foreign country.

In addition to friendships with North American colleagues, Katya was building friendships with nationals. Katya indicated that as she developed relationships with Cambodian people she developed better cultural understanding. She asked questions such as, "Why do you do this?" and "Why is it like this?" which caused her to "understand things a lot better."

### Assimilative Thinking

Gemma, the instructor who had been in Cambodia the longest at almost 3 years, commented that she measured her adjustment to her foreign experience based on her response to traffic. She realized that she was adjusting when she did not "even think twice when someone beeps at you when you're driving." Adjustment was also evidenced when Gemma began to think in the Khmer language. For example, she explained, "[W]hen someone asks you, 'What do you want to eat?' I was like, yeah, sometimes I think of something in Khmer [that] I couldn't even translate into English."

## Challenges to Cultural Adjustment

The faculty members mentioned several deterrents to cultural adjustment, including their physical appearances, conflicting values, team culture, and lack of proximity to other Westerners.

### Physical Appearances

The international instructors in this study were Caucasian and indicated that their ethnicity and appearance contributed to their alienation in Cambodia.

## 44   *Alexander Jun, et al.*

For example, John observed, "I'm like a foot taller than everybody, and so I still get looks everywhere I go. I mean, so obviously [I] still feel like I'm being a total foreigner." Ted believed that his ethnicity drew attention. He explained:

> I feel like a huge foreigner . . . because even riding on my [motorbike] you know people whizzing by, and they're all dark-skinned and I'm like, yeah, I think I stick out here a little bit, my white skin. So every time I see a police officer, I'm thinking, this may be my guilty conscience, but I think they're going to target me because I'm white.

Katya also felt like a foreigner based on her skin color. She commented on cultural perceptions of whiteness:

> I will never totally blend in to Cambodia because of my skin color. Yeah, I feel like a foreigner every day. People are always commenting on my looks because I look so different from them. Like, oh, your skin is so white. Your nose is so long, you're so beautiful. So just that simple reminder that like I look so different than all of them basically.

Katharine indicated similar experiences related to national perceptions of beauty; however, her white skin also inspired her to make changes to her attire. She explained:

> As you notice, I'm wearing long leggings and a sweater, despite the fact that it's 90 degrees outside. I do that partially because . . . for whatever reason, I am very attractive in this culture. Like, I did not have this problem at all in America, and so a lot of boys, when they see me on the street, they're like . . . hello, beautiful lady. And if it's moto drivers or took-took drivers, they'll catcall me, [and say] hey, where are you going? Borderline harassing me. And so if I cover up most of my whiteness, the level of that tends to go down.

Maggie said candidly, "Yeah, I feel like a foreigner, well, I'm tall, I'm white and I'm blonde. So it doesn't matter what I do, I stick out like a sore thumb."

### Conflicting Values

The international professors encountered another challenge to their acculturation as they grappled with the educational values they observed in their students and their students' families. For example, Gemma indicated,

> I feel like, there definitely is not the value placed on education by parents in this country that there is in the U.S., especially students going to university. Their parents [in the United States] are expecting them to go to class, maybe they're not [going to class], but their parents expect them to. Here [in Cambodia], parents will call in the middle of the class and be like, come home, I need you. And so I've asked, is it an emergency,

## A Portrait of the Life and Work of Expatriate Educators 45

and they're like, I don't know. Well, does your mother understand that you have class? Oh yes, but she just wants me home.

Katya also commented,

[T]he view of education by a lot of Cambodians is really different. Like a lot of our students . . . don't really value education for its intrinsic worth. In other words, I want to learn more and be a more knowledge-able person. They want [a] certificate. So they will study at two schools because two certificates is (sic) better than one. They won't come to class because they don't need to come to class to get their certificate; they can just pay money and get it later. They don't need to come to English class, because they can come to the final exam, and they already know English, and they can pass it. . . . It's a different view of education.

### Team Culture

As part of the NGO, the international instructors worked within a profes-sional culture. Although Katya expressed her appreciation for her team-mates, she had to adjust to the team culture and other expatriate faculty members' perspectives. She explained,

[I]t was a little bit hard for me at first is when I got here; I was so enthusi-astic about Cambodia and learning about the culture and language, and when some teammates did not share that enthusiasm—and like for them, it's really hard to live here, and they didn't want to learn the language, or they'd complain about Cambodian culture. That was really hard for me because I was excited and I don't want people to make me feel unhappy about living here . . . before I came in, some people on the team [also] had interpersonal problems with each other, and nothing to do with me, but coming to a team like that. Yeah, so that was just an adjustment.

Maggie was also challenged by the adjustment to team dynamics. She said, "I felt like I was prepared to walk onto a team that was healthy and vibrant." However, Maggie "didn't have a healthy and vibrant team at the time." Interteam conflicts complicated Maggie's adjustment to life and work in Cambodia. However, by relying on her "experience with short term work and also cross-cultural dynamics with teamwork," she successfully "implement[ed] some of that short-term stuff that just made people think a little more and move forward in their conflicts." Not only did Maggie adjust to the team culture and thus ease her adjustment to international life and work; she was able to assist other members of the team as they navigated conflict and acculturation.

### Multiple Locations

Ted and John were two of the newest teachers working for the NGO and were the only international professors teaching at CISA. They were

## 46  Alexander Jun, et al.

challenged by communication dynamics that the instructors working at the CC campus did not face. The NGO's cooperation with the CC campus was well established, whereas their cooperation with the new CISA campus was relatively recent. Ted indicated that communication between the international professors on the two campuses was beginning to develop. He explained that leadership from the team working on the CC campus tried

> to give us insight into the culture. They have someone assigned to monitor our adaptation to the culture, so like taking the language lessons and [asking], "Are you getting out into the culture? . . . What are you doing to learn the language, what are you doing to acclimate yourself to the culture and what are your goals for the next six months?"

Although communication was improving between the international instructors on both campuses, it also appeared that adjustments were necessary to create a single team culture. For example, John indicated that there had been international professors at the CC campus

> for 12 years, and so there's a system there that's worked, [and] a lot of the kinks have been ironed out. Honestly, I feel like our leadership forgot some of those kinks from like when they first showed up here, and so it was like oh, why doesn't [the faculty members at the new campus] figure this out; why hasn't this happened yet? It's like, well, it's our first year, just building that relationship so . . . I think there's just a lot of miscommunication in general.

### Summary

Findings from multiple interviews with international professors produced rich descriptive themes and helped create a portrait of the life and work of international professors working in higher education in Cambodia. Themes related to preparation and adjustment included orientation provided by the NGO, personal efforts made by the faculty members, previous transnational experience, and degrees of pedagogical preparation ranging from formal teacher education to no formal preparation to teach. Elements and evidence of cultural adjustment included independence and routines, local language acquisition, relationships, and assimilative thinking. Challenges to cultural adjustment included physical appearances, conflicting values, team cultures, and working in multiple locations.


## DISCUSSION AND LESSONS LEARNED

Perhaps most striking in the data were the international professors' different degrees of adjustment stress and the relationship of that stress to the amount of time spent in countries outside of the North America. For individuals such as Katya and Maggie, life in Cambodia provided a relatively new experience; however, their years of living and working outside of North America helped them embrace cultural differences and minimize adjustment stress. This is insightful when one considers the varieties of cultural adjustment stresses noted in the literature (Crabtree & Sapp, 2004; Shin et al., 2007). Findings from this study suggest that expatriates can mitigate those stresses by having previous international experiences. While this may appear self-evident, it is important for educators and institutional leaders to consider incorporating cross-cultural immersion experiences as part of their pre-field preparation to help foster success for international instructors.

Professional preparation to teach also appeared to mitigate adjustment stress in this study. Newness to the teaching profession confounded some of the international professors' ability to discern cultural dissonance and added to adjustment stress. All but one instructor had only recently become a teacher, and those instructors were sometimes uncertain whether to attribute particular work-related challenges to the unfamiliar host culture or simply to the hazards of an unfamiliar profession. This finding suggests that international instructors may benefit from increased teaching experience and pedagogical education prior to departure. When that is not feasible, host or sending institutions may offer specialized professional development concurrent with instructors' terms of work.

The experiences documented in this study are reminiscent of challenges associated with the national service initiative, Teach for America, where training is intensive but brief and often inadequate for success. In situations where gaps in educators' personal and professional development are identified, sending organizations could collaborate with other organizations (e.g., teacher education institutions, cultural stress management institutions, and host country institutions) to understand instructors' needs and provide opportunities for continued professional development.

One theme present in the literature, but absent from our findings, was the confusion caused by culturally different communication styles and expectations in the workplace (Bodycott & Walker, 2000). The international faculty members in this study had a circumstance that is perhaps unusual in overseas teaching contexts: They were represented by an expatriate colleague who served as the ombudsperson for the university administration. Because of this arrangement, most of them had little direct interaction with the university administration. Furthermore, while they were eager to spend time with local colleagues, opportunities to do so were rare. Their local counterparts seldom had time to engage with the international professors, due in a large part to their part-time teaching responsibilities at other institutions. Many of the expatriate educators in our study felt somewhat isolated from the university, which may bear a resemblance to faculty life in North America.

## CONCLUSION

Several universities in Cambodia have embraced globalization by requiring English as a teaching medium, recruiting foreign faculty, and adopting Western pedagogies. Although these universities are not yet fully involved in global knowledge production, they are positioned at the heart of change in their country. These institutions often recruit faculty with advanced degrees and enroll only a small proportion of qualified high school graduates. International professors who teach in these universities wrestle with translating their life and work amid vibrant cultural and academic exchange.

International instructors should prepare both personally and professionally for cross-cultural adjustment. International professors in Cambodia may need to adapt their pedagogies and develop new levels of independence and routines. They may also encounter issues of language acquisition and discover how success in this area can enhance their new relationships and experience and how a lack of language acquisition can promote isolation. Providing support for instructors who live transnationally and teach in higher education may include helping them learn to manage challenges related to their physical appearance and negotiate conflicting values. In addition, those who teach as part of a team or in multiple locations may need to adjust to different institutional cultures and to the team culture. Understanding the experiences of instructors teaching in foreign universities can play a vital role as countries grapple with globalization in their higher education institutions and prepare global leaders in their various disciplines.

## REFERENCES

Altbach, P. G. (2004). Globalisation and the university: Myths and realities in an unequal world. *Tertiary Education and Management, 10*(1), 3–25.

Bodycott, P., & Walker, A. (2000). Teaching abroad: Lessons learned about inter-cultural understanding for teachers in higher education. *Teaching in Higher Education, 5*(1), 79–94. doi:10.1080/135625100114975

Burton, D., & Robinson, J. (1999). Cultural interference: Clashes of ideology and pedagogy in internationalizing education. *International Education, 28*(2), 5–30.

Crabtree, R. D., & Sapp, D. A. (2004). Your culture, my classroom, whose pedagogy? Negotiating effective teaching and learning in Brazil. *Journal of Studies in International Education, 8*(1), 105–132.

Fowler, M. R. (2005). Transplanting active learning abroad: Creating a stimulating negotiation pedagogy across cultural divides. *International Studies Perspectives, 6*(2), 155–173. doi:10.1111/j.1528-3577.2005.00200.x

Garson, B. (2005). Teaching abroad: A cross-cultural journey. *Journal of Education for Business, 80*(6), 322–326.

George, P. G. (1995). *College teaching abroad: A handbook of strategies for successful cross-cultural exchanges.* Boston, MA: Allyn and Bacon.

Getty, L. J. (2011). False assumptions: The challenges and politics of teaching in China. *Teaching in Higher Education, 16*(3), 347–352.

Herman, W. E., & Bailey, M. P. (1991). Recommendations for teaching overseas. *College Teaching, 39*(3), 117–121.

Kuh, G., & Hu, S. (2001). The effects of student-faculty interaction in the 1990s. *Review of Higher Education, 24*(3), 309–332.

Shin, S. J., Morgeson, F. P., & Campion, M. A. (2007). What you do depends on where you are: Understanding how domestic and expatriate work requirements depend upon cultural context. *Journal of International Business Studies, 38*(1), 64–83.

Walker, A., Bridges, E., & Chan, B. (1996). Wisdom gained, wisdom given: Instituting PBL in a Chinese culture. *Journal of Educational Administration, 34*(5), 12–31.

# 4 The "Unusual" Professors
## The Experiences and Impact of Foreign Professors in Post-Franco Spain

*Alice Gail Bier, Xavier Coller, and Louis Lemkow*

## INTRODUCTION

The challenges that foreign trained faculty have in a host country's classroom are embedded within a complex, layered environment of host country and personal cultures, academic expectations, politics, social change, entrenched systems, and personal grit. The authors of this chapter were members of the Universitat Autònoma de Barcelona (UAB) community in post-Francoist Spain. Two foreign-trained professors and a student who studied with foreign-trained professors present different but interrelated perspectives on the integration and impact of foreign-trained faculty. The three stories provide insights into the struggles that foreign professors experience in becoming part of the academy, as well as the enormous impact they can have on the learning environment and intellectual growth of their students. The experiences of the professors also illustrate how institutional structures and differences in academic training create barriers to the integration of foreign-born professors.

## THREE STORIES

### Story 1: A Politically Well-Informed Young European Confronts a Different Political Teaching Landscape—Louis Lemkow

*Background*
Born in Sweden, educated in the United Kingdom, and having spent more than 2 years as a lecturer at what today is the University of East London, I began my academic career in Catalonia at the UAB, a young and progressive institution, at a time of flourishing activism and grassroots social movements. The authoritarian structures and organizations under Franco were being challenged with generalized demands for change throughout society. There were calls for drastic reforms of university governance and the introduction of democratic decision making at all levels of academic life.

I was eager to learn about Catalan identity and language, topics very much on the agenda of UAB politics, yet initially, I had only a superficial

The *"Unusual"* Professors 51

knowledge of Catalan and the academic norms and rules of conduct of the Spanish and Catalan university.

### Becoming a Permanent Member of the Academic Community

Outside the language-teaching field, foreign-born and foreign-educated academic staff were virtually nonexistent in the Spanish/Catalan university system, and even in 2014 they are still an oddity. To become a permanent member of the academic community in the early 1980s at the UAB, obtaining Spanish nationality and degrees (or foreign degree validation) was obligatory. These were highly complex and immensely time-consuming processes. Despite my radicalism and dislike of such unfair rules, pragmatism won the day. I acquired a Spanish nationality through marriage and invested the time to earn the necessary Spanish university degrees.

### Academic Challenges

While I initially taught in English in the Escuela de Traductores (School of Translators), I soon began teaching sociology using the expected *lección magistral* (formal lecture) in Spanish to journalism students. The shared political interests and activity I had with my journalism students in the rapidly unfolding events of the democratic transition helped me to connect with them. Teaching in a foreign language felt like walking through a minefield. It was scary but—once negotiated—exhilarating.

Handling the obstacles in a foreign language that I did not command added to the perceived dangers. I frequently misinterpreted what the students meant as I did not know the cultural subtleties. There are no shortcuts or textbooks to explain the complexities and subtleties of the host culture and society. Even with the best attempts to integrate and assimilate the unwritten and fuzzy norms and to avoid cultural "faux pas," it was a constant strain and tension to maintain my professional and personal dignity.

My foreign presence in the classroom and teaching style exposed students to a new, refreshing way to learn and see the world. I was viewed as especially "exotic" with my Russian surname, French first name, and strong, and an unmistakable, English accent. This, in general, worked to my advantage, providing me with some kind of "sympathy" points and elevating my status amongst the students.

### Differences in Political Views and Academic Traditions

While relations with my academic colleagues were mostly cordial, there were clashes due to different academic traditions and very different political environments. The Spanish/Catalan grading system was very baffling to me. When I proposed external exam grading, my suggestion was seen as authoritarian and a threat to *libertad de cátedra* (academic freedom). Spanish/Catalan university faculty were responsible for setting their grading standards with no external control unlike the UK system of external examiners. Furthermore, prestige among Spanish/Catalan professors was largely

# 52    *Alice Gail Bier, Xavier Coller, and Louis Lemkow*

a function of the numbers of students they failed. In the United Kingdom, faculty with unusually high fail rates were singled out for inspection by the authorities, while high pass rates and grades were considered an indicator of teaching excellence.

In light of the preceding, I proposed that those who taught the same subject matter, mandated centrally, might also share assignments, readings, activities, and tests. The reaction of my colleagues was hostile, as such a measure was considered to infringe on their academic freedom. In making my proposal, I had not considered the long-standing and deeply ingrained concerns about external political interference by the central Spanish Ministry of Education and ideological impositions that were part of the Francoist past.

The political agenda in the Spanish and Catalan context were, of course, quite different from those to which I was accustomed. My political focus based on union organizing in the United Kingdom was a mismatch with the highly participative systems of governance promoted in the Catalan university. The participative system was a radical break with the past, during which appointments had been politically motivated and undemocratic, and university governance was very authoritarian and top down. The new university governing body implemented democratic elections in which students, administrative staff, and faculty could vote for practically all positions of authority, including the *rector* (president). Furthermore, students and non-academic staff would be highly represented in the university's governing bodies. The irrelevance of my past experience was disorienting and a blow to my self-esteem. Learning to change and participating in the developing political process was a very rich and rewarding learning experience. I learned to incorporate new ideas and ways of viewing the changing political and social environment.

## Story 2: A New Foreign Professor Enters the Classroom—Alice Gail Bier

### Background

I came to the UAB as a foreign-born and foreign-trained scholar with a PhD from a private Ivy League university in the United States. Before teaching at the UAB, I had spent four years carrying out field research in various parts of Spain. By the time I joined the UAB in the early 1980s, I was fluent in Spanish and had a basic working knowledge of Catalan. I had also learned the rhythms of rural and urban lives, the hopes that Spanish-speaking migrant laborers had for their children, and the cultural conflict represented by their geographic mobility to Catalan-speaking areas. The knowledge gained from the richness of my research experiences gave me the confidence to take on a university teaching position at a Catalan university. Yet, I found that there was much to learn about teaching at a foreign university, including how to survive its political and social dynamics.

### The First Days in the Classroom

It was a hot, sunny day in early October, my first day as a university professor. From the raised platform, I looked out over 250 students crammed into two columns of tables with attached seats stretching to the back of the room. The cacophony of students, barely visible through clouds of cigarette smoke, ricocheted off the cinderblock walls. This scene was not the organized classroom of expectant students I remembered from my undergraduate days. I stood on the elevated platform with no podium to hide behind or give me more presence feeling exposed and vulnerable. Impossible to get the rapt attention of the entire class, I settled for the attention of the students sitting in the front rows. I began speaking loudly. The cacophony eventually dimmed to a low hum. Emulating my former professors, I wrote my name and contact information on the blackboard, laid out the course objectives, presented the syllabus for the yearlong course, and reviewed the required readings, homework, quizzes, and tests. After answering a few questions from the bolder students, I dismissed the class with great relief.

The next day, I began the first of the twice-weekly 2.5-hour *lección magistral* (formal lecture) in Spanish. The lengthy lectures were laboriously prepared from a multitude of unfamiliar sources. Students in the front rows would assiduously copy verbatim the overly prepared and stilted presentation, while those far in the back became restless and distracted. The rising volume of classroom conversation forced me to stop lecturing and bring the class to order before continuing. As the first weeks wore on, I continued to be nervous but also became more comfortable and confident in lecturing to the 240 students.

It came as a big surprise, given the hours invested in preparing the lectures, when a student appeared in the office and informed me that the class was going to hold a group criticism of me. I was stunned. After the student left, my office colleague, who had spoken barely two words to me since my arrival, looked up from his work and said the only words he would speak to me the whole year: "Don't worry, it has happened to me; it has happened to all of us. Just go, listen, and then carry on as usual." These few words of empathy provided some calm to my bewilderment. Standing in front of large group of students and awaiting their criticism, I felt like one of the innocents facing the firing squad in Goya's painting, the *Executions of the Third of May* (http://www.artmuseums.com/goya.htm). The "bullets" of criticism came fast and furious: Why was I teaching in Spanish rather than in Catalan, the language that would better support Catalan nationalism? After all, Franco's dictatorship was over. Why was I, an American, not teaching the English-language class, and the Catalan-speaking English professor teaching our Sociology of Business and Industry course? Some students complained they could not hear my lectures; others complained that I spoke too fast and that they could not take proper dictation. Students in the back complained they could not see because of the cigarette smoke. Students argued with each other over my Spanish-language abilities. An older student belonging

## 54  *Alice Gail Bier, Xavier Coller, and Louis Lemkow*

to a leftist political party accused me of teaching from a capitalist rather than a Marxist socialist perspective. Another complained about having to be responsible for required reading and written assignments—that he did not have time for homework because of family and work responsibilities. More than one student indicated that it was the professor who should be the source of all information and knowledge that was to be tested, rather than required readings or projects.

### Mutual Learning of a New Academic Culture

While some of the complaints were easily addressed, others went to the core of differences in academic expectations of teaching and learning between my own and the host country's culture: Smoking would happen during a break, not in class. I would request a microphone. We agreed that when I spoke they would not and vice versa. I spoke more slowly and taught students how to outline lectures and readings and how to take notes. I introduced them to in-class small group activities where they were expected to apply the learned concept, not just memorize it. This, however, was a huge shift for the students and created a lot of anxiety before evaluation periods. Other issues were not so easily resolved, but I did not give up.

### Stereotypes, Change, and Opportunity as a Foreign Professor

As a foreigner, everything I did or said was given additional scrutiny and compared with the teaching standard students had previously experienced and of which I was unfamiliar. The mantles of "foreign" and "American" were laden with stereotypes drawn from imported movies and TV shows, images enhanced in the student's minds by news of unpopular U.S. foreign policies and editorials unfavorable to the United States. A common view of the United States was that of an imperialist enterprise with low moral standards, high divorce rates and drug usage, and low K–12 educational standards. At the same time, there was interest in U.S. culture, material objects, and the quality of U.S. graduate education that was accessible through scholarships and grants. Meanwhile, Spain and Catalonia were changing rapidly, opening to new ideas, participating in European student exchanges, and expanding Catalan culture and language. Excitement and expectation were in the air for a new Catalan future. Students were curious about the new and different and were excited about finding it through the few foreign professors in their classrooms.

As I became more known through structured small-group interactions, after-class encounters, and student visits during my office hours, I became less intimidating to the students and less intimidated by them when in the classroom. I began to know the students' their hopes and dreams, their insecurities and questions, their struggles and those of their families. My very differences—approachable, young, female, and American—encouraged students to educate and dialogue with me about highly charged political and personal topics that they would not broach with a Spanish/Catalan professor. Being *foreign* opened doors.

### A Clash of Traditions, Shifting Expectations

The more interactive nature of U.S. classrooms did not translate well to the large classes I was assigned. I was also unable to embrace wholeheartedly the *lección magistral* format, which I found not only difficult to prepare, but also enormously boring. After my first year of teaching "Spanish style," I looked for ways to create smaller working groups of students within the large classroom and to introduce in-class "experiments," debates, projects, and group assignments. Some of the activities worked better than others. Whereas American students are not shy about expressing an opinion—even an uninformed one—my UAB students were more interested in supporting a particular political line or social correctness. In addition, debating ideas was difficult. My students had a great need for approval by their *compañeros* (fellow students) and wanted to avoid the feeling of *verguenza* (public shame) by presenting an unpopular position.

Introducing small-group projects and activities within the massive classroom had an interesting effect on the students and me. The first challenge was to convince students that they, not just the professor, were responsible for their learning. I found that a mix of the large lecture format, with small-group in-class activities followed by problem solving worked well. This mix combined both the Spanish learning style with new elements I introduced and was supportive of student anxieties as to where this new teaching method would lead.

At times, my students would do things that would make me realize my underlying insecurity as a new teacher. For example, the week after teaching a unit on roles and norms, I entered the classroom to find the entire classroom of 240 students kneeling on their chairs and facing backward, away from the teaching podium. Even when I began my lecture, the students did not budge. I felt sheer panic as a fleeting thought passed through my mind that I had totally lost control of the class. My initial reaction quickly turned to jubilation when I realized that the students were consciously acting out a lesson on social norms that we had just completed the previous week. In unison they were purposefully breaking a social norm of classroom behavior to demonstrate that they had learned the material and were able to put it into practice.

Another change happened as I became increasingly comfortable in the Catalan classroom: I found greater enjoyment in teaching. As I was adapting to some of the expectations and characteristics of the students, they were incorporating new viewpoints and approaches into their own learning.

My determined changes to the *lección magistral* format, however, did have consequences. In a social science research methods course for journalism students, where the national standard was that all 240 students were required to do a research project, I formed research teams and guided them through the process of conceptualization, field research, and the final report. The first half of the yearlong course consisted of *lecciónes magistrales*, while the second half was a mixture of formal lectures, classroom work, and in-class research team guidance. Both the department chair and the dean of the school invited me to their offices for an explanation of why I was "not teaching" my course. While working to engage the students in more meaningful learning experiences, I had clearly overlooked the importance of maintaining the *lección magistral* and the significance of rejecting the established way of doing things.

### Matches and Mismatches of Academic Training with Host Institution Expectations

In an academic system that valued long-term loyalty in research groups and well-defined theoretical orientations, my interdisciplinary academic training and the way I approached issues were viewed with suspicion. Because I had not risen through the training grounds of the same institution, I had not been incorporated into the existing academic silos. I was a native English speaker (something highly coveted), fluent in Spanish, and I could understand and read Catalan but had not mastered it sufficiently to lecture in that language. I did not endear myself to some of my Catalan colleagues because I was not fluent in Catalan, nor did I embrace many of the Catalan political platforms. However, in the classroom, a potential linguistic conflict was diffused for all, but the most regional nationalistic students by my offer to students that they could speak or write in Catalan, Spanish, English, or French, but I would lecture in Spanish.

Several factors helped my integration into my academic department and gave me a modicum of academic standing with my colleagues. My ongoing physical presence and participation in university and departmental activities made it hard for my colleagues to ignore me. Also, my research on internal migration and grassroots political movements was of relevance to current events, and I was invited to give lectures at various public events that my colleagues organized. Thus, they had a vested interest in me because I was also a source of information on how to secure certain grants for U.S. research or teaching opportunities. I gained academic respect through publications and a book on grassroots neighborhood associations, a topic of great interest in understanding the political transition.

### Sacrifices and Gains

My collegial acceptance came from simply being more available and from teaching the largest classes in the least desirable locations, with flexibility in last-minute scheduling. My trials of being a new teacher lessened over the years as I gained experience and grew to enjoy and find pleasure in my work. My knowledge of Spanish and Catalan cultures grew, as did my place within it. However, obtaining a long-term position within the Spanish higher education structure was to be elusive, largely because of bureaucratic or legal challenges—not to mention the ingrained biases against the stereotypical American or foreigner who thought differently and whose very existence challenged the status quo. Many students, however, were open to new ways of learning, thus making the challenges of being a foreign professor worthwhile. The following is the story of one of those students.

## Story 3: The Student Experience: Reflections on "Unusual" Professors—Xavier Coller

### Background

I came from a working-class family in Barcelona. Scholarships made university study possible for me. Spain was then a relatively poor country fighting to modernize, democratize, and achieve a well-being comparable to its northern neighbors. My parents saw higher education as the way for their children to create a better life than they had. I knew university study would be an adventure but did not expect the opportunity to study with foreign professors at the UAB. This was a very unusual situation there and even more so at other Spanish universities in the early 1980s. Being exposed to these "unusual" professors would be a life-changing experience.

### The Unusual Professor Brings Different Ways of "Looking" Into the Classroom

For young students at the time, these unusual professors were practically the functional equivalent of what the Internet is today. Foreign-born professors and those educated abroad provided windows through which students could learn from international comparisons and, above all, from ideas developed in other countries. I had my first contact with new sociological theories (e.g., sociobiology) in those classes. I was exposed as well to explanations that were not commonly used in Spanish classrooms because they had yet to be integrated into Spanish sociological thought. Certainly, these unusual professors added to the collective effort of other professors and raised the learning bar for students. As a result, we can generate better explanations of social phenomena and get closer to the giants whose shoulders we climb to see better.[1]

The foreign professors with whom I studied also introduced different teaching styles that still influence me today. I have vivid memories of the class participation and interesting discussions that these foreign-educated professors tried to encourage. The professors challenged us, helping us to better formulate our own positions. It was a different style of learning: more interactive formats (far from the formal lecture we also had in classes), in which students were required to think critically. Years later, I realized that method was used in all the doctoral courses that I took at a U.S. university. It is also something I try to do today in my own university courses in Spain, sometimes successfully.

### The Unusual Professors' Dilemma of Adapting or Innovating

To a certain extent, the unusual professors were active agents of a kind of university isomorphism. New ideas and new ways to impart them marked a certain difference from other professors. Over the years, little by little, these differences might dissipate with some organizational learning and emulation; however, inducing changes and challenging organizational cultures usually has professional and personal costs. These costs may become negative incentives for innovation. This is, I believe, the dilemma of the unusual professors: adapt or innovate. Some of us, students of the early 1980s, were very lucky that the foreign professors chose to introduce innovations in the teaching style and relationships with Spanish students.

The unusual professors brought us closer to distant realities, and they were more approachable and accessible to students who wished to learn more. It was not unusual to eat with these professors in the university dining halls, while that activity was unusual to do with Spanish professors. I clearly remember discussions on current events (considerations that made us see things differently) and, above all, I remember the fixation on Freud's social writings by one of those professors (I must confess that I have, until recently, required my students read Freud's *Civilization and its Discontents*). I remember also the dry sandwiches that we ate while discussing Freud or general politics. It was not unusual for the foreign professors to invite some of the students to eat at their houses at the end of the school year. I remember the first of these dinners; there were 12 students. We went into a home full of books. There were no pictures and no television. All the walls were lined with books. We sat on the floor, on chairs, on an old sofa, and we ate roast beef. For a boy of 19 from a humble family who had never left his country, this was an extraordinary adventure into a completely unknown world. In my family's home, we had a five-volume encyclopedia and about 30 books. Rarely did we eat any place other than at the table, and roast beef would have seemed an extravagance to my parents (it was to me then). I think it was the first time that I realized that New York existed as a reality beyond that depicted in movies and novels. We talked and talked until midnight. I had similar experiences at other dinners with foreign-trained faculty. I learned two important lessons that I have tried to keep alive each semester with my own students: Knowledge should not generate distance between people—on the contrary, we must make it accessible in an attempt to better society—and to debate with students is an interesting exercise from which any professor can (and must) learn.

### Inspiring Students Through New Ways of Being

One of the many intriguing aspects of my experience with these unusual professors was their accessibility. Typically, professors in Spain were available only immediately before or after class. There was little opportunity for a student to intellectually engage with them. With the unusual professors, one could visit them in their offices and call them at home (never before or after did a Spanish/Catalan professor give out his or her phone number). One could even become friends with the foreign professors. Through interaction with the unusual professors, students were exposed to a more intense international and multicultural air. In the conversations, critiques, intellectual exchanges and recommended readings, I was inoculated with the curiosity virus Bourdieu (1984) called *libido sciendi*.[2] There is no cure for this lifetime virus; it was the best gift that the unusual professors gave me.

The "Unusual" Professors   59

Looking back, one realizes that there are certain events that are turning points in one's life. I had several associations with the unusual professors. One was the possibility of developing stronger personal relations with them. They encouraged me to study English and, when I was old enough, to study abroad. I was very lucky. Thanks to the mentoring of a British professor, I went to Warwick University in the mid-1990s to do research for my Spanish dissertation. There, I met academics whose friendship I still value today and from whom I learned to be pragmatic when doing research. Thanks to the insistence of another unusual professor, I was able to obtain scholarships that allowed me to study for a doctorate in the United States, at Yale University. This was one of my life's turning points. Without a doubt, I would not have been able to do that had I not met these professors in 1983. At Yale, I was socialized into the academic profession, developed my sociological imagination, sharpened my critical sociological eye, and was motivated to raise myself onto the shoulders of giants. To my advantage, some of the possibly disconcerting situations I experienced during my studies were already familiar to me, because I had previously been introduced to those situations by the unusual professors with whom I had studied in Catalonia.

## Collective Thoughts on Being Foreign: Lessons From and for Foreign Faculty

### On What Is Foreign

The preceding three stories on the challenges and exhilaration of being a foreign professor and their impact on students provide a rich and multi-layered view of what it means to be a foreign professor, and the challenges and triumphs that can be achieved. Part of the complexity in understanding the interwoven histories lies in the perception of the meaning of *foreign*, who determines that meaning, and to what degree foreignness represents a challenge to existing assumptions. The foreign professor may view the host country's educational system as foreign, while the host academic community views the incoming professor as foreign. In time, as the foreign professor accommodates and adapts to expected academic behaviors, no matter how odd or illogical they may seem, he or she becomes less foreign to his or her colleagues and students.

### Isolation or Engagement of the Foreign Faculty

The life of a foreign professor, new to the institution and perhaps country, can be a lonely, anxious, and isolating experience. It can, however, also be exhilarating, intellectually fruitful, and tremendously rewarding in the role of both professor and researcher. The new foreign professor needs to cope with unfamiliar routines, with a lack of family and deep friendships, and with an unawareness of new professional expectations. He or she may be unable to access familiar academic resources or be aware of social and professional miscues. It is therefore no wonder that a foreign faculty feels tension and uncertainty.

60   *Alice Gail Bier, Xavier Coller, and Louis Lemkow*

Lemkow and Bier both talk about the exhilaration of teaching within the foreign environment and the thrill of reaching students. They also talk about the significant self-doubt felt initially when trying to understand and move within the administrative structure, build collegial friendships, and feel successful in the classroom. While dealing with all the hurdles a foreign professor faces, it is easy to forget the positive impact that person has on the people around him or her. As a student who received instruction and mentoring from the "unusual" professor, Coller talks about the excitement and wonder he felt. Lemkow and Bier had different strategies for overcoming many of the hurdles presented by teaching in a foreign environment. Bier and Lemkow's work and successes were not done in isolation but, rather, with the help of each other and from colleagues who, over time, got to know them and helped open opportunities.

In sum, all three authors over time created a community around them with varying interests and that included nonacademics, colleagues who had been abroad, colleagues with shared academic interests, and persons from different countries. It was also important to be present and available in the department, in the classroom, and at the university.

### Using Differences to Engage Students

The ability and importance of a foreign professor to bring new ideas and ways of thinking into the classroom cannot be understated, and should not be mired in the contemplation of, or barriers due to, "foreignness." Coller draws from his own student experiences to elucidate how foreign-trained faculty engaged and encouraged students in ways that were different from the tradition of Spanish academics who had not studied abroad. The foreign-trained faculty reached out to students beyond the classroom and engaged them in discussions over meals, in hallways, in the office, and at their homes. Foreign faculty at times tries to disguise their differences with their local colleagues, but it is often these very differences as Lemkow points out, which make them valuable to their students.

### Finding Foreign Faculty in the Strangest
### Places: Openness and Engagement

Teaching is primarily about one's students and helping them grow intellectually. Learning from foreign-born professors, however, can be puzzling, if not scary, because it can challenge the security of ingrained learning patterns. The strangeness and discomfort a student might feel in being taught by a foreign professor can come from a multitude of issues. These may include foreign accents, national origin, race, and idiosyncratic teaching methods. These factors can be compounded by the student's stereotypes. All three authors identified the importance for foreign faculty to participate in or create venues for discourse outside of the classroom (which help overcome stereotypes).

As a student, Coller found a new universe of learning when he accepted invitations from foreign faculty for dinner in their apartments where not just meals, but dialogue and dreams were shared. Lemkow and Coller both appreciated the role of social spaces (such as the cafeteria and snack bars) where, over a meal or a cup of coffee, conversations and the exchange of ideas took place among the foreign professor, students, academic colleagues, and administrators. These were the spaces for tabletop seminars and free-ranging discussions in which the foreign professor became more multidimensionally interesting. Individual students who were brave or curious enough to join in while eating an inexpensive "bocadillo de atun" (that dry sandwich to which Coller refers), offered a way for the foreign professor to gain insights into the students' lives. Few left the table without a slightly altered perspective.

Accessibility could also mean eating with students or attending campus events with them, or an open door during regular or expanded office hours. Openness, for Coller, meant the ability of the foreign professor to consider a student's idea or new ideas and ways of thinking, rather than to the thought traditions passed down from faculty to student without question.

The foreign professor brings, above all, a different academic culture, perhaps more international, more aligned with the spirit of the times—or perhaps more centered on what brings prestige to any academic institution: research. The professor brings to the host institution contacts and perhaps a good research network from which other local colleagues can benefit if they wish. However, often, local culture and traditions are strong barriers for innovation and change. All three authors observed that when new initiatives are introduced, colleagues might not be receptive if the status quo or privileges of some groups are affected. The integration of the foreign professor sits on the shoulders of the academic community—colleagues, chairs, deans, administration, and the student body. The presence of the unusual professor is one that can enrich the learning environment and bring institutions in closer contact with the global academic community.

## NOTES

1. See Robert K. Merton, (1965), *On the Shoulders of Giants*, New York: Free Press.
2. Pierre Bourdieu, (1984), *Distinction. A Social Critique of the Judgment of Taste*, Cambridge (MA): Harvard University Press.

# 5 Conversations on Ethnicity, Adaptation, and Belonging
## Autoethnography at the Base of the Ivory Tower

*Marcia D. Nichols, Aminul Huq, Bijaya Aryal, and Xavier Prat-Resina*

> *Aminul: Whoever learns and educates himself will get to ride cars and horses.* (Bengali Proverb)
> *Marcia: Wisdom is the principal thing; therefore get wisdom: and with all thy getting, get understanding.* (Proverbs 4:7)
> *Bijaya: A king is worshiped in his country, but a knowledgeable person is worshiped everywhere.* (Sanskrit Proverb)
> *Xavier: A drop hollows out the stone by falling not twice, but many times; so too is a person made wise by reading not two, but many books.* (Giordano Bruno, *Il Candelaio*)

Shakespeare's assertion that "we know what we are, not what we may be," may apply to anyone starting out on a new career path; however, it is especially salient for foreign-born professors—people outside the American mainstream culture—who seek to ascend the Ivory Tower. Although in many ways each is a stranger in a strange land, the authors, who work together within an interdisciplinary department at a midwestern state university and represent a wide range of disciplines (physics, chemistry, mathematics, and literature), share the same challenge of ethnic or outsider experience (Nepalese, Catalonian, Bangladeshi, and southern United States).

## INTRODUCING THE INTERLOCUTORS

When a person embarks on a new career, he or she often feels like a stranger in a strange land. This feeling is especially salient for outsiders to mainstream American culture who seek to become successful in American academe. It is in this connection that the Shakespearean quote looms large. For immigrant professors, self-identity is not a stable thing, but an ongoing, ever-developing process—one that emerges more through conversations within ourselves and with others in the societies in which we find ourselves.

We are colleagues in a close-knit, interdisciplinary department at a small, upper midwestern state university. Aminul Huq is originally from

Bangladesh. After finishing his undergraduate degree in mathematics from Bangladesh, he migrated to the United States to study, where received his PhD in combinatorics at a northeastern university before coming to his current institution. Bijaya Aryal is originally from Nepal. Before migrating to the United States as a student, he finished his master's degree in physics from Nepal. He received his PhD in physics from a midwestern university and taught at a different upper midwestern university before coming to his current institution. Xavier Prat-Resina is a Catalonian from Spain, where he received his PhD in chemistry. He completed a postdoctoral program at an upper midwestern university before coming to his current institution. Marcia Nichols is from a working-class, Appalachian U.S. background. She received her PhD in literature at a southeastern university and held a fellowship at a northeastern university before coming to her current institution.

Although in many ways we are each a stranger in a strange land, our shared belief in the power and value of education connects us across cultural boundaries. The opening quotations that we each shared from our home cultures claim great things for those who seek wisdom and knowledge. As academics, we each pursue different avenues of knowledge, delighting in the journey as much as in whatever the destination might be. As educators, we hope to inspire others by sharing our experiences.

In this chapter, we explore questions of identity and immigration with an autoethnographic lens to analyze a series of conversations about the experience of being foreign-born academics at a U.S. university. Whereas these conversations explore the different authors' experiences, of greater interest are the unexpected similarities. By applying the theory of a dialogical self to our conversations, we demonstrate how the commonalities of our experiences can bring together the foreign born and native born—as professors and as students—as we pursue our educational and professional paths. Because molecular ensembles are made up of individual molecules whose individual properties affect the properties of the ensemble as a whole, we believe that a microscopic study of individuals such as this one may result in a macroscopic pattern of immigration in general. First, we lay out our theoretical framework and our methodology before turning to how that methodology helps us understand the self-identifications of the immigrant professor and how he or she navigates through the inevitable culture clashes. Finally, we turn to how these clashes and the ongoing narrative of self affects the ways in which immigrant professors interact with students.

## METHODOLOGY

We have chosen to engage in a collective autoethnographic inquiry because we believe that it is the best method to highlight both the differences and the similarities of the formation of an immigrant identity within academia (Chang, 2008). Moreover, we think that the inclusion of the voice and

## 64   Marcia D. Nichols, et al.

experience of an American-born colleague who, like many Americans, has moved from her region of birth to a culturally distinct region highlights the common human experience of culture shock and feeling "immigrant-like" in one's own land. We recognize that one of the drawbacks of autoethnography is a lack of critical distance from the subject (Chang, 2008); nevertheless, we believe that our joint effort goes far in mitigating this gap. Besides, careful use of theories of self-identity also helps us to take a critical stance toward our conversations and our own experiences. Thus, we employ two basic, but interrelated, approaches to self-identity: dialogical self theory and the concept of a nostalgia-infused narrative self to illustrate and buttress our points.

## Dialogical Self Theory

Dialogical self theory attempts to navigate the thorny terrain of self-and-other and self-and-society by arguing for a decentered notion of the self made up of various, interacting I-positions. The *I*, or self, may own or disown these various positions, and that ownership or recognition is not stable nor constant. As Hermans and Gieser (2012, p. 2), explain, "the dialogical self can be conceived of as a *dynamic multiplicity of I-positions* . . . [which] fluctuates among different and even opposed positions (both within the self and between self and perceived or imagined others)." It is through the negotiation of these various internalized positions or "voices" that a sense of self emerges. Through these interactions and conflicts the "self" emerges as appropriating and owning some positions while disowning others. Thus, the self becomes a *narrative* one through the internalized voices others and Others—that is, both other people and those figures identified with socio-cultural alterity. In other words, the act of recounting one's life is the act of creating one's self identity, not merely comparing oneself externally to others. Narrative also allows for the active and continuous incorporation of alterity into oneself. As such, memories become a crucial nexus of identity. As one remembers, one creates actual others into internal "characters" (Hermans & Gieser, 2012, p. 2) that can function as different positions within the self (typically labeled by theorists as I-positions, third positions, meta-positions, or promoter positions) whose dynamic engagement results in a sense of coherent self-identity or *I* for the rememberer.

For every person, but perhaps more poignantly for the immigrant, memory is always tinged with a sense of loss. We term this sense of loss for the irrecoverable, *nostalgia*. Ritivoi, (2002, p. 29) defines nostalgia as "a reflexive stance, a vantage point from which we make sense of our experience and identity" through "comparisons between the past and the present." For the immigrant, nostalgia—this sense of loss—is heightened. The homeland is forever in the past—for even if one returns home, one does not return unchanged. Drawing an analogy from physics, where wave function is space and time dependent, a personal identity is also time and space dependent. Identity stretches across one's own life span, as well as forward and back

## Conversations on Ethnicity, Adaptation, and Belonging    65

into generational time. It also stretches across geographic space, as one both travels and meets people from various parts of the world. Thus, a person evolves within time and space. A person who migrates with extended family has to deal with their personal transformations and the transformations of their immediate families. At the same time, their extended families serve as a constant reminder of the lost homeland, even as the immediate family metamorphizes as it adapts to the new environment.

## Interlocuting Self-Identification

> *Aminul: Coming here forced me to learn more about my culture and religion. It made me identify more with them, so that I can actually talk to people and not sound like I don't know what I'm talking about. Back in my home country, you never encounter questions like, "So why do you pray five times a day?" Everybody knows why they pray. But, that doesn't also mean that everybody learns the reason behind why you pray five times a day. So, that type of question and other questions like that—not only about religion, but also about culture, Bangladeshi culture—I faced here. For example, a lot of would people ask me, "Are you an Indian?" and even after saying, "Oh no, I'm from Bangladesh," they would think that Bangladesh is part of India.*

An immigrant professor often develops extra personal identities that did not exist before moving to a foreign country, and nostalgia acts as a repository of their previous experiences, achievements, and even a sense of belonging—especially when confronted with their different identities. As such, the past acts as a powerful self-reinforcing tool. Ritivoi (2002, p. 30) suggests that "nostalgia [acts] as a psychological filter employed in establishing and maintaining a sense of personal identity." Aminul's quote (in italics) fondly recalls a cultural homogeneity that permitted him not to have to think about his religious practices. Coming to the United States resulted in the loss of that comfort and belonging. However, as he pointed out, it also resulted in greater ownership of his home culture. Dialogue with Americans caused Aminul to seek out information to defend or explain his beliefs and practices. According to dialogical self theory, this process would result in the internalization of the viewpoint of the Other. In seeking reconciliation between these conflicting positions, a third position emerged, in which "the original position is lessened and mitigated" (Hermans & Gieser, 2012, p. 15). Indeed, one sees this in Aminul's experience. In the interlocutors' conversation, he stated thus:

> me having two different identities, one being a Muslim, and also Bangladeshi. . . . , when you come here, and you encounter those

66  *Marcia D. Nichols, et al.*

questions, you have to defend two different identities. And I guess at some point, one of the identities (for me at least) prevailed [over] the other one—[which is] being a Muslim, as opposed to being a Bangladeshi.

Thus, before immigrating, Aminul's different identities as a Muslim and as a Bangladeshi were never in question or had defined boundaries, but because he was a migrant in the United States, his identity as a Muslim became of greater significance.

Nostalgia is also "a type of autobiographical memory" (Ritivoi, 2002, p. 30) that is crucial in the formation and maintenance of personal identity for foreign-born professors. As individuals work to discover meaning in their lives—to understand themselves better by making comparisons between the past and the present—they integrate experiences into a larger schema of meaning: with respect to nationality, culture, religion, and family values. For example, Bijaya also asserted that his traditional and cultural identity as a Nepali has been solidified after migrating, because of a new realization its importance now, more than ever. He explained that as a parent and as professor, he finds himself constantly comparing how he enacted those roles in Nepal versus the U.S. At the same time, however, he feels that this identity has been hybridized. (Babad, Max, & Benne, 1983; Surgan & Abbey, 2012).

Xavier's comments, on the other hand, suggest that his approach has been more of one of "restorative nostalgia [which] taps into nationalism and/or political conservatism" (Ritivoi, 2002, p. 32). He described how he felt the urge to build and preserve his identity as a Catalonian, by, for example, treasuring Catalan books, poetry, and songs, which before he had taken for granted. He also recounted an additional adopted identity—the "role of being the caricature of the lazy Spaniard"—as a form of subversive resistance to American preconceptions about his ethnicity (Babad et al., 1983; Ritivoi, 2002). Because that seemed to be a stereotype that he encountered within the United States, Xavier incorporated and embodied this stereotype as an ironic posture toward this negative expectation.

The final interlocutor, Marcia, appears to have taken more of an assimilationist approach (Bhatia, 2011), when she spoke about code-switching to evade stereotyping, "because a southern accent is very stigmatized in academia." For each of these individuals, relocating to a new geographic and cultural region resulted in a readjustment of their self-identifications. Although each followed a different strategy in reconciling the home culture with their new situations, they all experienced a sense of nostalgia for a simpler time in which their identities seemed less problematic. This nostalgia-tinged, self-narrative-creation seems to precipitate third positions in their developing senses of self.

## Culture Clashes

> *Bijaya: [O]ne of my peers in a class (actually I didn't know him person-*
> *ally, because it was just my first week) ... said, "Howdy." And*
> *I said "What?" and he said, "How're you doing?" So there*
> *are two things: one, English slang, and second, culture ...*
> *First of all, I didn't know what "howdy" meant. And even*
> *if I had known that it means "how're you doing?" even*
> *then, because I didn't know him personally ... and that*
> *was maybe the first time I saw him. ... And he said howdy*
> *just to say hello or hi, but in our culture, if you don't know*
> *people personally, then they don't even say hello.*

Immigrants inevitably undergo cultural clashes in their everyday and professional lives. Shock, confusion, and simple misunderstandings inevitably
arise as the newcomer attempts to navigate a new cultural terrain. As such,
culture shock is an important concept for understanding the psychological reactions if immigrants (Ritivoi, 2002). Cultural clashes originate from
exposure to sociocultural norms that are different from how one traditionally interacts with family, colleagues, and students. Thus, immigrants
constantly reminded that they have to evolve both with the times but also
geographically. On one hand, these cultural shocks can trigger nostalgic
responses such as those discussed earlier; on the other, the immigrant must
react and adjust to these occurrences on a daily basis.

In Bijaya's italicized quote stated earlier, he experienced culture shock
when a peer accosted him in idiomatic English. The friendly chattiness of
the American took him aback because he did not understand the purpose
of his peer's greeting. Additionally, the idiom itself seemed almost esoteric.
Although fluent in his second language, Bijaya had not been exposed to a
midwestern regional dialect before entering his graduate program. Thus,
he was challenged with entering a doctoral program while immersed in an
unfamiliar linguistic and social reality. Although familiarity quickly taught
him how to navigate that new terrain, he still vividly remembers that first
friendly clash.

Learning American English, in all its variants, is one of the biggest challenges faced by immigrant professors. Many immigrants are taught British
English (Hutchison, Butler, & Fuller, 2005). Not only is American English
different from the English these immigrants learned, American English is
often regionally marked by dialect and marked by slang that often changes
by the generation. It can be marked by various professional jargons and
can reveal a person's class, race, or ethnicity. As with many languages, its
tone, inflection, and volume can carry meanings that often escape nonnative
speakers. Such variations can cause untold difficulties as nonnative speakers
attempt to use it to navigate social and professional terrains.

68  *Marcia D. Nichols, et al.*

Cultural classes are inevitable, and unfortunately, not all have such humorous outcomes as Bijaya's. For example, during our interlocutors' discussions, both Aminul and Xavier spoke about being criticized for being "too loud." Both spoke of times when their loudness was taken to be offensive or rude by Americans, both inside and out of the classroom. However, Xavier staked this locus of misunderstanding as a point of resistance to the over-culture, proudly declaring, "I am generally loud and direct." He resisted becoming acculturated into midwestern indirectness that is considered polite and mannerly in his adopted region. Instead, by tapping into a restorative nostalgia, his original sense of self becomes entrenched. Aminul, on the other hand, reflected on his past to find the reason(s) why he is perceived loud in this culture as compared to his own and adjust his behavior. He realized that he was born and raised in one the of the densest cities in the world, where one must be loud to be heard over the noise of honking cars, yelling rickshaw pullers, day traders, and so on. For him, the issue of being loud is not to be taken personally, but a cultural practice that derives in part from a long history of illiteracy and political unrest. People, especially politicians, think that if they are not loud they will not be taken seriously, and protests must be done with violent confrontation and loud speech; this then tends to bleed over into everyday interactions. Another factor is that most classes have 100 or more students, and the teacher needs to deliver his lecture without any microphone. So how can you be a good teacher or leader without being loud?

## THE IMMIGRANT PERSONALITY IN THE CROSS-CULTURAL CLASSROOM

### Communication styles and the use of Standard American English

Adapting to idiomatic American English is a crucial factor for success as an immigrant professor. Often, that means recognizing and adapting one's natal verbal cues. Bijaya agreed with Aminul about classroom demeanor; he asserted that in his culture, being soft-spoken in class instruction is usually regarded as lazy or informal. In fact, teachers are expected to have loud and commanding voices; those who do not are suspected of being unable to control students and keep them attentive in lecture. However, during regular conversations outside the classroom, being loud generally is not received positively. Thus, Bijaya's adjustment was similar but different from Aminul's. For Marcia, while her experiences with culture clash have been less pronounced, she, too, has found adjusting to the indirectness of midwestern discourse difficult. Like Xavier, she has tended toward resistance, hanging onto the directness and humor of her home culture, using the persona of a "Southerner" to elicit acceptance of her difference by students and colleagues alike.

We have chosen to focus on linguistic challenges because of its potential to complicate other areas of life. For example, Schmid points out that "speaking

## Conversations on Ethnicity, Adaptation, and Belonging    69

accentless English has been identified as an essential component of loyalty to the nation and American identity" (2001, p. 172). Because Americans tend to make idiomatic English a metonym for patriotism and shared culture, speaking in accented English marks a person as a cultural Other.

Three of the interlocutors are nonnative speakers, and the fourth grew up speaking a heavily accented, idiomatic dialect. Thus, the linguistic challenges each has faced, from understanding idioms to managing voice tone and level, have caused each to question the way language has formed a part of their self-identities and how they convey those identities to others. The challenge of acting out the intonations and idiomatic speaking of English like a native speaker is crucial because speaking English often serves as a proxy for other sources of cultural conflict such as race or class (Schmid, 2001). Speaking accented English in a society in which some elements of mainstream media often preach fear of (non-White) foreigners and immigrants, political gaffes frequently involving racist remarks, and anti-Muslim or anti-Latino memes that get traded via social media and e-mail often marks immigrants as potentially dangerous Others. For the foreign-born professors in this study, navigating this environment has forced them to define their personal identity faster than they would have preferred. For such reasons, foreign-born professors often seek bridges between their native and new cultures to identify the common platform of discussion or acceptable behaviors.

Because speaking English properly is seen as necessary to escape suspicion and to be accepted into mainstream American society, these linguistic challenges are formative in the lives of immigrant professors as they navigate culture and academia alike. Their linguistic choices and language fluency will influence the ways that their administrators and colleagues perceive and interact with them. More important, however, is the way that language comes into play in the classroom as immigrant professors struggle to connect with and instruct native-born speakers.

### Interacting With Students

> *Aminul: Back home, our teachers would say, "Well, this was a stupid thing to do, you know." "You are stupid." And we wouldn't care. [Bijaya chuckles]*
>
> *Xavier: [interrupting] But would the students tell you, "Uh, you made a mistake on the whiteboard . . . [Bijaya interrupting: They do.] Are you stupid?"*
>
> *Aminul: No. no. . . . So, we can point out the mistake, but usually people, uh, don't do it right away, or something like that. But, from the teacher's point of view, if you are doing something wrong, they're not only blunt, they may also call you, like you know, "Why are you doing it like you're stupid?" But we wouldn't as students.*

70   *Marcia D. Nichols, et al.*

> *Xavier: You wouldn't reply back.*
> *Aminul: No, no; we wouldn't reply. Or, we wouldn't even take that personally.*

### Communication Challenges

A huge challenge for immigrant professors has to do with communicating with students (Hutchison, 2006; Hutchison, Butler, & Fuller, 2005). Students frequently complain about accents, intonations, or idiomatic language, seemingly failing to consider the foreign-born professor's position of teaching in a foreign language. For example, Aminul described how, on his student evaluations from his first semester of teaching at a U.S. university, he received comments like "He cannot speak English" and "I don't understand what he says." He was baffled and more so after the course coordinator assured him that he spoke as good as an American. The next day he casually mentioned the comments to a number of fellow American colleagues, one of whom he knew received the teaching award the year before. To his surprise they all told him, "Relax; I received that comment too. Just ignore it." Students found unfamiliar regional American dialects as confusing as his foreign one! These inexperienced American students were uncomfortable being faced with Others in the forms of their professors. They, too, were facing the cultural clash of entering a new environment with new social rules. Much like their mathematics professor Aminul, they were learning how to communicate in a new idiom. To move forward, both professor and student must see things from each other's perspectives. (Ritivoi, 2002).

Aminul's confusion also stemmed from the experience of receiving student evaluations, which is not a practice in Bangladeshi institutions. Institutional practices in U.S. schools vary greatly from those in other nations. In the earlier conversational excerpt, Aminul and Xavier discussed the clash of expectations Aminul faced when beginning to work in a U.S. institution. Aminul had been used to a directness from professors in Bangladesh that would be perceived as rude and belittling by American students. For Aminul, telling a student that some mistake was "stupid" was merely an educative and supporting gesture, whereas American-born students found such comments insulting and offensive. He had to learn to adjust his manner of feedback to avoid negative student evaluations or, as Marcia put it, to avoid having them "call their mom, and their mom's gonna call your boss."

For Xavier, this top-down approach was equally baffling. His home culture had fostered a "more open" and "very relaxed environment" where students would both take and give constructive criticism. Possibly because of historical reasons, such as trying to break from a previously very rigid and stratified society, Spanish education eliminated most formalities between professors and students at all levels. Xavier was used to openly interacting with students with the common understanding that if he was being direct with students, they could also be direct with him. This was not the case in his current U.S. institution: students insisted on addressing

## Conversations on Ethnicity, Adaptation, and Belonging 71

him as "Dr. Last-Name," and his directness would come off as somewhat aggressive.

Communication with students can also be stymied because of different conceptions of two key components of academia: the concepts of success and time. For many American students, success seems to be defined by the grade earned in a course rather than the knowledge gained, whereas for some of the interlocutors, this was a counterintuitive definition of success. Xavier argued that

> it's such a narrow definition of what being successful is . . . even with my kid . . . he has to meet the standards right away. There is a normalcy that he needs to follow; otherwise, it seems that there is [or he has] a disorder—[that] there is something wrong happening . . . I find that very, kind of, counterproductive.

For Xavier, success should be more about the journey and less about the end results. He observed that he often finds himself "going against this discourse, and I talk about it in class, but also outside" in an attempt to convince students to change their notion of success—including advising them to take or continue taking a course that the student has no chance of receiving an A (or even a passing grade). His insistence that the experience is worth more than the final grade often baffles students and student development staff alike. While all the interlocutors agreed that learning for learning's sake was worthwhile, the end result, at least in the form of a money-earning job, mattered more for some of them. Both Aminul and Marcia argued that success needed to include the ability to earn enough money to live comfortably or, at least, as Aminul put it, "to keep from dying from shame."

### Communication, Timeliness and Its Implications

Timeliness is often also a source of conflict between the interlocutors and their students. This again related to what some of the interlocutors saw as an overemphasis on technicalities rather than on the task of learning. For example, Bijaya found students' focus on deadlines confusing and strange:

> So when I go to class, as a teacher, I find the students' expectations different from what I would do, back in Nepal. [H]ere the students are given some structure, and they want to follow them . . . for example, if they are given some deadlines. Deadlines are very important here . . . so they are more task-oriented and more schedule-oriented. Like, "I have to do this, this, [and] this," And "Give me the instructions; I have to follow those." So, sometimes if we are not so flexible in that area, that could be problematic. . . . So I used to misunderstand what that means, because my focus was on the teaching, and not on the technical aspects: Only about learning, not the technical aspects, like these scheduling things; like when is the deadline? When is the due date? [Those] kinds

# 72 *Marcia D. Nichols, et al.*

of things are very, very important here. Because my expectation and their expectation were different, that is why sometimes it was difficult to communicate also.

Marcia suggested that this may have to do with a different conception of timeliness—that for most Americans, a strict clockwork-like schedule was the cultural norm. Classes start and end at precise times, as does work for most adults; television shows follow suit, along with businesses, radio shows, and even traffic lights. A focus on such details becomes ingrained as necessary for success—for earning the A or the paycheck. These conflicting concepts of time can put the foreign-born professor at confused odds with his or her native-born students. In fact, such conflicts can complicate methods of assessment, because assessment methods seem so commonsensical or ubiquitous that it is easy to forget how culturally inflected they are (Hutchison & Bailey, 2006). The immigrant professor must learn to adjust to American temporal regularity or face being labeled as unproductive or inefficient by colleagues and as pushovers or disorganized by students.

### Building Bridges With Students

Notwithstanding the preceding points, daily interactions with students compose some of the first bridges to immigrant professors' current and past life experiences. Both Aminul and Xavier mentioned that this bridge can be built from two different viewpoints: by communicating on a personal level with students through common interests and by setting up a relaxed environment that will promote open and honest conversations between students and the professor. To do the first, as Bijaya pointed out, requires learning about local sports, music, movies, and other popular cultural references. Even one's go-to metaphors often need to be revised. He explained that

> some of the metaphors I used in Nepal . . . are not effective here. I have to figure out [new] metaphors or analogies or things like that. Or Humor. When I first came here, the professor would say something and 70% of students would laugh, and I wouldn't get it. And when I understood, I still didn't think it was funny.

Fortunately, humor is cultural, and the longer one sojourns in the new land, the more common experiences and points of reference the immigrant professor comes to share with his students. For example, now Bijaya uses baseball as his go-to sports reference rather than the cricket he used in Nepal.

The second bridge—open and honest communication—requires foreign-born professors to be cognizant of the differences between their native university environment and that of the United States. When immigrants begin building this bridge, it helps to remember that its construction can be delayed because of differences in cultural expectations. This bridge requires an awareness of how one's preconceptions about Americans in general might undermine their perception of their current students' needs. For example, Aminul shared that the perception of everyone from his country is that the United States is a rich country; therefore, everyone is rich. Often, foreign-born professors' knowledge of cultural norm in the U.S. stems from the media—which do not necessarily convey or match social realities. For example, in Bangladesh, anyone who owns a car can be safely considered as rich or at least an upper middle class, whereas in the United States, virtually everyone can own a car if they so wish. Thus, the appearance of students being rich can make it challenging for immigrant professors to identify students' financial and economic situations and support or advise them accordingly.

Immigrant professors often come to the United States with existing narratives that clash with what they learn about and experience. For Aminul, talking with Marcia about the poverty she experienced in the rural South, such as living in a house without running water during her early childhood or the shame she experienced as an older child standing in line with her mother at the food bank of a local church, forcefully helped him understand the inaccuracies of media portrayals. While many people in the United States do live comfortable lives, too many others struggle to survive. Thus, a car is frequently less a symbol of wealth than a necessary and burdensome tool for survival. Learning to listen to students with credulity and empathy is something every professor, foreign born and native born alike, must do to lay the foundation for open communication.

In summary, if the student interactions described by the interlocutors in this section are viewed in terms of dialogical self theory, we would hypothesize that they have resulted in the formation of different I-positions. If these positions are like characters in a story (Hermans & Gieser 2012), then each of these interlocutors might develop promoter positions, such as the mentor professor from the culture of origin or the admired U.S. colleague. Moreover, other I-positions could develop, like that of the U.S. student rather than that of the student from the home culture. The dialogue among these various voices, along with the immigrant's cultural and religious I-positions, would then work to form the identity of the foreign-born professor. He or she would fluctuate between these different positions, depending on the social environment. In one interaction, the voices from the home culture might be stronger than the integrated voices from U.S. culture or vice versa. It is through the hybridization of, or resistance to, these positions that the self-identity of the foreign-born professor emerges.

## LESSONS LEARNED

Developing a self-identity is an ongoing and lifelong process. For the immigrant, that process is chronicled by cultural clashes as he or she navigates the uncertain terrain. The immigrant is faced with both the potential loss

## 74 *Marcia D. Nichols, et al.*

of the home culture and the rejection by the new culture. For immigrants in general, these clashes and fears cause a nostalgic longing and respect and heightened value for the home culture. For the immigrant professor, such collisions bleed into the classroom setting. In the classroom, immigrant professors face daily cultural clashes, from interacting with students dressed in ways the student might consider indecent, to interpreting unfamiliar idioms, or handling student complaints of using alternative value systems.

For us, the interlocutors, these clashes have informed our classroom demeanor and behaviors. We have had to learn how to cope with adversarial students, with behaviors at odds with our religious mores, and with confusions occasioned by communication breakdowns. These notwithstanding, our conversations reveal that our struggles are not unique. Through conversations about our individual experiences, we are able to offer each other needed support, understanding, and encouragement. We form a new community that, while it can never replace those lost, can supplement and enrich our private and professional lives. We may come from various parts of the world, but each of us holds as fundamental truths the opening proverbs from our home culture. These proverbs reaffirm each other. Each states a firm belief in the value and power of education. We come together as dedicated educators who want to instill these beliefs in our students. As we work on effectively communicating with and instructing our students, they, too, come to be sources of support, as they and we discover common ground and thrill in the discovery of *new* intellectual grounds. In the pursuit of *new* knowledge, all of us—foreign born and native born, student and professor—are truly strangers in a strange land.

## REFERENCES

Babad, E. Y., Max, B., & Benne, K. D. (1983). *The social self: Group influence on personal identity*. Beverly Hills: Sage.

Bhatia, S. (2011). Acculturation and the dialogical formation of immigrant identity: Race and culture in diaspora spaces. In H. J. M. Hermans & T. Gieser (Eds.), *Handbook of dialogical self theory* (pp. 115–131). Cambridge: Cambridge University Press.

Chang, H. (2008). *Autoethnography as method*. Walnut Creek, CA: Left Coast Press.

Hermans, H. J. M., & Gieser, T. (2012). Introductory chapter: History, main tenets and core concepts of dialogical self theory. In H. J. M. Hermans & T. Gieser (Eds.), *Handbook of dialogical self theory* (pp. 1–28). Cambridge: Cambridge University Press.

Hutchison, C. B. (2006). Cross-cultural issues arising for four science teachers during their international migration to teach in U.S. high schools. *School Science and Mathematics, 106*(2), 74–83.

Hutchison, C. B., & Bailey, L. (2006). Cross-cultural perceptions of assessment of international teachers in U.S. high schools. *Cultural Studies in Science Education, 1*(4), 657–680.

## Conversations on Ethnicity, Adaptation, and Belonging 75

Hutchison, C. B., Butler, M. B., & Fuller, S. (2005). Pedagogical communication issues arising for four expatriate science teachers in American schools. *Electronic Journal of Science Education*, 9(3). Retrieved from http://wolfweb.unr.edu/homepage/crowther/ejse/ejsev9n3.html

Ritivoi, A. D. (2002). *Yesterday's self: Nostalgia and the immigrant identity*. Lanham: Rowman & Littlefield Publishers.

Schmid, C. L. (2001). *The politics of language: Conflict, identity, and cultural pluralism in comparative perspective*. Oxford: Oxford University Press.

Surgan, S., & Abbey, E. (2012). Identity construction among transnational migrants: A dialogical analysis of the interplay between personal, social and societal levels. In H. J. M. Hermans & T. Gieser (Eds.), *Handbook of dialogical self theory* (pp. 151–168). Cambridge: Cambridge University Press.

# 6 Voices From Behind the Scenes
## How Foreign-Born English Teachers Find Their Place in the French Education System

*Claire Griffin*

## INTRODUCTION

Since the early 1990s, European citizens have been allowed to sit the competitive examinations that provide access to qualified teacher status within the French education system. This change has attracted British and Irish candidates who were not born or socialized in France. Sometimes, it takes them years to decode the system. These teachers discover that their professional integration depends on their capacity to adjust not only to the requirements of French schools but also to the French approach to teaching and learning English. Foreign-born teachers bring with them a set of internalized rules, norms, and values that have a national dimension (Schnapper, 1992). So how do they negotiate the journey toward being a "teacher-citizen" (Tardieu, 1999) in a different school context? How do they achieve positive, professional integration within the French education system where teaching is part of a historical, political and sociocultural process that they themselves never experienced from the inside, either as children or teenagers? How do they cope with being stereotyped by others in the workplace, and what role do stereotypes play in the professional integration of foreign-born teachers? What lessons can we learn from the real-life stories of foreign-born teachers?

## METHOD

The quotes used in this chapter are drawn from a series of interviews of foreign-born English teachers who participated in the author's doctoral inquiry into the professional identity of native English-speaking teachers (NESTs) from the UK and Ireland who teach (or have taught) in French secondary schools (Griffin, 2012). The research project was designed from a grounded theory (Charmaz, 2006; Corbin & Strauss, 2008; Glaser & Strauss, 1967) and an interpretative perspective (Kaufmann, 2007) using mixed methods. Interviews were analyzed using the Australian qualitative data analysis software NVivo. The researcher interviewed 24 foreign-born language teachers, 21 of whom were native English speakers from the United Kingdom and Ireland and 3 of whom were native speakers of other European languages (Italian, Greek, and German).

## The Obscure Art of Labeling: A Permanent Challenge for Foreign-Born Teachers

One of the most baffling aspects of education systems worldwide must surely be the ever-changing, ever-more-complex set of acronyms originally designed to simplify the way we navigate through the mazelike reality of state-organized learning and teaching. Foreign-born teachers who enter the maze as adults just do not possess the stock of knowledge that their French coworkers gleaned as students, making deduction and inference more difficult for them. The obscure codes are there as a permanent reminder of their inescapable difference: Even as they learn to crack them, they discover to their dismay that old codes are no longer in currency, having been usurped by those of a new political cycle. The same applies to technical, didactic, or administrative jargon, which Anita, a NEST, finds particularly tedious at times:

> **AN76:** *they use a lot of jargon which I didn't necessarily understand, so I had to really concentrate and sometimes I thought "Oh, you're so stupid, Anita. What are they talking about?" but because they're using, they liked, especially in the IUFM [teacher training university institute] to use very didactic vocabulary which I had to learn off by heart which I never used again afterwards [laughs], stilted language, um, even today when I get some papers put into my locker-hole\* sometimes I have difficulty understanding it because of the wording, stilted language.*

This teacher's initial reaction is to feel inadequate, but little by little, she devises an adaptive strategy (Manço, 2002) which enables her to cope with the feeling of alienation triggered by the technical language of official circulars and administrative orders or memoranda:

> **CG77:** *What do you do to understand it? Do you just put it to one side or do you ask someone to help you decode it?*
> **AN77:** *I usually put it to one side.*
> **CG78:** *You do?*
> **AN78:** *Yes.*
> **CG79:** *Um, in the first few years, did you have the same reaction?*
> **AN79:** *No, I asked questions the first few years. Now I sort of prioritize things, well I was reading a paper yesterday and it won't affect my pupils or my personal situation, it's all to do with the uh, management of private schools in the region,*

78   *Claire Griffin*

> so nothing really I could say would change much anyway so
> I just put it to one side.

**CG80:** So you're kind of resigned to the fact that some aspects of
school life are a bit hermetic to you because of the language
barrier at a certain level?

**AN80:** Yes. Managerial level, definitely.

Anita realizes that her avoidance strategy is not ideal, but she acknowledges the fact that such a compromise is necessary if she is to maintain a balance in her work. Although Anita would like to understand everything, she admits that she cannot: "It's not true" (**AN86**). A simple adaptive strategy facilitates self-preservation (*conservation de soi*), (Camilleri, Kastersztein, & Lipiansky, 1990) and has prevented Anita from reaching a crisis point in her professional identity as a teacher.

The temporary opaqueness of a "host" education system leads inevitably to the impression, every so often, that the foreign-born teacher is an "outsider." Jason, a young NEST in his 20s, implies in his interview that he has come through this period of strangeness and that it is now more or less behind him: "*Um, because I—it was completely new for me, I did feel a bit, you know, a stranger or a foreigner to that.*" The deictic *that* refers implicitly to the absent noun group "French schools."

It takes a long time for a novice to adapt to a new profession, and the process is a nonlinear one involving the whole person (Lave & Wenger, 1991). If the concept of *legitimate peripheral participation* (Lave & Wenger, 1991, p. 49) can be positive in that it implies a dynamic movement toward increased participation, it can nevertheless refer to a certain feeling of helplessness or powerlessness. Close analysis of the data points to a pattern of different forms of peripheral participation. Indeed, some participants are fully aware of being at the periphery of things, using the term "periphery" itself or semantically similar ones such as "edge." Susan, a British NEST from Scotland, reflecting on the cultural content of English lessons, asserts that "*you're always on the edge even when you're joining in . . .*" (SU136). NESTs always have an offbeat take on things, being somewhat out of step with their French coworkers. However, their standpoint is also likely to differ from that of a British or Irish national who has never emigrated.

Clara, an Irish-born NEST in her late 60s, was always on the edge in her professional life. She explains that she held this peripheral position because she failed to understand the intricacies of the French education system. Clara's case is an extreme example of how some foreign-born teachers fulfill their daily teaching tasks without having a firm grasp of the local context or the larger-scale political issues that affect and determine educational policy and planning.

> **CG62:** So what was it like being a[n] NS inside the French system?
> When you started teaching and also throughout your career?

**CL62:** *I'm not sure what it was like because, um, even though I took my job very very seriously, I was extremely busy, I had a terribly busy life and **I did not worry really about all sorts of things that French people worried about simply because I didn't know what they were talking about.** I mean it took me years to cop on to this, um, you know you'd get this sheet of paper about your assiduité and your rayonnement de prof and I thought "What the hell is this?" but I had no idea. **The whole French system was something that was beyond me, in a way. I was on the periphery of it.***

Clara seems to have been well integrated as far as actual teaching and socializing with her coworkers were concerned, yet when it came to understanding the subtleties of the system, she was often at a loss. We may wonder if her resistance was not in fact a kind of protection against too much of what Jacques Demorgon (Demorgon & Lipiansky, 1999, p. 204) calls *interculturation*, which could potentially have led to the feeling that her original Irish identity had been dissolved in a life of Frenchness. Clara also rejects certain French attitudes she has witnessed in staff meetings or read in school reports (she often found teachers' comments too deprecating).

The negative implications of peripheral participation come through in the interview of Lucy, a British NEST in her mid-40s. Lucy makes a connection between the fact that she has never stood for election on the school board and the "jargon" she has habitually heard used in the workplace. She also criticizes her coworkers' loud attitude in meetings, which has often made her feel invisible and unheard:

**LU71:** *I've personally, **I've never got involved**—I was inspected last year and the inspectrice she asked me if I was involved in the* conseil d'administration, des choses comme ça—*I've never, **I've always avoided getting involved in things like that because of the jargon that goes on and because of the French set-up in that** . . .[stops and then continues] successful French meetings are full of various people that speak very loudly at the same time and I find it very difficult um, one, I find it very difficult when you're in that situation trying to get a word in edgeways, um, but also actually being heard I find, and I've got a colleague who's German—the German teacher, she's German as well—and she feels exactly the same as me, in that sometimes, **we do actually feel invisible.***

Here, Lucy tends to "other" her French coworkers and brings a German colleague into the discourse to corroborate what she is saying, with her use of the pronoun *we* having more clout than the pronoun *I*. Lucy is far from what Altay Manço (2002) calls "pragmatic detachment," a competency that often comes in useful to people from different sociocultural backgrounds.

80   *Claire Griffin*

Her testimony underscores the dangers of disempowerment and acculturation stress, which can develop into a phobia. In Lucy's case, she protects herself by not exposing herself to situations that could potentially reinforce her own sense of isolation. Peripheral participation, therefore, serves many purposes: It can be the result of deliberate positioning and help foreign-born teachers to strike a balance between the ongoing exigencies of adaptation and the need for self-preservation. However, if peripheral participation is the result of a professional *malaise*, it can deeply affect a teacher's professional identity, self-esteem, and sense of purpose.

## Stereotypes in the Workplace (1): Can Stereotypes Facilitate Integration? The Case of Adele.

One of the foreign-born teachers I interviewed in order to triangulate the primary data about NESTs working in France was Adele, a native Italian-speaking teacher in her 40s. Adele was practically the only foreign-born teacher to acknowledge the importance of what she called "my stereotype." Indeed, many of her nonnative coworkers (i.e., French-speaking teachers) thought that she was "joyful," always "in a good mood," and "loud" (see "I make a lot of noise" [AD29]):

> **AD28:** *When I arrive somewhere, it's always "Wow, Italy's so great, it's amazing, the Italian language is beautiful." So I'm lucky to speak a language and to come from a country whose culture French people really appreciate, even in troubled political times, but generally speaking, half of the work has already been done, and I do correspond completely to the stereotypes people have.*
> **CG29:** *Could you explain?*
> **AD29:** *Oh, yes. I'm joyful and good-humored, no, no, but I'm really aware of that! . . . When I walk into a staff room, people can hear me coming. I have been known to sing in the corridors, hum. So I correspond to the stereotypes people have about Italians.*

Adele cashes in on the way French people stereotype Italians and Italian culture and is fully aware that it works to her advantage. Yet the stereotype has its limits when it comes to her fellow Italian teachers, as illustrated by a brief anecdote from her recent professional life. During a meeting, Adele tuned into an interesting subtext that one of her coworkers was conveying to the other teachers at the meeting. Adele says she always tries to be frank about things including her understanding of certain professional issues. However, at this particular meeting, her colleague seemed to be implying that Adele didn't understand *because she was Italian or foreign.* This incident got Adele thinking about relations in the workplace between native Italian-speaking teachers and their nonnative counterparts.

## Stereotypes in the Workplace (2): Hannah and the Third Reich

Hannah's stereotype is quite different, and it took her many years to come to terms with it. As a native German-speaking teacher, she feels at home with her social identity but admits that it has often been hard to accept the fact that German as a second language does not have a good reputation in French schools: Both students and parents tend to think that German is difficult and exclusive. The most salient point of Hannah's interview addresses how she progressively learned to distance herself from the way French people stereotype Germans and the German language. When she began teaching German in France, Hannah used to visit primary schools to attract prospective learners who would soon be starting a new foreign language in the first year of high school.

> **HA110:** *Germany is the country of the Nazis, it's the Third Reich with all the connotations, these difficult languages that aren't fun to learn. . . . There you are, having to face this prejudice all the time was hard and it's true that in the early days, I found it really hard to deal with. In the first years of my career, I went round the local primary schools to find new recruits for German and it was in a rather disadvantaged suburb and the children would say, "Heil Hitler," to me when I walked through the classroom. So there you are! I found that really very hard to deal with.*

Foreign-born teachers who teach their native language and culture to young learners who tend to soak up stereotypes and prejudice before they can open up to others may well find that stereotypes are hurtful. It is difficult not to be affected by them personally. The modern language teacher is implicitly a kind of unofficial ambassador of the countries whose language they teach (Zarate, 1993, p. 11); as such, language teachers need to make allowances for the impact that their own identity and affiliation can have on their students: "Measuring the effects induced by one's own cultural affiliation, and including students' and teachers' identities in the teaching process should be a full-fledged objective in language teachers' training" (Zarate, 1993, pp. 43–44). Hannah's initial shock forced her to take a step back from her own affiliation, her own German identity and culture, and to try to make sense of the stereotyped representations that her French students had of Germany. Talking about her experience with other people really helped Hannah to move beyond this initial crisis. For teachers who are unprepared for this sort of thing, it can be very unsettling:

> **CG113:** *How did you manage to work through that?*
> **HA113:** *Well, I talked a lot about it with other people. And also, I think I realized that I had to stop taking everything personally. OK I'm German, but I have nothing to do with what happened 60 years ago.*

82   *Claire Griffin*

> **CG114:** *Detach yourself a bit more from it then?*
> **HA114:** *Yes, I can't embody that. And I think to myself that Germany has also produced so many other brilliant things in literature, in philosophy . . .*
> **CG115:** *That is hidden by all the rest?*
> **HA115:** *That's right! Now, I try to look at it like that.*

Hannah has learned to detach herself from the image of Germany that young learners often have, to concentrate her efforts more on all the other aspects of German culture and history besides the Third Reich. It is crucial that foreign-born language teachers learn to understand the stereotypes that they trigger, often unwittingly. They also need to show tolerance for learners' "interpretive rights" (Zarate, 1993, p. 99) and by doing so, they can hope to find a comfortable professional identity that gives them enough space and distance to understand the perceptions of others without taking everything personally.

## The Challenge of One's Own Language

As we have seen, foreign-born teachers face challenges in different areas of the field, including understanding professional codes, learning how to protect themselves from negative stereotypes and the preconceived notions that some people may have about their language, culture, or country. Kath Woodward (2002) reminds us that identity is closely linked to place: After all, these native speakers can only be labeled as such because they no longer work in spaces where their native language is the norm.

The way we relate to language is at the heart of our identity, which can vary according to the language we speak at any given time. We may feel different when we speak in English, our initially dominant, first language, as compared to when we speak in French, the learned second language. If second-language users are able to reinvent themselves through another tongue, in a creative way, it is also true that second-language users sometimes feel "reduced" (cf. Peter Harder, 1980, on the "reduced personality" of the second-language learner) or lost, a bit like Jacques Derrida, who always held on to his French-speaking identity (cf. Derrida, 1996, *in* Phipps, 2007). Living between the English and the French-speaking world naturally leads us to wonder about "where [we are] in between" (Phipps & Gonzalez, 2004, p. 28). After a time, being in between can affect the very language a person learned as a child, and that has become a central component of their professional identity if he or she is a NEST working in another country. The "initial linguistic gift" (Griffin, 2012) that helps NS candidates through the rigorous French teaching examinations can change over time. Some teachers are aware that their accent has changed or is "lost" or that their English has become stilted because of having to make adjustments to cater for French-speaking learners. Clara, a retired teacher in her late 60s, elucidates this connection: "*I had to articulate, um, my accent, although I never lost it, has changed, um, I've maintained a very stilted type of English because of the need to be understood."* Paradoxically, Clara goes as far as to say that she feels more comfortable speaking in French than in English: *"Funnily enough, um, speaking in French, um, I find easier now than speaking in English."* Anita, a teacher in her early 50s, feels that she has totally lost her original accent: *"I do feel that whatever accent I had in the beginning has been totally lost."* Teaching has also affected the quality of her English: *"Teaching has made my English a bit poorer."*

The contact between the two languages has other linguistic and cognitive effects. Jenny, for example, finds that French has affected her brain: *"I'm getting polluted, my brain is getting polluted"*; *"sometimes I don't hear the mistakes* [the students make]." Jenny, an Irish NEST in her early 40s, is not too worried about her Dublin accent, which still comes back quickly when her mom comes to visit. Kate, a British NEST in her mid-30s, is aware that her spoken English is slower than before. She has also become self-conscious about the mistakes she makes in English. Janet sometimes struggles to find her words, and Emma knows that she uses Gallicisms quite frequently. Caroline, a recently retired teacher from the United Kingdom, cites the example of idioms she finds harder to retrieve because she so rarely uses them. The following anecdote is a hilarious illustration of the tricks our brain can play on us when we are between two languages:

> **CG91:** *What do people say to you about your English?*
>
> **CA91:** *They, they, not about my English but they say of my children that they have a slight French accent which I don't hear; I'm so used to hearing them speak that I don't see it as a French accent.*
>
> **CG92:** *And what about you? I mean do you never get comments, either about your accent or about the expressions you use?*
>
> **CA92:** *Oh I said something would cost a bob or two and of course that's sort of . . .* (laughs). *Because of course shillings and things have long since gone. Probably there are things I say, I make mistakes, I know what I did, it was terrible, I completely confused two expressions—you know when people have a toast, they say "bottoms up" . . . and I said, "up yours" or something.*

Caroline acknowledges the fact that her second language (French) affects her first language (English), yet she has not noticed a change in her accent after several decades of living in France. In his book *Bilingual: Life and Reality*, François Grosjean (2010) debunks some of the myths people tend to have about bilinguals. A lot of people assume that a bilingual speaks the two languages with no accent: *"An accent is one of the things that we notice most in someone's speech and we always have an opinion about it"*; *"Having a foreign accent in one or more languages is, in fact, the norm for bilinguals, not having one is the exception"* (Grosjean, 2010, p. 77).

84    *Claire Griffin*

Notwithstanding Grosjean's assertion, several participants in the study seem not to believe in the unchanging nature of accents. Kate, for instance, does not believe it when people back home in the United Kingdom say that she sounds French: "*Maybe they say I'm French or something like that. I think it's a load of rubbish. I don't think I sound French at all. Not even when I speak French!*" Bess goes one step further, rejecting the very idea that she might one day speak English with a French accent: "*I do not want to have a French accent when I speak English ever. Because it would be denying my ultimate identity. It's the only thing that's left. I think it's important for the kids too.*" Bess's determination to keep her English intact points to a telling need for self-preservation in a world that has required her to constantly adjust to fit in. Bess appears to be very well integrated, and it is interesting to see that she is strongly attached to certain aspects of her English-speaking identity: Asserting one's first-language identity seems vital for some im-/migrants when it comes to finding and maintaining a healthy equilibrium.

In sum, it seems clear that the "initial gift" or linguistic capital we set out with needs to be maintained, renewed, and kept alive, not only as a crucial component of our identity but also because as teachers, we have a duty to keep in touch with current, real language use. This capital is indeed a treasure that needs special attention lest we lose touch with it forever, only to lose ourselves in the process. Moreover, we may wonder whether this initial asset is still an advantage when it becomes altered to the extent that it is no longer an authentic model for language learners.

## The Challenge of Finding One's Place

Finding one's place is not a linear process, and the participants who have worked in a number of different schools all highlight the impact that changing schools can have on the way a teacher integrates, socializes with co-workers, and generally gets involved. For a few foreign-born teachers, leaving the secondary school system for a job at university has appeared to solve all their worries: They had found K–12 classroom management challenging at times and felt relieved teaching in French universities, where they thought they would have more to offer the students (3 of 21 participants), and one teacher totally changed her approach to teaching. These examples show that finding one's place can sometimes mean making rather extreme decisions: On one hand, it has meant moving away from the secondary system altogether (Kate and John); on the other, it means teaching "outside the box" (Janet), which requires courage.

### LESSONS LEARNED

At the end of each interview, participants were asked to share what advice they had for newly qualified NESTs like themselves who were embarking

*Voices From Behind the Scenes* 85

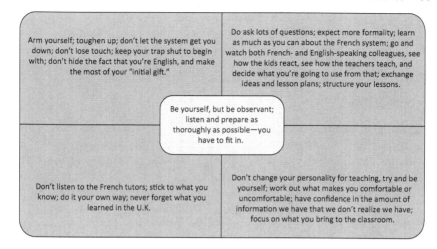

*Figure 6.1* Participants' Advice for English-Speaking Immigrant Teachers

on a career in France. Their advice has been presented in a matrix (see Figure 6.1) in which two poles are clearly visible: that of acculturation, mostly in the center and in the top right-hand box, and that of self-preservation, whereby an individual holds on to original values and identities. At the center of the matrix is Susan's guiding principle: "Be yourself, but be observant."

Susan herself admits that she has completely dampened down any remaining Scottishness, presumably in an effort to reinvent her identity. Her imperative "be yourself" is at the center, not because it implies that we never change, but as a professional guideline for foreign-born novice teachers who might feel trapped inside a conformist professional identity they assume is necessary to fit in. What we see in the bottom left-hand corner is of a more static nature. The advice offered depends on the personality of each participant. Jessica, for example, admits to being a bit of a clown and advises newcomers to "make it lively." Jenny, whose year of training had been a rather negative experience, advises people not to listen to the French tutors, which may or may not reflect what newcomers need to hear as they strive to construct their own professional identity. We have here little snippets of what Connelly and Clandinin (1999) call "stories to live by"—the stories of bi- and multilingual teachers living their professional lives between different languages, cultures, and spaces in a highly complex world.

Claire Kramsch (2009, pp. 4–5) reminds us that learning a foreign language is an embodied reality that changes the way we look at what is familiar to us. She stresses that for language learners, identification with this new, embodied reality (i.e., language learning) affects not only the mind but the body (and the heart) too (Kramsch, 2009, p. 18). So just how far can you go without losing yourself in the process? In Figure 6.1, we can detect echoes of a similar tension between the "mold" of acculturation and professional

## 86  *Claire Griffin*

compliance, and first-language identities that some teachers strive to preserve, to such an extent that they cannot detect any change in the way they speak English after many years of living in France (Helen).

## CONCLUSION

Foreign-born teachers may find it hard to decode the "host" education system for years, because of what Claire Kramsch refers to as the lack of an "extended self." Indeed, they are constantly learning new words (educational and pedagogical terms, acronyms, etc.), which they sometimes struggle to connect up to their own network of stored memories (cf. Kramsch, 2009, p. 71). It therefore seems inevitable that foreign-born teachers should have a restricted vision of their new professional world, at least to begin with. On the other hand, their in-betweenness can be a real asset if it leads to a positive form of empowerment: showing empathy toward others, finding one's voice, building a specific, enriched standpoint beyond a binary opposition of two worlds. Foreign-born teachers can potentially compensate for any lack arising from their different primary socialization (in Ireland or the United Kingdom in the case of this particular inquiry), by positioning themselves as "multilingual subjects," as social actors with plural standpoints.

## REFERENCES

Camilleri, C., Kastersztein, J., & Lipiansky, E.-M. (Eds.). (1990). *Stratégies identitaires*. Paris: PUF.

Charmaz, K. (2006). *Constructing grounded theory: A practical guide through qualitative analysis*. London: Sage Publications.

Connelly, F. M., & D. J. Clandinin. (1999). *Shaping a professional identity: Stories of education practice*. London, ON: Althouse Press.

Corbin, J., & Strauss, A. (2008). *Basics of qualitative research: Techniques to developing grounded theory* (3rd Ed.). Los Angeles, CA: Sage.

Demorgon, J., & Lipiansky, E.-M. (Eds.). (1999). *Guide de l'interculturel en formation*. Paris: Retz.

Glaser, B.G. & Strauss, A.L. (1967). *The Discovery of Grounded Theory: Strategies for Qualitative Research*. Chicago: Aldine Pub. Co.

Griffin, C. (2012). *L'identité professionnelle des professeurs d'anglais "locuteurs natifs" exerçant en France depuis le traité de Maastricht. Entre conservation ontologique et acculturation : les limites du "capital natif."* Doctoral thesis supervised by Claire Tardieu. Université Sorbonne nouvelle – Paris 3.

Grosjean, F. (2010). *Bilingual: Life and reality*. Cambridge, MA: Harvard University Press.

Harder, P. (1980). Discourse as self-expression: On the reduced personality of the second language learner. *Applied Linguistics, 1*(3), 262–270.

Kaufmann, J.-C. (2007). *L'entretien compréhensif* (2nd éd.). Paris: Armand Colin.

Kramsch, C. (2009). *The multilingual subject*. Oxford: Oxford University Press.

Lave, J., & Wenger, E. (1991). *Situated learning. Legitimate peripheral participation*. New York: Cambridge University Press.

Manço, A. (2002). *Compétences interculturelles des jeunes issus de l'immigration. Perspectives théoriques et pratiques*. Paris: L'Harmattan.

Phipps, A. (2007). *Learning the arts of linguistic survival: Languaging, tourism, life*. Clevedon: Channel View Publications.

Phipps, A., & Gonzalez, M. (2004). *Modern languages: Learning and teaching in an intercultural field*. London: Sage.

Schnapper, D. (1992). *L'Europe des immigrés*. Paris: Éditions François Bourin.

Tardieu, C. (1999). *Le professeur citoyen*. Bourg-la-Reine: Éditions M.T.

Woodward, K. (2002). *Understanding identity*. London: Hodder Education.

Zarate, G. (1993). *Représentations de l'étranger et didactique des langues*. Paris: Didier. Coll. CREDIF essais.

# 7 Challenges and Self-Efficacy of Female East Asian–Born Faculty in American Universities

*Hyeyoung Bang*

## INTRODUCING FEMALE ASIAN-BORN PROFESSORS

A large number of international faculty are hired by American higher education institutions. The highest numbers are from China (22%), followed by India (9.4%), South Korea (9.3%), Japan (5.4%), Germany (5%), and Canada (4.5%) (Institute of International Education, 2008). According to these data, about half of international faculty members hired by U.S. universities (hereafter referred to as America) are from Asian countries, and 80% of these Asian-born faculty are from East Asian countries. Many studies have been conducted on international students and their challenges in higher education in the United States (e.g., Bang & Montgomery, 2013); however, few have investigated the perspectives of international faculty, especially female East Asian-born professors (hereafter referred to as FEA faculty).

Coming from East Asian societies that highly respect educators for their knowledge, age, and authority, FEA faculty experience sociocultural differences when teaching in American universities—teaching environments that value egalitarianism, and individualism (Dedoussis, 2007; Hofstede, 1991). In particular, FEA scholars can be very apprehensive about their competence in U.S. academia because of their emotional and communication acculturation concerns (Bang & Montgomery, 2013), as well as deep cultural differences in academia. Because of such barriers, many find themselves working extra hard to fit in and yet often find themselves dissatisfied because of loss of self-efficacy and confidence, discrimination, disrespect, and mistrust.

This chapter discusses the challenges experienced by four South Korean and three Chinese female professors, ranging from 32 to 44 in age. At the time of writing, all had fewer than six years of teaching experience as tenure-track assistant professors in American universities. In addition, all of them came to the U.S. for their master's or doctoral degrees, and none of them held U.S. citizenship. The points in the stories either involve similar experiences or can be attributable to one person.

## At Issue: Respect Versus Egalitarianism

FEA faculty are from cultures that respect educators because educators are viewed as the custodians of knowledge. At the same time, educators are normally older, and elders are accorded respect. On the other hand, Western culture, including American culture, values egalitarianism and individualism and may not necessarily see educators as figures of authority or respect, unless they earn it (Hofstede, 1991). This differentiated view poses a challenge (i.e., a sense of disrespect and mistrust) when the FEA faculty work with American students and consider themselves as figures of authority but the American teaching context views them as facilitators and colearners (Robertson, 1999). Not surprisingly, therefore, many FEA faculty reported that their teaching efforts do not produce the same positive outcomes as their research.

Several scholars (Alberts, 2008; Hutchison & Jazzar, 2007; Thomas & Johnson, 2004) have noted numerous examples from their interviews with international professors about how such professors have experienced conflict or had a misunderstanding with their students because the professors had different cultural expectations. Many professors reported that the students lacked respect for them, challenged their authority, and displayed what the professors perceived to be inappropriate behavior in the classroom (Thomas & Johnson, 2004).

## Assessment Issues: Consumerism, Performance Goal Orientation, and Grading

Higher education institutions in America respond to business and market pressures, and that tends to compromise traditional academic values, as opposed to the maintenance of rigor of programs. For many students, the purpose of attending a university is often solely for acquiring a degree or certificate for work, rather than for pursuing knowledge and wisdom. This partly forces students to work for high grades rather than content mastery.

Several FEA faculty think that their teaching experiences in the United States have been rewarding but also traumatic. A lot of aggression and disrespect occur after taking tests or getting grades for assignments, especially in the latter part of each semester. Although this probably happens to many American (i.e., non-international) professors, the forms of the aggression and disrespect might be more exaggerated toward foreign-born professors. In addition, the FEA faculty feel even more uncomfortable with American students' obsession with, and expectation of, higher grades and their informing professors of the grades they desire. FEA faculty understand the value of a higher grade but find students' audacity to determine their own grade unacceptable.

Regarding assessment, FEA faculty have observed the following tendencies in American students:

- If they come to the class, they should get a good grade, no matter how little they worked in the class.

90    *Hyeyoung Bang*

- If they did not get a good grade, it is the instructor's fault, regardless of their efforts.
- If they followed the rubric or grading scheme, they should get an A, no matter the quality of their work.
- If they did not get the grade they deserve, it is legitimate to argue with the professor for a better grade.
- If they argue with the professor for a better grade, they can get something out of it.
- Because they pay for the degree, they should get it, whether or not they work for it.
- Because they have paid tuition, deducting points for absenteeism is "stupid" and does not make sense; after all, it is *their* money.

The gap of understanding academic standards between foreign-born professors and American students can be significant, and this can create conflicts, frustration, and resentment toward professors. Hutchison and Jazzar (2007) argue that this is an area of conflict between international and American students, because while international instructors believe that 70% is a strong grade, Americans believe 70% to be a failing grade. Stout's (2000) argument on *a feel-good education* could support some of these points. A feel-good education in America encourages a narcissistic attitude by providing generous grades even when students perform poorly. Having been educated under demanding academic standards, however, FEA faculty encounter discrepancies when confronted with such situations.

Ultimately, therefore, FEA faculty view the grade of A to mean *excellent* work. In one situation, although an FEA faculty provides plenty of explanation about assignments, rubrics, and guidelines, as well as sample assignments, to prevent these complaints, she, almost without exception, expects to hear complaints about grades at the end of each semester, often leading to poor teaching evaluations. International professors therefore often find themselves tiptoeing around students so as not to jeopardize international professors' course evaluations, which have an impact on the tenure-promotion process. The more we worry about this, the less effective we appear, as instructors. The result is that our self-efficacy is negatively impacted.

Many international faculty, including FEA faculty, are viewed as less knowledgeable, are questioned about their qualifications, and receive more negative comments by American-born students (Lee & Janda, 2006; Vargas, 2002). Coupled with their teaching evaluations, therefore, one can generally state that because of perception issues and different understandings of assessment and academic standards, the FEA faculty are often confused and become pessimistic about their potential success in American higher education.

## Resistance to Constructive Criticism or Instruction

Students' ability to take constructive criticism is another cultural difference. As Stout (2001) argued, American education emphasizes a feel-good education, and many American students expect no criticism, nor do they like to be criticized. This does not boost the self-esteem of such students; rather, it has the potential of damaging it because such students are not accountable for their own learning, and they attribute their own failure externally (Weiner, 1986). The FEA faculty have encountered many students who cannot take even small amounts of constructive criticism. The FEA faculty believe that one of their responsibilities is to correct students; on the contrary, several FEA faculty have students who do not hesitate to resist and confront them in the classroom when corrected. In one interesting situation, when an FEA faculty tried to help her students to be better counselors, one female student got very angry and screamed at her: "I am a good counselor. What do you know? You don't even speak proper English." She later learned from other faculty that this student apparently was a *good student* among her American professors.

## International Faculty: Bullies' Targets?

In the same vein as resistance to instruction from foreign-born professors, it is interesting to hear stories from international faculty about how often they appear to have been "bullied" by their own students. For example, in one FEA faculty's classes, students organized themselves as a group not to respond to her lessons. In the same class, she was nearly physically hit by one of her male students while lecturing about multiculturalism. This male student did not agree with the content (he felt like his White privilege was threatened) and decided to attack his professor. He jumped up out of the chair, almost swinging his fist at her. She should have reported and expelled him from the class; however, new FEA professors may not know what the disciplinary rules are and their power to report and potentially have students expelled if abused. Furthermore, the FEA professors are also not used to that kind of practice, because such behavior would rarely happen in East Asia.

Class attendance is another issue the FEA faculty often face. When one of the FEA faculty started teaching undergraduate courses, she did not create an attendance policy because she thought that all students should be accountable for their own learning. However, she quickly learned that an attendance policy is crucial; otherwise, students would manipulate her intention. She had two students who were failing because they had missed a lot of the class sessions and had learned little as a result. One of the students threatened that if she did not give him a passing grade, he would report how awful this professor was to the university authorities. The faculty could not believe that was happening in a college class. At first, the student threatened to get a passing grade, and then he begged her to forgive him and give him a passing grade.

The preceding discussion generally raises the question as to whether FEA faculty are easier targets for students to blame because they are foreigners and females. I personally wonder if this happens often to American

## 92  Hyeyoung Bang

professors. If this happens frequently to American professors too, then it is a serious problem in American higher education.

## Challenges When Dealing With Graduate Students

That undergraduate students pose greater challenges than do graduate students may be due to their maturity levels; however, my colleagues and I have encountered passive aggressive behaviors and attitudes from graduate students as well. Examples include switching their thesis advisors, getting recommendations from other American professors, reporting any issues to program directors rather than dealing with instructors directly, and avoiding and ignoring the faculty's urge to think seriously about graduate assistant responsibilities.

In connection with these behaviors, an FEA faculty once had four master's students, two of whom switched their thesis chair from her to an American faculty member without consulting her. This might have been due to their mistrust in the faculty's credentials, a language barrier, or a perceived incompetence in her ability to advise their thesis. In another case, a hard-working FEA faculty spent a lot of time preparing her courses, as well as trying to connect her students to paid internships. She put a lot of effort into getting to know her students. Her students knew and appreciated that; however, when they needed recommendation letters, they went to White American professors. When she found out this, she felt heartbroken.

One of the FEA faculty is in charge of a counseling center where many students do not take responsibility for what they should do. Some, including her graduate assistant, ignored her directions and guidance and refused to respond to her e-mails. This made her feel cheated and devastated because she felt ignored and disrespected, and the resulting frustration often made her cry.

## The Need for International and Global Education in Higher Education

Unfortunately, many international faculty members experience prejudice and discrimination (Lin, Pearce, & Wang, 2009; Ngwainmbi, 2006; Thomas & Johnson, 2004). Some experience discrimination in institutional and departmental rewards such as salary, rank promotion, or tenure. Corley and Sabharwal (2007) found that foreign-born scholars were paid less, despite their higher scholarly productivity. Lin et al. (2009) found that international faculty members are less likely to be tenured and have lower salaries. In addition to interviewing faculty members, Alberts (2008) found that several American students had been advised by their peers not to take classes with foreign-born professors because of their accents; however, it was also found that majority of the students actually enjoyed having a foreign-born professor and that the accent was not a hindrance to their learning. Thus, the research suggests that there exist biases among students that are based on their attitudes about foreign-born professors.

Because my experiences in the classroom have been challenging, I wanted to understand my students' perceptions of international faculty. Thus, I had related discussions with my students in various class sections (twice in 2010 and once in 2013). The following are some perspectives from my students (please keep in mind that these opinions are from more outspoken or more expressive students and not from everyone):

1. Students avoid instructors whose names sound even remotely foreign.
2. Students have negative opinions about hiring international faculty: They think that it is a waste of the institution's money and that institutions should spend more money on domestic student achievement issues and hire more American professors.
3. It is hard to understand the accents of international faculty. This is especially true regarding mathematics courses taught by international faculty, described as "the worst nightmare."
4. Communication is an issue: It is hard to make personal or close relationships with international faculty. American professors try to build personal relationships while foreign professors just teach and leave.
5. International professors have different academic standards and expectations. Students fear that international faculty expect more from them, with little handholding.
6. Positive comment: International faculty bring different perspectives and contribute to U.S. education and scholarship. International faculty use various teaching materials and activities to reduce the language barrier. Communication may be an issue in the beginning, but if students want to understand the material, they can ask questions and pay close attention.

It was shocking to me that some American students think that hiring international faculty is a waste of money and does no good for American higher education. Some students believed that institutions pay more money to international faculty and provide free tuition for international students. This shows the need for high-quality and accurate global and multicultural education. Students do not appear to know how many Americans are hired by international corporations. It appears that they hold some resentment toward international scholars because of misinformation, and according to the FEA faculty, this mind-set is more prevalent in institutions in rural and predominantly White regions.

One of the FEA faculty complained that this mind-set was present not only among students, but also among her White colleagues, and this made life very unbearable, threatening, and disheartening. As one of the first international or minority faculty hired after her university was forced to be more multicultural, she did not receive any support from colleagues and received no respect from students. Her students would gang up on her and plan collectively to not respond to her instruction. She was bullied, rejected, and humiliated by her students, partly because she was brought to teach multiculturalism, and the predominantly White students saw this as threatening to their community. They did not perceive learning about multiculturalism from an Asian female professor as necessary and did not believe that it helped their career training. She was horrified and felt unhappy and unsafe living there. Since the time she was interviewed for this chapter, she was desperately trying to leave the community even if she had to give up her job and has since moved to a more urban, diverse university.

## COLLEAGUES AND SCHOOL PERSONNEL: BOUNDARIES AND EMOTIONAL SUPPORTS

The FEA faculty found their local colleagues as sympathetic to their situation and helped them in many ways; however, they also tried not to get help from colleagues because they believed that if they asked for help, they would need to explain their situation, and it may sound as if they were whining and were not happy to be in the United States. Thus, one FEA faculty stopped talking altogether about her students or classes when she realized that it was not really helping her.

Cultural differences make the FEA faculty feel that they only know their American colleagues on a superficial level. For example, although one of the FEA faculty tried, she was not successful in making friends. She invited colleagues to her home for meals and even went to visit a Christian church even though she is not a Christian, just to make connections with her colleagues. Although she is a very active and outgoing person, the cultural gap is so huge that she has a hard time finding friends. In the small college town where she teaches, there are many fundamentalist Christians (students as well as colleagues) who do not tolerate multiculturalism or anything *exotic*, including foreign people and food. She is one of the few faculty members with an international or diverse background. Because of her different values, she has not made any friends and she feels lonely. Although she has a lot of issues with students (aggression, violence, disrespect, challenging authority, ignoring her orders), none of her colleagues has tried to help. Her colleagues' general attitude when she raises issues seems to be "I don't have any problems, and so you shouldn't have any."

Like the FEA faculty, many international faculty members are challenged emotionally as well. Evidence shows that many feel isolated and have feelings of loneliness and alienation (Collins, 2008; Thomas & Johnson, 2004). Collins (2008) surveyed 30 foreign-born faculty members from a variety of institutions in terms of size and location. Of her 30 participants, 63% reported they were feeling isolated and were not coping well with loneliness (Collins, 2008). Numerous studies also indicate that there is little support to help international faculty deal with their feelings of isolation (Bazemore, Janda, Derlega, & Paulson, 2010; Collins, 2008; Thomas & Johnson, 2004). Professors from Thomas and Johnson's (2004) study complained of a lack of collegiality among their American colleagues. In comparison to their experiences in their respective countries, international faculty have found that American university departments often lack a communal meeting place for faculty to interact, and American faculty members tend to isolate themselves in their offices and rarely interact socially. The lack of collegiality among their American colleagues "may reduce job satisfaction and feelings of belongingness to the university" (Bazemore et al., 2010, p. 85) which could potentially create high turnover among international faculty members. According to Collins (2008), many faculty members expressed their disappointment in how little support they received from both the university and their colleagues. In fact, 22 of 30 participants in Collins's study rated their international office negatively, and two thirds expressed a lack of support from their department chairs. These research findings are in agreement with FEAs' experiences.

## JOB SECURITY: HIRING AND THE GREEN CARD APPLICATION PROCESS

Another challenge for FEA (and other foreign-born) professors is related to the hiring process and the consequent visa and green card acquisition processes (*green card* is the term for the legal document that gives the possessor the rights of permanent residency in the United States). Because it is rare for administrators and classified staff to deal with the unique challenges related to hiring and obtaining a visa and green card for international faculty, there is a lot of confusion and delays in obtaining the H-1 visas. This can potentially result in illegal employment, and the opportunity for applying for a green card may then be lost, which could result in placement in a rehiring pool and potential loss of employment. Because many administrators do not know the faculty advertisements requirement by the U.S. Department of Homeland Security, some international professors have found themselves in a rehiring pool as job candidates. In one situation, a university had to repost the advertisement, and the professor had to leave the job because the university decided to hire someone else from the new pool.

Normally, international faculty have to apply for their green card within 18 months before their H-1 visa expires. If they miss the chance, they have to reapply for the H-1 visa, which is a costly, hectic, and complicated process. A few faculty were in this situation and learned about several previous cases in which international faculty were forced to move or give up their job because of such visa mishaps. One FEA faculty contacted her university's attorney about the issue and was informed that there was nothing the office could do because the office existed to protect the university, not the faculty.

96  *Hyeyoung Bang*

The attorney also warned the FEA faculty that there was a chance that she might not be hired back if she decided to sue the university.

In another case, an FEA professor's college did not act quickly enough to help her to get an H-1 visa, and although she had urged the college many times, she ended up working for a month without a proper working visa. This incident not only put her in a dangerous position of either being arrested or deported from America but also put her in a situation where her students did not respect her because she was not properly introduced to them because of the legal issue. After that incident, several of her colleagues approached her and offered to hook her up with an old male friend to help her get a green card (she is a young and beautiful woman). She was offended and disappointed by her colleagues because they had not even recognized that what they were doing essentially amounted to sexual harassment. Interestingly, Pike and Johnson (2003) reported the images of Asian women as being "hyperfeminine: passive, weak, excessively submissive, slavishly dutiful, sexually exotic, and available for White men" (p. 5). I wonder whether this stereotype may have inspired the FEA faculty's colleagues to behave that way.

Studies have reported similar issues regarding the green card application process. For instance, in her survey of 30 international faculty, Collins (2008) found that 28 reported that one of the biggest challenges they faced was obtaining the green card. As noted earlier, the application process is extremely time-consuming and expensive. Partly for this reason, some faculty remarked that they had sacrificed some of their career goals to acquire a green card because they were required to stay at the same institution until the process was complete. This restricted them from taking better positions at other universities (Collins). In addition, because the application process is time-consuming, faculty with heavy teaching loads were limited with respect to their research productivity, which is necessary for career advancement (Collins).

## EMOTIONAL WELL-BEING AND COPING STRATEGIES

Not many people can imagine how stressful it can be for international faculty. Not surprisingly, discrimination and prejudice can have psychological effects. For example, faculty who believed their stereotyped status affected their everyday lives were more likely to report lower self-esteem, lower feelings of well-being, fewer positive feelings toward the university, and less teaching effectiveness (Bazemore et al., 2010).

Most of the colleagues I have mentioned in this chapter seem to manage through the psychological stresses; however, they experience varying stress levels, emotional discomfort, depression, anxiety, anger, and distress. When faced with discrimination and disrespect, they feel devastated, hopeless, depressed, and less eager to teach, which dramatically influences not

## Challenges and Self-Efficacy of Female East Asian–Born Faculty 97

only their self-esteem but also their physical function. I, too, often feel so tired after classes that I cannot do anything else the rest of the day. I have to either sleep or watch a movie to relax my nerves. One of my FEA colleagues, who has now received tenure, informed me that she had to drink alcohol whenever she had to teach. Many FEA faculty reported that they have cried, screamed, and drank to release their stress. They have had second thoughts about teaching in America and have dreamed about returning to their own countries.

Most colleagues realize that recognizing the challenges of being an international professor and working harder and harder is the best way to overcome their situation if they want to keep their job in the United States. Rather than complaining about our situation, participating in professional development and similar workshops is one way of improving our teaching skills. Additionally, making lessons more interesting using a variety of materials, putting a smile on our faces and being nice no matter what prejudice we encounter, and exchanging our experiences and information about how to deal with our challenges could help us to overcome our hardships. Perhaps that may be the healthiest way of coping with being an international professor.

## LESSONS LEARNED: EMPOWERING INTERNATIONAL FACULTY'S SELF-EFFICACY

This chapter addresses some of the challenges FEA faculty have encountered in U.S. institutions of higher education. While some aspect of these challenges might be unique to FEA faculty, I believe many international faculty face similar challenges. FEA professors come from collective societies and a tradition of respect for educators, resulting in differing expectations and interactions with students. For these reasons, they, as well as other international faculty, need to adjust their expectations of their students and their teaching styles and social interactions to make sense of their new teaching environments.

With a desire to increase global and multicultural education in their classrooms, higher education institutions in the United States have put a strong focus on recruiting international faculty members (Bazemore et al., 2010; Mamiseishvili, 2009). Foreign-born professors bring with them important global knowledge, unique perspectives and experiences, and diversity to the campus environment, making them beneficial for the students. During the 2007–2008 academic year, the Institute of International Education reported that 126,123 international scholars were teaching or conducting research in U.S. higher education institutions, an 8% increase from the previous year (Institute of International Education, 2008). With a growing presence and significance of international faculty members on American campuses, it is important to understand the experiences of this particular population to further recruit and maintain these faculty members.

98    *Hyeyoung Bang*

This chapter indicates that American institutions need to emphasize the importance of international and multicultural education, partly because many American students do not understand what international scholars bring to the United States and how many American citizens work for international organizations in other countries. Their knowledge gaps can potentially pose cruel threats to international faculty, both physically and emotionally, as shown in the examples in this narrative. Some colleges do not even require any international or multicultural courses or related opportunities, which compromises students' understanding of global issues at large, and international faculty and their everyday hardships in particular.

Professional development sessions and mentoring programs for international faculty could be offered so that international faculty can understand where their students' attitudes are coming from, and help them prepare or intervene positively when they encounter such attitudes and behaviors. When I was struggling with students' attitudes, one of my White colleagues shared her story about one of her students who had a behavior issue, and that story helped me understand that American faculty also deal with similar issues. The professional development sessions can address the issues mentioned in this chapter. For example, information on how to deal with students' performance goal orientation, including dealing with issues with grading by providing clearer expectations and detailed guidelines would be useful. In addition, mental health supports for international faculty would help them to cope with their stresses.

## REFERENCES

Alberts, H. C. (2008). The challenges and opportunities of foreign-born instructors in the classroom. *Journal of Geography in Higher Education, 32*(2), 189–203.

Bang, H., & Montgomery, D. (2013). Understanding international graduate students' acculturation using Q methodology. *Journal of College Student Development, 54*, 343–360.

Bazemore, S. D., Janda, L. H., Derlega, V. J., & Paulson, J. F. (2010). The role of rejection in mediating the effects of stigma consciousness among foreign-born university professors. *Journal of Diversity in Higher Education, 3*(2), 85–96.

Collins, J. M. (2008). Coming to America: Challenges for faculty coming to United States' universities. *Journal of Geography in Higher Education, 32*(2), 179–188.

Corley, E., & Sabharwal, M. (2007). Foreign-born academic scientists and engineers: Producing more and getting less than their U.S.-born peers? *Research in Higher Education, 48*(8), 909–940.

Dedoussis, E.-V. (2007). Issues of diverse in academia: Through the eyes of 'third-country' faculty. *Higher Education, 54*, 135–156.

Hofstede, G. (1991). *Cultures and organizations: Software of the mind.* Maidenhead: McGraw-Hill.

Hutchison, C. B., & Jazzar, M. (2007). Mentors for teachers from outside the U.S. *Phi Delta Kappan, 88*, 368–373.

Institute of International Education. (2008). *Open Doors 2008: International scholars.* Retrieved October 1, 2014, from http://opendoors.iienetwork.org/?p=131567

## Challenges and Self-Efficacy of Female East Asian–Born Faculty    99

Lee, G.-L. & Janda, L. (2006). Successful multicultural campus: Free from prejudice toward minority professors. *Multicultural Education, 14*(1), 27–30.

Lin, Z., Pearce, R., & Wang, W. (2009). Imported talents: Demographic characteristics, achievement and job satisfaction of foreign born full time faculty in four-year American colleges. *Higher Education, 57*(6), 703–721.

Mamiseishvili, K. (2009). Foreign-born women faculty work roles and productivity at research universities in the United States. *Higher Education, 60*(2), 139–156.

Ngwainmbi, E. K. (2006). The struggles of foreign-born faculty. *Diverse: Issues in Higher Education, 23,* 28.

Pike, K. D., & Johnson, D. (2003). Asian American women and racialized femininities: "Doing" gender across cultural worlds. *Gender & Society, 17*(1), 33–53.

Robertson, D. (1999). Professors' perspective on their teaching: A new construct and developmental model. *Innovative Higher Education, 23,* 271–294.

Stout, M. (2000). *The feel-good curriculum: The dumbing down of America's kids in the name of self-esteem.* Cambridge, MA: Perseus.

Thomas, J. M., & Johnson, B. J. (2004). Perspectives of international faculty members: Their experiences and stories. *Education & Society, 22*(3), 47–64.

Vargas, L. (Ed.). (2002). *Women faculty of color in the White classroom.* New York: Peter Lang.

Weiner, B. (1986). *An attributional theory of motivation and emotion.* New York: Springer-Verlag.

# 8 The True Meaning of Integrity
## Reflections on a Professional Life in Japan

*Robin Sakamoto*

## INTRODUCTION

Japanese universities are in dire straits. In 2011, 39% of private universities were operating with student enrollment under their capacity level, including 32 universities that were operating at less than 50% capacity (Breaden, 2013, p. 36). A career in higher education would seem perilous to the bravest and ludicrous to any of the less than 5% full-time foreign faculty in Japan. Notwithstanding these circumstances, inclusion and contentment can be achieved. This chapter examines how, after close to three decades of perseverance, a U.S. woman has broken through the bamboo ceiling as a professional workingwoman and mother of three to become the second foreign female to serve as dean of a Japanese university.

It was not until 1982 that a law allowing foreign nationals to be hired as faculty with full voting rights at national universities in Japan was passed (Chung, 2010). Without any awareness of how this would affect my entire life, I arrived in Japan 3 years later to teach junior high school English. I had a brand-new bachelor of arts, a teaching license, and 2 weeks of intensive Japanese that I had naively thought would be enough on the assumption that if Japan was hiring native speakers of English to teach junior high school, everyone must speak English. "Culture shock" is far too mild of a phrase to describe what happened when I began teaching in a remote rural area of northern Japan with a population of 30,000 and one foreigner—myself. However, had it not been for this experience, I do not think I would have acquired the needed integrity to pursue a career in Japan.

Anyone who has lived in a foreign culture for a long enough time to acquire the language knows that there are some words that simply cannot be translated. I had long admired the word *integrity* and had envisioned myself becoming a person of integrity in my professional life. Imagine my surprise, therefore, when I found that the Japanese translation of *integrity* was "foolish diligence." It seemed to take the entire aura away from the word and replace it with something far less meaningful. Yet now, when I look back on the nearly 30 years of my professional life, I realize that the Japanese definition of integrity I learned those first formative years

*The True Meaning of Integrity*   101

in rural Japan is the one that has paved the way for me to succeed as an immigrant.

To move through culture shock, one does need to be diligent. Learning a new language, educational system, sense of values, and culture takes hard work; however, the lesson that was much harder for me to learn as a young, educated, White woman was humility. I simply had not been aware of how privileged my life had been in the United States and how totally unprepared that privileged life made me for my new life in rural Japan. In my new environment, I became illiterate overnight, had only cold running water until I figured out how to use the hot water heater, and had no central heating system for my apartment or a flush toilet. Nothing was familiar, and I simply could not make it through a day without asking countless others for help. I had to accept the fact that, in my new surroundings, I had much more to learn than I could possibly teach.

In the classroom, I was considered an authority when it came to English, as I was a native speaker, but when it came to teaching, I had so much to learn about learning styles, classroom management, and the day-to-day life in a school system very different from my own upbringing. In addition to my teaching at the junior high school, I studied Japanese at the local elementary school, starting at the first-grade level. I spent 1 day a week getting to know people in my community. I made school lunches in the cafeteria, saw how sake and tatami were made in local family-run businesses, and hiked nearby mountains with my middle-aged neighbor. At the end of my 2-year contract, I felt that I was just at the point where I could begin to contribute to this community, and extended my contract for a year. Following that, I taught at a nearby high school for 2 years prior to beginning my university career.

What had felt like "foolish diligence" was actually opening very rewarding opportunities that I could truly appreciate with a humble heart. Had I not lived in that community for those years, I doubt I ever could have learned this lesson. But as I later discovered in my graduate studies, I had also learned a great deal about interactive acculturation.

## THE DUALITY OF ACCULTURATION

As my Japanese-language skills progressed, I found that above and beyond effective communication, I had to acculturate to my new environment. The depth of that acculturation was also very much a negotiation between my desire to be a contributing member of the community and the level to which the community wanted to accept me. It was thus with great joy that I came across the work of Adam Komisarof, whose research focuses on interactive acculturation among Japanese and Westerners.

Komisarof (2012) asserted that acculturation is a dual process, and "to better understand how Westerners build satisfying relationships with Japanese, the *compatibility* of acculturation strategies between Westerners

## 102 Robin Sakamoto

and Japanese is more important" (p. 221). I believe that this holds true for any immigrant. The amount of acceptance you experience will depend on the extent to which the surrounding community wants to accept you. In my first years in Japan, the remote area where I lived really did want to accept me, and I wanted to be accepted. This compatibility allowed me to become a member of that community. I now illustrate how the patterns found in Komisarof's research apply to my various experiences as a university professor.

My first university position was in a department of education working with students who would become junior high school English teachers. There was one other non-Japanese faculty member in the department, and I worked there for close to 10 years. During that time, I felt "pleasantly" accepted, in that I was included in many on-campus events and was invited to present with fellow faculty members at academic conferences, and it was here that I began to do my own research and start publishing. I felt supported and respected by the department. This would reflect a stage of "integration" in which "everyone mixes together in the same bowl or society, but retains their culturally unique 'flavor'" (Komisarof, 2012, p. 216). I was accepted because I had unique qualities that were desired by the department and hence utilized. At the time, I was also interested in maintaining my own cultural heritage because I was conducting research, publishing, and finishing my dissertation, all through U.S. universities. This worked for me and my department, but after a decade I was still completely unaware of the intricacies of running a Japanese university. I was not included in faculty meetings and hence was not going to advance beyond being a "native speaker" English teacher. As long as I was comfortable in that role, this worked, and I might have stayed there forever, had it not been for the restructuring of Japanese national universities, which resulted in my position no longer being available because of a lack of funding.

At this stage of my life, I was the mother of three children and had just recently completed my PhD, had a few publications and a decade of experience at a national university. I felt that I had the qualifications needed to move to another university, but because of cultural barriers, it ended up taking me longer to find a tenured position than it took to complete both my master's and doctoral degrees. The following 7 years saw me commuting to Tokyo and staying away from my family half the week, teaching at four of the six most prominent universities in the Tokyo area as an adjunct faculty member.

Those 7 years were very frustrating for me, and only through "foolish diligence" could I keep going. Not only was I ready to integrate into a university as a full-fledged academic, but I also wanted to do more. I felt more than ready to assimilate into the role of a Japanese professional workingwoman. Alas, as I was adjunct faculty, there was simply no desire on the part of the universities where I worked to see me as anyone significant. This stance, which fit into what Komisarof called *separation*, is characterized by

The True Meaning of Integrity    103

a lack of acceptance by the host community and results in delegating the foreigner to a marginal existence. It is unlike the integration I had experienced in my first university, where, even though I was seen as different, there had been acceptance. According to Komisarof (2012), "Integration and Separation share some similarities: in both cases, the immigrant, expatriate, or sojourner is seen as culturally distinct . . . these types differ in that Integration entails social acceptance while Separation does not" (p. 217).

Ironically, I was working at the best universities in Japan and so theoretically, my abilities were being recognized. However, I was continually denied access to any level of involvement with my colleagues. What was most frustrating about this period was that I knew I had the qualities necessary for acceptance but could simply not break through the cultural barriers to prove it.

## Employment Pursuits and Hardships

Employment in Japan is done en masse during the third year of university when students apply, interview, and commit to a company for full-time employment upon graduation. Once accepted into a company, people will devote their entire professional life to that company. For academics in Japan, there is a strong tendency to follow one's advisor and work in the same university or acquire a job through that advisor's connections. It is looked on as an asset to have graduated from the university where you become employed. In fact, one online application for a university to which I applied had a form that had already listed the name of the university-affiliated high school, as well as the 4-year and graduate school names of the university. One simply was expected to insert the name of the department. The only way I could submit the form was to print it out, remove the school name, and then scan the "revised" document. I learned the hard way that without the connections that Japanese academics have, it is very difficult for a foreigner to receive a full-time tenured position, no matter how qualified he or she may be.

I eventually received a full-time limited contract at a very well-known university. I became fairly close to some of the tenured Japanese faculty, and in the very first year of my employment learned of a tenured position opening up in that department. I applied for the position but did not get beyond the very first step. I rationalized that I was still too new in the university environment and that this served as a catalyst for me to really try to assimilate as a Japanese working professional. I worked very hard and remember one evening in particular when I was still at the copier with a Japanese colleague at four o'clock in the morning! I felt the acceptance I had not had as an adjunct faculty member, yet I knew I was on a limited contract. Both that year and the next, I again applied for tenured positions, never getting beyond the first step. When I confidentially asked my mentor what was wrong, I was told that the university had a policy of not hiring staff from those working in contract positions. If I really wanted to work there, I should leave and work somewhere else for a few years and then reapply.

During this time, I was pursued by recruiters from two universities. One looked quite promising, and my application was previewed by someone on the faculty, so I thought that the application process was a mere formality and that I would soon be offered a tenured position. Alas, once again, I was not even granted an interview. When I inquired what was wrong, I was told that too many of my publications were coauthored. I later learned that the position went to someone with fewer publications than I, but who was male and had attended prestigious universities in the United Kingdom. I felt very frustrated at this time, and at one point even considered returning to the U.S.

The second university that approached me did so through a colleague. The position was not announced publicly, and after an interview I received tenure at the rank of professor. It was as if all those years of "foolish diligence" had somehow borne fruit. I felt again the humility from when I first came to Japan. Here was an institution willing to take a risk on me, an unknown quantity, simply on the basis of a colleague's recommendation. I vowed to give them my undying loyalty and to work as hard as I could in appreciation for that confidence. Ironically, during my second year there, I was approached by the university where I had worked on a limited contract and offered a tenured position. With the utmost satisfaction I used a U.S. cultural metaphor "three strikes and you're out" and replied that it had had three opportunities to have me on the faculty and had "struck out."

I recall these experiences here because it was only through the accumulation of these many years of job searching that I realized just how difficult cultural barriers can be. It was necessary not only to be in the right place at the right time but also to find a working environment in which I had the ability to "fit" at the level of acceptance being offered. Perhaps most important, I also had to feel that my ability to contribute would be recognized at a level that would be emotionally satisfying for both parties.

I am now once again in what Komisarof (2012) characterized as a compatible acculturation scenario. Unlike when I was integrated into university life as a valued outsider, I am now in a stage of assimilation which means that my colleagues "support the active societal participation of the non-dominant group but reject the maintenance of their heritage cultural identity, while Assimilators from the non-dominant cultural group pursue close relations with the dominant group while renouncing their own heritage culture" (Komisarof, 2012, p. 217). Although I feel the word *renounce* is a bit too strong, I currently act far more in a Japanese mode than the mode of my heritage culture. In return, with my recent appointment as dean, I have been granted an active voice in the running of the university, and my colleagues expect me to work the same, if not more, than they do. I am challenged daily as to how much I will adapt, and yet the payoff for that adaptation is the societal inclusion that has long eluded me. It has also

*The True Meaning of Integrity*  105

been at this level of inclusion that I have begun to understand the social agency of foreign immigrant professors.

## SOCIAL CAPITAL OF FOREIGN IMMIGRANT PROFESSORS

Poole (2010) provides an ethnographic study of the Japanese professoriate. His model, while using terminology perhaps unique to Japan, examines how a professor builds collateral both within and outside the university and how this is valued by the university. In this section, I illustrate, through concrete examples, how this model can be expanded to reflect the experience of immigrant professors in any country.

The Japanese use the term *uchi* to explain things that are within one's direct home environment, as opposed to *soto*, which is used to explain things that are outside. Poole (2010) took this terminology and applied it to a university setting. In Figure 8.1, I take his original model and define the four categories he calls 1, 2, 3, and 4 with my own terminology to show how I believe the model can apply to university professors in any setting.

The role of a university professor is not limited to the classroom. The term *uchi* refers then to the work that a professor does within the university itself. This may, of course, include teaching as well as administration work, participation in on-campus activities, and student advising. This would be separate from the *soto* work a professor performs, which may or may not take place directly on campus but has an outside focus. Examples of this kind of work are research, conference presentations, publications, and grant procurement. Both of these types of work become social capital for the university, and a professor can perform various amounts of both types of functions.

In this model, professors could progress from any category to another during the course of their careers. In the case of Japan, there is an implicit assumption that Category 1 would be better than Category 4. This is due to the cultural mores that employment in Japan is usually spent at the same company or, in this case, institution. Therefore, a professor in Category 1 would be a "lifer" or devoting his or her entire career to the university through active involvement in all of its inside activities. I have named this category "The Cheerleader."

*Table 8.1*  Social Structure of Community

| Social Agency of Professors | Social Structure of Community | |
| --- | --- | --- |
| | *uchi* | *soto* |
| Inwardly oriented | 1 The Cheerleader | 3 The Nine to Fiver |
| Outwardly oriented | 2 The Card Player | 4 The Substitute Teacher |

Source: Adapted from Poole (2010).

## 106   *Robin Sakamoto*

## The Cheerleader

The Cheerleader has an overflowing amount of school spirit and is very visible on campus. Whether the team is winning or losing, cheerleaders support and cheer until the last minute, with a smile on their faces. I believe this is the hardest category for a foreign immigrant professor to achieve. Although one can be in a state of integration or assimilation, the dominant cultural group—by its very nature as the "natives"—will still harbor thoughts that prevent a foreign professor from being, or viewing themselves, as an "authentic" cheerleader. This could stem from physical characteristics, such as my blonde hair and blue eyes, which simply cannot make me the cover girl for a Japanese university. The differentiator, however, can be more subliminal, and colleagues may secretly doubt if the foreigner is really dedicated to the university "for life." There is an underlying suspicion that at some point, the foreign professor will "go home" and leave the university behind. No matter the amount of "foolish diligence," to become a cheerleader as a foreign professor may be a bit too much of a challenge for any foreign professor. Thus, we find ourselves placed (whether justly or not) more often in the category of "The Card Holder."

## The Card Holder

The Card Holder is more outward looking than the Cheerleader. These professors work hard for their institution but also keep track of the cards they hold and whether they can, or need to, fold and leave for another university. Hence, they are more actively involved in research activities, publications, and securing funding and networks that may or may not lead to future opportunities. No matter the state of their acculturation, a foreigner will hold a card that members of the dominant group do not. Based on cultural mores, this foreignness can be either positive or negative social capital. In my case, I can teach content courses in English that provide added social capital for my university as they internationalize their curriculum. Depending on the amount of merit this brings to the university, I may receive privileges that other colleagues may not in the hopes of "keeping me happy."

I believe that a tension arises when the foreign immigrant professor wants to be a Cheerleader but is regarded as a Card Holder. The ability to truly network with colleagues may be difficult because of cultural barriers. Anyone familiar with Japan will know that a large amount of information disclosure and decision-making takes place after hours, over drinks. This is called *nomification*, which stems from the Japanese verb *nomu*, meaning "to drink," and shows that social capital can be gained by spending large amounts of time after hours with colleagues. This has been the hardest form of social capital for me to accrue, although I believe that I am finally beginning to authentically do so.

One evening, I was working late with junior faculty and found out the very next day that the male professors had all been out together drinking.

I felt that this was unfair and that I was not being given access to important information that would help me to become involved with the administration of our university on a deeper level. I cornered one of my colleagues that day and told him that if I did not know him so well, I would have assumed that I was being discriminated against for being a woman. He assured me that was not the case, and the next time there was an after-hours meeting, I was sought for and invited. In some ways, it was a case of needing to be careful what you asked for, because not only was I the only woman at our table, but in the entire establishment. Not only that, but while I did gain valuable information, sometimes ignorance can also be preferred in certain matters. Nevertheless, I did feel a level of rapport with my colleagues that I had not before and think I may have come one step closer in showing them my sincere dedication to our university.

There are, however, many professors who choose not to become involved in the politics of the university and have no desire to be included in the "inner circle" of activities. Their placement on the outside can fall into one of two categories based on their orientation.

## The Nine-to-Fiver

"Nine-to-Fivers" are happy at their institution and do a good job. They may be involved in student advising and feel a very close relationship with colleagues; however, they have either consciously or unconsciously chosen by their actions or are regarded by others as not wanting access to the innermost circles of university life. This category may be where most foreign immigrant professors find themselves. This category can be very rewarding, as one may be viewed as a contributing member of the university community. Because of outside circumstances or family situations, any professor may even choose to become a Nine-to-Fiver for a while until things settle down, and they can go back to contributing the extra hours and dedication needed to be a Cheerleader. Because this model was written for a Japanese audience, there is an implicit assumption that a professor will want to be a Cheerleader more so than a Nine-to-Fiver. I wonder, however, if this would be a universally accepted assumption elsewhere.

There are similarities between the Integration phase and the Nine-to-Fiver. At the national university where I worked, I was very pleased with my university and would have been happy to work there longer, if funding had been available. I was not at that time considering being in the "inner circle" of administration, nor was I being included in faculty meetings or other more "intimate" activities. This conscious decision to orientate oneself positively within the university community is in direct contrast to "The Substitute Teacher."

## The Substitute Teacher

The Substitute Teacher, as defined by Poole (2010), encompasses professors who, although they "may be conspicuous in their relative absence on campus,

108　*Robin Sakamoto*

it is not their physical but structural invisibility that is striking—invisible in terms of the standard definition and classification, the symbolic capital of a 'good' professor within the community" (p. 129). In the adjunct faculty positions I held, my placement in this category caused me the most frustration. I felt I was a "good" professor, yet the institutions where I worked viewed me simply as a "substitute" teacher. I was put in charge of classes but was not seen as making any contribution to the university as a whole. For this reason, although I was physically present on campus, I was an invisible asset, as compared to the "real" professors. This resulted in my having an outward focus (of trying to find a "real" job as soon as possible), instead of the inward focus of a Nine-to-Fiver.

As noted earlier, Poole (2010) wrote his model for a Japanese audience, but I believe that it can be more universally applied as a guide for foreign immigrant professors as they try to negotiate their social capital. By becoming cognizant of such categories and how they are perceived by their colleagues, it provides the foreigner with the ability to access alternative ways of thinking and acting to move to a better "fit" within the institution.

## LESSONS LEARNED

Thirty years on, there are still many areas in which I hope to develop as an accepted professional in my chosen field of academia. However, it has also given me an opportunity to reflect on the lessons I have learned through being here which might or might not have been learned had I never left the United States. I find comfort and encouragement in the theories and models I have presented in this chapter and hope that readers will come away with new ideas and ways to continue on their own journeys as contributing professionals in an adopted homeland. I also would relish the opportunity for this book as a whole to serve as a catalyst for further discussion.

I began my professional career aiming to become a person of "integrity." That path has taken me in many unexpected ways, but any success I have achieved has been because of "foolish diligence." There were many times when I thought about taking the easier route, but I simply could not. I truly believe that I have unique social capital to contribute to this society, and those times when I have felt most like giving up, I take a minute to look back and see where "foolish diligence" has brought me. I refuse to quit believing in myself: If I do not believe in what I have to contribute, how can I possibly expect others to give me a chance?

Besides the experiences noted thus far, I have had other professional opportunities to work on projects in the Ukraine, Uganda, and the Philippines. These experiences have helped me further appreciate the lesson in humility I learned when I first came to Japan. I am humbled by the many people I have met who simply were not given the opportunities I have received, through no fault of their own. You can dedicate your whole life

The True Meaning of Integrity    109

to hard work and simply never be in the right place at the right time. When I feel frustrated or discouraged, I think of the millions of others who are working even harder than I do and not giving up.

I have also learned to laugh at myself often and to try to view how my actions must look to someone from Japan. I had the unique opportunity to return to that remote village twenty years later and meet with many of my former colleagues. To hear their stories of when I first arrived in Japan from their perspective made me see things in a completely and often unflattering view. While I know in my own mind what I am trying to accomplish, to others it might seem to be just plain crazy.

One of my daughters recently returned from a study abroad experience in Madagascar. She told me that in the village where she lived, she was known as the "crazy foreigner." I asked her how in the world she got that nickname, and she told me that it came from her habit of running in the morning. She got up at dawn and went jogging, which to her was perfectly logical. On her first morning, she had barely set out when somebody started running behind her. Soon, more and more villagers were following her. It is impossible for us to imagine who was more surprised at the encounter—my daughter being followed by many villagers on her morning jog or those very same villagers when she got to a halfway point and decided to run back. According to her, the people in the village kept looking around, trying to find out what it had been she was running to or from, for nobody would just take off running without a logical explanation.

I think of her story often, and it always brings a smile to my face. How I must look the same to my Japanese observers! In my own mind, I have a logical understanding of what it means to be a social asset to my university—the goals and objectives I hold as a professional and what I hope I will be able to accomplish in my professional lifetime. But from a Japanese perspective, I must appear at times like someone who is expending unknown quantities of energy for no logical reason.

My "foolish diligence" has indeed brought me to a very special place as a contributing foreign immigrant professor of my university. I hope that the lessons I have learned and expressed in this chapter will aid others to reach their full professional potential without necessarily being branded as "crazy foreigners."


## REFERENCES

Breaden, J. (2013). *The Organisational dynamics of university reform in Japan: International inside out.* New York, NY: Routledge.

Chung, E. A. (2010). *Immigration and citizenship in Japan.* New York, NY: Cambridge University Press.

Komisarof, A. (2012). *At home abroad: The contemporary Western experience in Japan.* Tokyo: Reitaku University Press.

Poole, G. S. (2010). *The Japanese professor: An ethnography of a university faculty, AW Rotterdam.* The Netherlands: Sense Publishers.

# 9 Moroccan Imams and the "Girl Professor"

## Positionality and *Epistemai* in a Classroom-Based Cross-Cultural Exchange of Knowledge

*Emilie Roy*

I am a scholar of Islam specializing in the anthropological study of West African religious institutions. I have a PhD in religious studies from a Canadian university, and for my doctoral dissertation, I studied the role of Islamic schools in Mali in educating young, democratic, Muslim citizens. On graduation, I was hired at Al Akhawayn University, a small Moroccan Anglophone university created on the model of the American liberal arts colleges, to teach in the Master of Arts in Islamic Studies (MAIS) program, designed from the perspective of the social sciences and humanities, as opposed to pure theology or religious doctrine.

I felt that I have been well trained to teach in such a program, and the "fit" could hardly have seemed better—until I met the students. The candidates in this program are not "average" students; they are imams: an all-male cohort of graduates from the Moroccan national seminaries, trained in the traditional Islamic educational system. These men had memorized the Quran at an early age, had studied Islamic theology and philosophy in one of the most renowned institution of higher learning in the Muslim world, and have had little or no exposure to any other religious tradition or academic field of study. My students are traditionally trained Moroccan imams in their late 20s and early 30s who are being confronted, for the first time, with a professor like me. I have been as much of a shock to them as they have been to me over the past years of working together.

Through a careful negotiation of our differences and commonalities, we nevertheless have created, in cooperation, a positive learning environment where the expertise of all parties was recognized and where fruitful exchanges were made possible. In this chapter, I explore the various ways in which issues of *otherness* flared up and have been managed in the university's classroom. I discuss the meeting of utterly different people and academic traditions: the struggles we have encountered—accepting me not only as their professor but also as an expert on the (anthropological) study of Islam—and the successes that followed. The discussions surrounding *otherness* in anthropology and in ethnography offers a suitable lens through which one can appreciate the negotiation of positionality in situations requiring cross-cultural exchanges and understanding.

## VULNERABILITY AND ACCEPTANCE: *OTHERNESS* AS A LEARNING OPPORTUNITY

Ethnographic fieldwork requires, at least since the 1970s, that attention be paid to some epistemological questions regarding subjectivity and positionality that arise from the research. Positionality is the idea that "gender, race, class, and other aspects of our identities are markers of relational *positions* rather than essential qualities. Knowledge is valid when it includes an acknowledgement of the knower's specific positions in any context" (Maher & Tetrault, 1993, p. 118). The researcher is expected to pose "racially and culturally grounded questions about themselves. Engaging in these questions can bring the researchers' awareness and consciousness known (seen), unknown (unseen), and unanticipated (unforeseen) issues, perspectives, epistemologies, and positions." (Milner, 2007, p. 395) Like any anthropologist entering her field site, the professor in a cross-cultural setting needs to engage in a self-reflecting exercise on her identities and the roles she takes on in the context of the research (or classroom, as the case may be)—and how participants or students do the same. The reflection surrounding one's positionality—of one's characteristics that impact the dynamic of exchange between researcher and participant—transfers well to the setting of my classroom. Awareness of positionality is therefore helpful in analyzing interactions in cross-cultural classroom settings.

## My Classroom Experiences

My experience of fieldwork in Mali has proven to be a good preparation for a classroom where the students and the professor are well aware of their alterity to one another. Indeed, for many of my students in the MAIS program, as for many of my interviewees in Bamako, some "facts" about my person were impossible not to notice, and that led to certain assumptions about who I was (or am): a young, single, Francophone, Canadian female professor who is ostensibly not Muslim. With students who were often older than me—Arab, male Muslim scholars in their own right who had studied Islamic sciences in one of the most renowned university in the Muslim world, one can only imagine the instructor–student relationships that were about to unfold in the classroom.

It may therefore come to nobody's surprise that, following our first class encounter, common stereotypes about my identity crystallized, and our relationships were inevitably affected by the students' perceptions of me. It is clear that my own attributes, and my students' subsequent judgments about them, mediated the dialogue that was possible and eventually emerged between us. A variety of assumptions about who I am as a professor was made by a number of students and necessarily influenced our classroom encounters. Many of these assumptions were, from my own perspective, either condescending or downright insulting; however, making the most out of these assumptions, accepting the students' perception of me, as well as

112   *Emilie Roy*

my own vulnerability, was key in creating channels of communication with some of these students. In the context of ethnographic research, as in the classroom, difference can be used to one's benefit.

## Making the Most of One's Vulnerability

The image constructed by some of the students assumed me to be an incompetent, inoffensive, harmless, and rather helpless researcher/professor. This assumption proceeded from the differences in academic background between my students and me and is discussed further later. Suffice it to say here that my students are theologians who study Islam as a set of unalterable and true beliefs found in a revealed text and then developed through a rigorous method by religious specialists informed by faith. On the other hand, I study Islam as a broadly encompassing set of practices informed by the specific cultural context in which they are found. From my students' perspective, therefore, I do not actually study Islam per se and am consequently not qualified to teach it. It is also possible that I adopted a demeanor that allowed them to construct such an image: I have been keenly aware from the beginning of class that my students were religious experts in their own right who, in many regards, were much more knowledgeable than I was. My own awareness of being a young, non-Muslim, foreign professor proposing to teach Islamic studies to a group of imams was sufficient to make me vulnerable in the classroom.

The uncomfortable position I found myself in nevertheless had positive consequences, and I highlight here the ways in which a vulnerable position may be used to create a positive classroom atmosphere: First, this impression of me, as developed by some students, allowed me to enter into a different kind of relationship with these students. If these students did not consider me as having valuable knowledge to share, they did, however, consider that *I* had a great deal to learn from them. Lines of communication therefore opened quickly with these students who did not recognize my own expertise. That initial one-way sharing of knowledge, although not ideal, nevertheless allowed for communication to happen.

Second, and proceeding for the previous point, I did not pose a challenge to these students and, therefore, engaging with me from a perceived position of superiority seemed to make them feel quite confident in class. My own acknowledged vulnerability in the classroom has been necessary for some of the students to feel at ease themselves insofar as my *otherness* was not perceived a threat but rather as something that was to be overcome. And overcoming of our differences, making me less of an *other*, necessarily required us to communicate—to exchange experiences and knowledge; it required us to cooperate towards a common goal: understanding each other.

Third, the unintended consequence of this shared objective in the classroom was a willingness to participate in debates in class. The students wanted me to understand them, so they stated and argued their opinions

Moroccan Imams and the "Girl Professor"   113

and shared their ideas with me and their fellow students quite candidly. By explaining their positions and sharing knowledge with me, they bridged the perceived gap that separated us at the beginning. We entered into an academic conversation where we discussed, together, what the study of Islam is and how different methodologies necessarily offered a different perspective on this point. We reconciled our differences by accepting our different academic backgrounds and therefore the different results of our respective research. Once it was accepted that I, as a social scientist and not a theologian, studied certain aspects of Islam (practices mostly) through rigorous methods (ethnography) and from a scientific perspective (anthropology), I was deemed a worthy interlocutor. My knowledge in my field could be recognized by the students because it was now clear that it in no way competed with, or annulled, their own knowledge.

Indeed, their view of me as vulnerable and my (reluctant) acceptance of this quality are integral parts of the relationship we established in the classroom. Anthropologists in the field are familiar with this perceived vulnerability and their need to accept. However much one might feel the need to shatter this image as dismissive, even insulting, it can nonetheless prove useful in making the anthropologist more approachable insofar as it displays the "appropriate" respect the anthropologist owes to his or her interviewees:

> Vulnerablity [*sic*] is such an elemental part of fieldwork . . . ; if the fieldworker is too good, too smart, too sophisticated to be treated in this way, people will never talk to them. And that is the heart of participation observation research—the researcher shows respect for the people he or she is working with by doing what they do, especially when asked to join them. (Lukens-Bull, 2007, p. 182)

Granted that vulnerability is an inherent part of being a professor in a foreign environment; however, displaying and accepting this vulnerability in the classroom may also prove a successful strategy for the professor in the foreign cultural and religious environment. Indeed, very much like the anthropologist in the field who needs to learn from his or her interviewees, the professor in cross-cultural context also needs to learn from his or her students to teach them more effectively. My seeming acceptance of the mostly condescending attitudes (from my point of view) exhibited by some of my students—that temporary position of perceived "inferiority"—facilitated the start of a dialogue between my students and me. This required me to accept their own expertise, which is indisputable, in the traditional Islamic sciences and in their knowledge of Moroccan culture. I therefore had to accept that they had something to teach me. This recognition of their expertise and my willingness to learn from them opened lines of communication. These students felt comfortable to engage in the classroom, adding to the discussion of the material, which, in turn, allowed me to respond, adding new elements from my own expertise to the ongoing debates.

114   *Emilie Roy*

For me as a young foreign professor, the temptation can be high to present oneself as exaggeratedly authoritative to compensate for the inherent vulnerability discussed above. However, I have found that by admitting to the limits of my knowledge and by allowing the students to teach me and learn from them, I was able to exchange with my students in a way that was beneficial to both of us. By allowing the students to educate me in their own field of expertise, I recognized and allowed them to see my inherent position as their *other*—as having a different set of skills and a different area of expertise. This, in a roundabout way, established me as an expert in the social scientific approaches to the study of Islam; it established me as one who possesses specialized knowledge of my own that could be shared. In this way, my students and I created a class environment where the exchange of ideas from various perspectives—mine and theirs—became the norm, an environment where engaging ideas on Islam and practices of Muslim worldwide could flow back and forth between the students and the professor.

## CULTURALLY AND RELIGIOUSLY INFORMED KNOWLEDGE: LEARNING ANOTHER *EPISTEME*

The acceptance of an utterly different professor, however, is only part of the challenge of teaching in a cross-cultural context. The specific knowledge held by the professor must also be accepted as worthy of study—as appropriate knowledge. Here, philosophical perspectives on the nature of knowledge are useful. For my students and me to communicate effectively through our different cultural, religious, and educational backgrounds, an understanding of our respective fields of knowledge was necessary. The MAIS program in which I am a professor aims at introducing the students to an academic field that is new to them. Religious studies and the social scientific approach to the study of religion are parts of the liberal arts educational tradition. The contemporary academic study of religions is rooted in an intellectual tradition dating back to the Enlightenment. It has a "distinctive multidisciplinary orientation and multicultural focus" (Taylor, 1998, p. 15) that seeks to emphasize the value of the plurality of religious traditions while also avoiding simplifications and reductionist perspectives of the complexity and, sometimes, confusion of the subject and the object of study.

### The Master in Islamic Studies Program

As a student in Canadian universities, and as a professor in the MAIS in Morocco, I have been trained and fully participate in a specific understanding of knowledge not originally shared by my students. The MAIS program here aims, through various courses and the acquisition of skills and knowledge, to introduce a specific *episteme* to the students, an *episteme* with which most of them are unfamiliar:

> By *episteme*, we mean, in fact, the total set of relations that unite, at a given period, the discursive practices that give rise to epistemological figures, sciences, and possibly formalized systems . . . The episteme is not a form of knowledge (*connaissance*) or type of rationality which, crossing the boundaries of the most varied sciences, manifests the sovereign unity of a subject, a spirit, or a period; it is the totality of relations that can be discovered, for a given period, between the sciences when one analyses them at the level of discursive regularities. (Foucault, 2010, p. 191)

The Intended Learning Outcomes for the MAIS program are in line with a liberal arts *episteme* and specifically with the academic methods for the study of religion within it. Students in the program must complete a number of courses that introduce them to the academic field of religious studies. As the professor for the mandatory course Social Sciences Approaches to Religion I first encountered the students.

Our students begin the program fully grounded in an *episteme* that proceeds from an Islamic theory of knowledge, but over the course of their studies they are expected to become familiar and at ease with the academic study of religion in a liberal arts tradition. The students first arrive in the MAIS program with the perspective that *knowledge* is Truth of divine origins but are introduced, through the courses previously mentioned, to secular knowledge: knowledge without divinely inspired truth claims.

## Bridging the Epistemological Gap

When they first enter the program, the MAIS students are fully participating in an economy of knowledge in which concepts, beliefs, and practices fit neatly and without qualifications into the dichotomous categories of "true" and "false." The sacred text is unchangeable; its content, as well as its form, is perfect and always true without qualification: It is a "manifestation of things as they are," and people use them in an economy of knowledge where they are of the highest value (Lambek, 1990). Knowledge, from within the faith is clearly defined:

> The Holy Qur'an makes it clear that knowledge is a characteristic of God Himself and that all knowledge comes from Him" (Q. 35:28). This applies whether the knowledge is revealed (*naqliyya*) or humanly constructed (*'aqliyya*), and it means that knowledge must be approached reverently and in humility, for there cannot be any "true" knowledge that is in conflict with religion and divine revelation, only ignorance. (Halstead, 2004, p. 520)

116   *Emilie Roy*

This *episteme* where knowledge is necessarily true (as opposed to ignorance, which proceeds from false knowledge) limits the *connaissances* that can indeed be part of the realm of knowledge. Out of the realm of true knowledge is *jâhilîyah* (ignorance) which, if it were to be studied, would simply lead to more ignorance. The students therefore arrive in the MAIS program with a specific understanding of knowledge that proceeds from this Islamic *episteme* through the traditional Moroccan Islamic educational system.

In contrast to my students, I am the product of an academic tradition where knowledge for the sake of knowledge should be pursued and where ideas of absolute truth or falsity based on faith have mostly been purged in favor of scientifically proven data. I have been trained to study religious practices as they happen, without judgment regarding their correct performance or underlying belief system. I fully participate in the anthropological tradition where beliefs and rituals are "true" insofar as they are real factors and produce actions in the lives of real people and religious systems are worth studying because they inform various aspects of their lives, regardless of whether the researcher considers them True with a capital *T*. Debates about correct or incorrect religious practices are relevant to my field of study only insofar as the researcher seeks to understand *why* and *how* these interpretations of correctness have emerged in a particular context. As a social scientist teaching in Islamic studies, it was my task to make my students familiar with this *episteme*, this academic tradition.

As part of the MAIS program, popular practices, heterodox beliefs, and a great diversity of concepts related to the field of religion are to be studied, understood, and investigated. To fully transition to the academic study of religion in the liberal arts model, the students are required to become familiar and conversant with *connaissances*—bits of knowledge—which may be classified as false or incorrect in the Islamic *episteme* in which they have so far participated. Eventually, the student is expected to come to the realization that "false" knowledge in their *episteme* might be accepted as part of useful ("true") knowledge in the new *episteme* they are introduced to. The slow transition between two heterogeneous *epistemai* is the goal of the program.

## *Salât* Prayer in Illustration of *Epistemai*

The academic practice of associating information that could be labeled as both "true" and "false" under the same concept would run counter to the Islamic theory of knowledge with which the students are familiar. One such concept extensively discussed and debated in my course, Social Sciences Approaches to the Study of Religion, was that of *rituals* as encompassing the practice of *salât* (prayer).

For the students, salât as a practice is entirely part of the Islamic *episteme* and defined as worship, which itself necessarily implied the inherent truth of the action. Ritual, on the other hand, is a concept encompassing various

*Moroccan Imams and the "Girl Professor"* 117

performances that necessarily are not all true in the way some of my students understand it and, as an anthropological category, is devoid of any criteria of truth or falsity. In anthropological studies, the concept of ritual is effectively used to qualify performances that the students' epistemological tradition require to be classified as false. The student's immediate reaction to the study of rituals was to "dissociate *salât* as 'true' knowledge/practice from ritual as beliefs/practices based in ignorance of the truth (Monette & Roy, in press). This reaction was completely unexpected to me and left me baffled: I did not understand what the problem was with the definition. I had expected a fairly straightforward discussion on Rappaport's (1999) definition of rituals, which is certainly complicated when encountered for the first time but not out of reach for students at the master's level. In the academic field of religious studies, salât can be understood as fully participating in the broad definition of ritual developed by Rappaport (1999) as "the performance of more or less invariant sequences of formal acts and utterances not entirely encoded by the performer" (p. 24). After discussion, it became clear that most students understood Rappaport's text and definition but that some of them did not *accept* it—and I could not grasp why.

This breakdown of communication and understanding in the classroom rooted in the differences in *epistemai* between a foreign professor and her students can be a precursor to new and enlightening exchanges. In anthropological theory, these unexpected moments when problems in cross-cultural understanding emerge are called "rich points." Those moments are often accidental, and they imply the vulnerability that I have discussed previously: Communication fails because one or both parties in the exchange have no sense of the other's perspective. The salât-ritual moment was a rich point in my classroom: it required me to delve into my students' understanding of salât to attempt reconciliation with my own understanding of *ritual* based in the academic tradition of religious studies. When the two *epistemai* collided during this discussion, the only way to bridge the gap was for me to understand my students' position and their difficulties with the new material I was presenting. Only after doing so was I able to reexplain the concept of ritual in religious studies effectively. I needed first to learn from my students' perspective to teach them a new one in a way that was acceptable to them.

The MAIS program is designed to educate the students in the fields of knowledge *about* religion in a form that is consistent with other Religious Studies and Islamic Studies programs in modern higher educational institutions worldwide. The students are expected to become conversant with the network of authorities who produce academic discourse *about* religion. The preceding is not to say, however, that the student must depart from his Islamic epistemological tradition and mode of knowledge but, rather, that, through progression in the program, the two *epistemai* should be reconciled. They are not to be considered as mutually exclusive but, rather, as complementary modes of knowledge. The program aims at rearranging in a novel way, and not replacing, the vast bank of *connaissances* gathered

118    *Emilie Roy*

by the students during their prior education through a growing familiarity with a new *episteme*. The role of the professor, in this context, is to serve as a bridge between the two *epistemai*. The professor faced with a foreign *episteme* ought to learn from her students, to become familiar with their form of knowledge, to better able to impart new ways of thinking about these *connaissances*. The students, although there to learn, should not be expected to cross that bridge by themselves. With the passing of time, there appears to have been a successful reconciliation of the concepts by introducing the students to the new (to them) discursive practices of the field of religious studies—because I found ways to communicate with them and to understand their challenges.

## An Example of Success

In the course of the MAIS program, the success of the students in undertaking this epistemological shift becomes evident through academic projects they have undertaken. One student, let's call him Hicham, is developing a master's thesis that clearly exemplifies the successful transition from one *episteme* to another. Hicham is quite representative of the group of students discussed in this chapter. A young man in his late 20s, he has pursued all of his education in Arabic within the traditional Islamic schooling system. He has, over the years, received a thorough education in the traditional Islamic sciences and graduated from the Qarawiyyine University with enough distinction to be hand-selected by the Ministry of Religious Affairs to pursue a master's degree in Islamic Studies at Al Akhawayn University. Like his colleagues, Hicham was first exposed to the social sciences approaches to the study of religion via my course and has since taken other courses rooted in the social scientific method. Hicham's master's thesis, still a work in progress, is indicative of this transition from one *episteme* to another, and the final product (the thesis itself), when completed, will be a tool, for me as his supervisor, to assess this transition. Hicham's research will explore the revival of Sufi practices in Morocco as encouraged by the official definition of "Moroccan Islam" developed by the government through the Ministry of Religious Affairs. His work will entail participant observation, as well as interviews with young Moroccans between the ages of 20 and 30 at the shrine of Moulay Abdessalam Ben Mchich Alami. Hicham, through in-depth interviews, seeks to examine the role of such practices in the life of young people.

This student's work exemplifies the switch to an epistemological frame of reference discussed earlier. Hicham's master's thesis demonstrates his growing familiarity with the methods and the *episteme* underlining the social scientific study of religions. The topics he has chosen to investigate display an excellent understanding of the questions that social scientific studies seek to address: There is no mention or discussion of "true" or "false" beliefs and rituals—simply an exploration of the religious life of a group as they

Moroccan Imams and the "Girl Professor" 119

actually live it. The quality of the work speaks to our common success at establishing dialogue in the classroom that, in turn, has allowed the students to understand and adopt a new way of thinking based on a different form of knowledge.

There was indeed a time when exploring the social impact of a heterodox religious institution would have fallen outside the purview of the study of Islam per se; however, the students are now capable of analyzing people's religious practices as having value in and of itself, and as being part of the academic study of Islam. They have therefore clearly recognized and accepted the expertise I have in anthropology and integrated the knowledge and ultimately made it their own. As a professor, for me, my role is to help the students in their general intellectual transition and to ascertain, in the end, not only that I understand their Islamic epistemological field of knowledge but also that they understand the discursive tradition of religious studies. Bridging the cultural and epistemological gap is achieved, ideally, by the professor coming to class with a foreign *episteme*, becoming familiar with the students' *episteme*, learning *from* them, and sharing *with* them.

## LESSONS LEARNED: DEVELOPING UNDERSTANDING AND TRUST

My experiences recounted in this chapter have taught me several lessons. I made the case that the recognition of alterity in the classroom, as in the field, allows for the possibility of dialogue. As any anthropologist knows, one is first and foremost a student in the field and can only obtain valuable information from one's respondents if they are first conceived of as having something important to contribute to the conversation. In the same way, positive, cross-cultural dialogue in the classroom can only happen when both professor and his or her students recognize each other as valid interlocutors—as possessing *connaissances* worth sharing. This, in turn, can only happen after the field of knowledge, the *episteme* in which the other participates, is recognized as worth engaging with. In the context of the classroom, like in fieldwork, the professor is required to recognize and take this alterity into account to establish his or her own position, and by acknowledging it, one can successfully engage with it.

I have also learned that, to establish a relationship with my students based on respect and trust, I needed, like an ethnographer in the field, to acknowledge a position of relative vulnerability. As much as my perception of myself as an expert with a PhD in the field seemed sufficient to justify my acceptance as the professor in the classroom, this necessarily proceeds from a point of view where this expertise is recognized; notwithstanding this fact, I was forced to realize that there is no reason for someone participating in another *episteme* to necessarily maintain the same recognition. Like the ethnographer who has to "enter" the field and subsequently constantly

## 120  *Emilie Roy*

negotiate his or her position in the field, so a professor in a cross-cultural context has to negotiate his or her position in the classroom. The normality of my position in the classroom could only be accepted by my students *after* we acknowledged each *other's otherness* and therefore the possibility to learn from one another.

As a non-Muslim, a young woman, and a foreign-born scholar, teaching highly knowledgeable Moroccan Islamic scholars has proved to be a challenge for both me and my students. Nevertheless, in the classroom and beyond, we have succeeded in establishing a mutually respectful relationship that allows for the recognition of differences in expertise and therefore for an exchange because of our difference(s). Our particular experience of cross-cultural communication can potentially serve others in similar situation by extracting from it some general principles I now try to apply in all my class and all students, be they scholars in their own right or not:

a. **Be yourself.** Teaching is an act, and all teachers, to a certain degree, put on a mask when teaching; however, I have learned to be myself, as much as possible. For me, as a professor who is different from the majority of my students, the temptation is twofold: (a) to pretend to participate in "their culture" more than I actually do and (b) to try to meet their expectations of what a professor should be. In my case, the second temptation was simply not an option, but I do think neither is sustainable in the long term. I, as a competent scholar and overall decent person (as are most professors, regardless of background), should suffice.

b. **Do answer personal questions.** Proceeding from the first point, I present myself as the person I think I am and will answer questions about myself, my cultural background, my and training, accordingly. The *other*, when known, is much more approachable. The questions may come across as expressing doubt about my relative position of authority as a professor and possessing a particular expertise of my own, but these doubts are better dealt with when verbally and clearly discussed, and then possibly dispelled, rather than by keeping silent. For example, a 30-minute discussion erupted around my marital status, which was prompted by a student who stated quite bluntly, "We never had a professor like you. We don't know what to call you." Doctor or Professor, my actual academic titles, did not come to the students' mind right away, and they were debating among themselves whether to call me Miss or Mrs. Roy. This question may come across as rather insulting in my own cultural environment but required much discussion in the Moroccan cultural environment.

c. **Recognize the students as experts** in some specific areas and value their knowledge. They often know things that the professor teaching in a different cultural environment may not. In my case, my students are recognized religious experts, and getting them talking about what they

*Moroccan Imams and the "Girl Professor"* 121

know establishes lines of communications and a habit of exchanging valuable knowledge.

d. **Learning is a two-way street.** Proceeding from the previous point, it helps to note that, for a foreign-born professor who is in a different cultural environment, there is much knowledge to gain. Creating a classroom environment where exchange of knowledge was both possible and valued has made me a better professor and a more knowledgeable person. It has therefore allowed me to teach the material I was paid to teach in the first place.

In conclusion, foreign-born professors should be open-minded in their new teaching contexts to become successful.

## REFERENCES

Foucault, M. (2010). *The archeology of knowledge.* New York, NY: Vintage Books, Random House.

Halstead, M. J. (2004). An Islamic concept of education. *Comparative Education, 40*(4), 517–529.

Lambek, M. (1990). Certain knowledge, contestable authority: power and practice on the Islamic periphery. *American Ethnologist, 17*(1), 23–40.

Lukens-Bull, R. (2007). Lost in a sea of subjectivity: the subject position of the researcher in the anthropology of Islam. *Contemporary Islam: Dynamics of Muslim Life, 1*(2), 173–192.

Maher, F. A., & Tetrault, M. K. (1993). Frames of positionality: Constructing meaningful dialogues about gender and race. *Anthropological Quarterly, 66*(3), 118–126.

Milner, R. H. IV. (2007). Race, culture, and researcher positionality: Working through dangers seen, unseen, and unforeseen. *Educational Researcher, 36*(7), 388–400.

Monette, C., & Roy, E. (in press). The Al Akhawayn University Master of Arts in Islamic Studies. In Beirut (Lebanon) (Ed.), الدراسات الإسلامية أمام تح\*\*\*ي [Islamic Studies in the contemporary world: التنوع الثقافي في العالم المعاصر A cross-cultural challenge]. Adyan Foundation. (Refereed).

Rappaport, R. A. (1999). *Ritual and religion in the making of humanity.* Cambridge: Cambridge University Press.

Taylor, M. C. (1998). Introduction. In M. C. Taylor (Ed.), *Critical terms for religious studies* (pp. 1–19). Chicago, IL: University of Chicago Press.

# 10 Not so Fast

## Navigating the Complexities of Teaching in an American University as a Foreign-Born Teacher Educator

*Eucabeth Odhiambo*

Foreign-born faculty consistently experience issues of race, gender, and prejudicial perceptions, resulting in complex relationships between the foreign-born faculty and their students. As a foreign-born educator, I erroneously believed that my educational background and international teaching experiences had prepared me to work anywhere in the world, including the United States. However, my professional journey has led me to a personal awaking, compelling me to look at the world from other perspectives. In this chapter, I examine my journey as a foreign-born educator going through social-cultural experiences, student–teacher relations, and grading and assessment issues. I share how my personal and professional development is discrete but intertwined and how I have had to reexamine my own perspectives. I discuss the complexity of my interactions with my students and how I have learned to successfully navigate the teaching journey and cope with the resulting stresses.

Foreign-born college faculty members, while providing their services in numerous higher education institutions across the United States and all over the world, continue to experience many challenges, including a lack of respect from students and discriminative work environments. They seem to receive the paradoxical message "We want you here," on one hand, and "You do not belong here," on the other hand. As a foreign-born faculty member who has experienced this paradox, I strongly believe that by sharing my voice, I will bring to light the specific issues in the hopes of stimulating a conversation, and therefore fulfilling the "potential for empowering unheard voices" (Dyson & Genishi, 1994, p. 4) to eventually bring change.

In my personal journey as a foreign-born faculty member, I have experienced many challenges including challenging student relationships and rewards along the way. Overall, the challenging teaching experiences have had an impact on me psychologically, physically, and emotionally. My journey has involved hard work, personal commitment, dedication, cultural interactions, learning, expectations, resistance, frustration, and continued efforts to meet my responsibilities efficiently and effectively as a teacher and scholar, while delivering dedicated service to the university. This journey has not been altogether lonely and isolated but has been shared with others on the same path. As Mayher (1990) noted, "by transacting with these stories of unfolding journeys, we can enrich and enlighten our own parallel, but necessarily individual, roads" (p. xv). In this journey, I have learned many lessons—lessons I believe are positive outcomes of these adverse experiences.

## MY JOURNEY AS AN INTERNATIONAL TEACHER EDUCATOR

As agents of learning and contributors to diversity, foreign-born faculty are confronted with the reality of interaction between their culture and that of the host country. The teaching journey for them is complex in that it involves first, acquiring knowledge about ethnic and cultural diversity and at the same time confronting their own racial and cultural biases. Second, it is a journey where one learns to see reality from a variety of ethnic and cultural perspectives. Finally, this journey involves challenging inequities in the place of work and working collaboratively with others with similar concerns to bring about change (Nieto, 1999, 2000).

### Embarking on a Difficult Journey

My teaching experience in Kenya was an eye-opener: I was teaching in a K–8 international school with children from a variety of backgrounds and cultures. It was challenging and at the same time rewarding. I progressed from crying every evening after a full day of teaching two grades in one room to leaving the school reluctantly for another job.

From Kenya to Bangkok, Thailand, where I worked with children from all over the world, I learned to take into consideration my students' culture, and to listen and teach them in ways that they would understand. Teaching had become a personal engagement for me, and I put in a lot of hard work and commitment towards teaching in a culturally responsive way.

### Culture and Pedagogical Shock in Student Life

Based on my previous experiences (attending a Christian school with many American teachers, teaching at an international school, and then teaching in Thailand), I did not expect much of a culture shock here in the United States. Furthermore, I thought that I had learned enough American culture through my geography lessons in high school; however, these were not enough to prepare me for some of the cultural and pedagogical shock I experienced. I believed that the American culture would accommodate mine, and me theirs. On my part, I was ready to accommodate any differences.

Pedagogically, my shock was based on the style of teaching that I experienced under some professors. Their teaching was very casual and lacking in the use of teaching resources, despite their ample availability. Another shock was the assessment process for students' academic work: I thought

124　*Eucabeth Odhiambo*

that grades were given for substandard work. However, I appreciated and learned to use different pedagogical styles than what I grew up with.

Culturally, everything was different. I thought I knew English until I got to the United States, where people spoke a different kind of English. I had to find out the American word for items I had learned the British way. The people, food, social relations, and academic culture were all different. However, the shock that I have continued to struggle with is the lack of respect for international faculty by students. Initially, as a graduate assistant, I thought that as long as I identified the problem and solved it, all would be well; after all, there was nothing new about a few students who were disrespectful; therefore, as an international faculty, I expected that such happenings would be rare and of very little consequence. I expected to be respected as a scholar. Reality, however, set in when I embarked on my new journey as a professor.

## Accent Issues and Micro-Aggressions

I accepted a tenure track position before graduating from my doctoral program. I was ecstatic. Things got off to a good start for me at this new institution. I did not know what to expect from the faculty or students, but was confident that things would work out; after all, I thought to myself, the students would know that I was new and would surely be patient with me. Yet within weeks of starting classes, I observed a strange atmosphere in my classroom that I could not explain. My students seemed standoffish; I felt unable to reach them. Then I learned that students had been visiting the department head's office complaining that they could not understand my accent. My department head told them that my accent was understandable and that they needed to talk to me first about any issues they were having. Not a single student came to see me. Students wrote in my evaluation that my accent was too thick to understand and questioned why the department employed people who could not speak English.

Things never settled for me after that in terms of student relationships. My first semester was the beginning of many similar and even worse interactions with students. This was the beginning of my experiencing what Solorzano, Ceja, and Yosso (2000) call "micro-aggressions"—"subtle insults (verbal, nonverbal, and/or visual) directed toward people of color, often automatically or unconsciously" (p. 60). Over the years, these micro-aggressions have been initiated both covertly and overtly. Students have engaged in micro-aggressive behavior such as speaking with subtle tones, mumbling during class, addressing me disrespectfully, expressing themselves inappropriately in written communications of different kinds, engaging in blatantly disrespectful speech, and making inaccurate remarks and maligning me in course evaluations.

Fortunately, not all of my students have behaved this way. Usually, just a handful of students are displeased. These students, unfortunately, tend to infect the whole class. The complex part of these aggressive actions is that

## Not so Fast 125

many students smile and say, "Thank you for your help, Professor," but represent themselves oppositely in their evaluations, which are eventually reviewed by the promotion and tenure committees.

## Teaching Challenges: Instruction, Assessment, and Disrespectful Student Behavior

My teaching style is a mix of lectures, group activities, short student presentation, and discussions. I, like most of my colleagues, use a variety of assessments in my courses so that students are able to leverage their strengths, that is, test, projects, presentations, and the like. I use rubrics to break down assignments such that students can see where their points are earned. For each assignment, there is a detailed procedural explanation on how to complete it effectively and, in so doing, make the best grade. Additionally, I briefly explain all assignments at the beginning of the semester, and then I go into detail before the assignment is due. I have an "open door policy": Anytime my door is open, students are welcome to come in beyond the time I am available for my regular office hours. With that, I feel that I provide various avenues of communication in case one fails. Unbelievably, I have been accused of not explaining the assignments clearly, for taking points off without explanation, for poor communication, and for not providing rubrics.

It was only after a couple of years of poor student behavior toward me and low evaluations that I was convinced there was more to this than just my performance as a teacher. At first, I thought that generally, all professors will experience such unfavorable relationships with students when they start their careers; after all, I reasoned, these students were intelligent and wanted a good education, and so they were not going to let any professor give them less than the best. I had high expectations for my students and invested a lot of time in my work. I was very willing to listen to "questions." I always proceeded to give a clear explanation as to why points were taken off, for example. In fact, I would go back to the notes or the text. However, I soon realized that most did not even take the time to read my feedback or even check the text or notes to make sure that the answer was correct. Worse still, they argued about how hard they had worked only to lose points. At times I gave points back. Such experiences sent me looking for what my colleagues were doing and if they were experiencing such challenges. They had fewer experiences of that type. Additionally, they indicated that students never refer to such minor problems in their evaluations of them. They knew that students were less tolerant of foreign faculty and hoped things would improve for me.

My expectations have not been well received by some students. I consistently receive complaints about "hard tests" and "expecting too much from assignments." Over the years, I have had to deal with defiant, rude, and disrespectful student behavior in my classes. Others challenge what I say both directly and indirectly. Some question the validity of my assignments,

126 *Eucabeth Odhiambo*

even after explanations and documentation are given. These behaviors have greatly bothered me, and I have often wondered what one can do or, better, what measures to take toward a college student who does not respect the professor, despite her myriad actions? This is a dilemma Sue et al. (2007) call "'the catch-22' situation: Damned if you say something and damned if you do not say something" (p. 279). My colleagues have suggested that I throw such students out of my class. I have never brought myself to ask a student to leave my class. Why have I not done it? I think it would work against me. Because I am consistently dealing with grade issues as explained earlier, I have to choose my battles.

However, the question remains: What can I do to turn these negative relationships into positive ones? It is more complicated when we consider that micro-aggressions are more than just disrespect; they are subtle behavior such as snubs or dismissive looks, gestures, and tones often delivered unconsciously (Rowe, 1990). Such experiences are similar to what Sue et al. (2007) call "microassaults."

## More Teaching Challenges: Student Evaluations

During my first year, I actually thought that students had been trained to identify the characteristics of good teaching and to give constructive criticism, but to my amazement, I was being evaluated by 18- to 20-year-olds who were not familiar with constructive feedback. Worse still, my teaching career was going to be largely measured by what they said. For me, student evaluations had become the pink elephant in the room. By my fourth year, I realized how problematic my evaluations would be for tenure and promotion; I needed to do something. How was I going to change such mean, hurtful, and unconstructive criticism? The comments in my course evaluations included the following and their like: "she is the worst teacher I have ever had," "her accent is so thick," "she is the worst professor in this department."

I shed tears at the end of many semesters wondering what to do. I asked myself if I was really in the right profession. Did other professors experience the same thing as I did every semester? They looked happy and seemed to have positive interactions with students. I wondered what I had done to deserve all these contrary interaction. What was I missing? I had spent many sleepless nights creating interesting lessons, yet, at each semester's end, many students did not appreciate the very things I had strived to do for them. Had they colluded to write their comments about me?

On the other hand, some students shared how frustrated they were with the amount of time we "waste[d] in class explaining assignments to people who [did] not read the assignment sheet." Others came to my office upset with their classmates for being mean to me. Such words of consolation gave me the motivation to continue teaching in higher education. I became more resolved each new semester to continue teaching and to not to quit.

Over time, I began to analyze the evaluation questions students were asked to respond to by the college administration. Take the question, "What aspects of this course would you change?" Astonishingly, students were interpreting this question as an opportunity for them to criticize me personally. In fact, I, the instructor, was one of the "things" in the course they would want to change. Their behavior during the semester was evidence that students had already judged me as something to change. This question, although gender and race neutral, was a poorly worded question and elicited aggressive responses from students. Evaluation questions need to be properly worded. Wiener (2013) noted that "we don't learn a lot from student feedback when we don't ask good questions" (p. 1).

Having not been given the opportunity to record their thoughts about the improvements that have taken place during the semester, students have definitely forgotten their experiences by the end of the semester and are in a rush to finish and go home. All they can offer is vague statements that could be interpreted in multiple ways and often negatively. For example, what does "lack of communication" mean? Does communication refer to my accent, written or verbal explanations, written exchanges such as email communications? Are the comments pervasive perceptions too complex to explain?

I have started conducting informal evaluations on everyday learning experiences and on how students view these experiences as having an impact on their own learning. I give them these evaluations during the semester and use their feedback to improve instruction. At the same time, I use them as evidence of my professional engagement.

I continue to do everything I can to teach in ways that address my students' needs. I consistently analyze problematic areas identified by students. The difference now is that I document my efforts and use a variety of methods to do so. I ask questions about course activities, assignments and specific learning events in my midterm and end-of-semester unofficial student evaluations, while students can recall what they are learning (see Weimer, 2013).

I am confident that if I were as terrible a teacher as my student evaluations demonstrate, the department would not have kept me this long. I am proud of the growth I have made with the support of my colleagues and by my hard work, commitment, and faith. I focus now on things I can do differently rather than on ways I can get students to view me differently. Students, I know, will always view me through a different lens than their American-born White professors. They will judge me harshly and, at times, intentionally seek to undermine me and make my life difficult.

## THE EFFECTS OF MY CHALLENGING JOURNEY

### Negative Effects

The challenges I have encountered in my higher education experiences (what I have so far referred to as micro-aggressions) have had some negative effects on me. The effects of these micro-aggresssions have been psychologically, physically, and emotionally taxing. Solorzano, Ceja, and Yosso (2000) reported in their study of this phenomenon that micro-aggression results in a negative racial climate and creates negative emotions such as self-doubt, frustration, and isolation.

The psychological impact of micro-aggressions has been the focus of several studies (e.g., Spanierman & Heppner, 2004). Racial micro-aggressions create psychological dilemmas that can lead to racial anger, mistrust, and loss of self-esteem for persons of color, unless they are resolved. Furthermore, there are consequences for both the perpetrator and the target person (Spanierman & Heppner, 2004; Thompson & Neville, 1999). Sue et al. (2007) noted that micro-aggressive acts are difficult to identify when they can "be explained away by seemingly nonbiased and valid reasons" (p. 275). Individuals who are the targets of micro-aggression are left with vague feelings that they have been disrespected (Franklin, 2004; Reid & Redhakrishnan, 2003). For me, as such a target, I have repeatedly tried to figure out what I had done wrong to be treated so negatively. In fact, I have not always been certain that I have been discriminated against by my students. I have had this vague feeling that something was wrong by the way a student responded to me verbally or nonverbally, yet I could not specifically identity the problem. I often wondered if I was just being oversensitive. I did not think that such treatment could happen to me, just because of my membership in a minority culture.

Sue et al. (2007) identifies four psychological dilemmas individuals like me can experience in higher education: (a) clashing racial realities (i.e., variation in the ways people of color and white people perceived realities; Jones, 1997), (b) bias that is invisible to the micro-aggressor, (c) the minimization of negative impact by the micro-aggressor of the negative impact of racial micro-aggressions, and (d) the catch-22 situation, for the targeted individual, of responding to micro-aggressions (which means that any response is likely to yield negative results).

Regarding the second psychological dilemma (the invisibility of bias to the micro-aggressor), my students often explain how they had acted in good faith and are offended when I ask them if they behave the same way in other classes. They do not seem to realize that they are behaving differently in my class than they do in other classes. This general response, I have learned, is actually predicted by research. Empirical evidence shows that micro-aggression can happen automatically as a result of cultural conditioning (Abelson, Dasgupta, Park, & Banaji, 1998). Sue et al. (2007, p. 278), citing the works of Jones (1997) and Keltner and Robinson (1996), suggested that "the most accurate assessment about whether racist acts have occurred in a particular situation is most likely to be made by those most disempowered rather than by those who enjoy the privileges of power." Students typically discount their micro-aggressive acts. Some indicate by e-mail or verbally that I am overreacting to their micro-aggressive acts.

Others claim that their behavior is not as bad as I say it is and that I am overreacting when I call them into my office to discuss the issue or identify their behavior as unprofessional. Sue et al. (2007) further noted that usually, "whites consider micro-aggressive incidents to be minor, and people of color are encouraged (oftentimes by other people of color) to not waste time or effort on them" (p. 278).

Regarding the catch-22 dilemma, Sue et al. (2007) notes that series of questions immediately floods the mind of the target during a micro-aggressive act:

> Did what I think happen really happen? Was this a deliberate act or an unintentional slight? How should I respond? Should I sit and stew about this or confront the person? How will I prove to administrators that the micro-aggression actually happened? Is it really worth my effort? Should I just drop the matter and pretend it didn't happen?" (p. 279)

I have often felt that I could not prove I had actually experienced a micro-aggressive act. For 8 years, I would start talking about such experiences and then invalidate them, convincing myself that they didn't happen. Many times I asked colleagues or friends what I should do. I wondered whether I should stew in on the matter or confront the students. My actions were always delayed because I was not sure about what to do and many times my actions did nothing to improve the situation. The two questions continue to bother me: Is it really worth the effort? and Will my actions change students' behaviors and perceptions of me? The catch is that inaction on my part—that is, not doing anything about such acts—can in itself, as Sue et al. (2007) concluded, be psychologically harmful, but, as noted earlier, taking action often yielded no results.

Negative psychological effects are often accompanied by negative physical effects because the body and the mind are often affected simultaneously. In other words, psychological harm often manifests as physical harm, for example, illnesses that come as a result of stress, depression and the like.

Emotionally, it is difficult to express what I have gone through and, to a small extent, continue to go through each semester. Students' comments in everyday communications as well as on course evaluations seem to convey the same message: "You will never be good enough. We will always find something against you." I have felt alienated and defeated. Over the years my mentors have encouraged me that things would get better. Their support has meant a great deal to me.

## Countering the Negative Effects

One may wonder how it is possible to survive such stressful conditions. First, my faith in God has been an important sustaining force in my life. My faith has contributed to my being positive about life. I always look for the best in life. I learned not to look at myself and my challenges but to find ways of changing my situation. Second, my family has always supported and believed in me. Third, my colleagues, including administrators, continue to encourage and support me in different ways.

Additionally, my daily stress reliever has been my consistent exercise routine. Furthermore, I am very goal-oriented and focused on success. Success for me is knowing that I have done my best and that my students have left my class as better people and can become successful practicing teachers—knowing that I did not reserve myself from giving my all while doing my favorite thing, which is teaching.

The most positive things that have kept me going are the tangible and intangible rewards. My rewards have been very elusive in the sense that they are sometimes hard to identify, specify, keep, and even show. These rewards are in the form of supportive students who have kept me going. They share their appreciation verbally, through their work and effort; in the lobbies and corridors, as they share with me what they are doing; e-mails that say, "Thank you for a wonderful semester"; cards at the end of student teaching; and so on. It is my hope that these unsolicited feedback will one day prove what I know in my soul.

## LESSONS LEARNED

I have learned many lessons from my challenging journey as an international teacher educator. Five factors have stood out, namely, confidence, strategic response, immediate action, mentors, and objectivity. These are integral to one's success as an international teacher educator.

Through my challenging experiences teaching in higher education, I have learned that confidence is a critical ingredient for surviving this journey. Furthermore, adopting strategies that my colleagues use in challenging situations have enabled me to figure out how to work with my students in ways familiar to them. For example, the strategy of asking students who have specific questions regarding assignments to meet with me after class and to do so only after they have reviewed the assignment instructions has worked well for me. In this way, they are clear about the requirements before conferencing with me, and they can easily identify the problem and are able to ask specific questions. They may even find that there is no need to meet with me after all. Additionally, using these strategies has also helped me confirm that students' responses towards me are more than just responses to my teaching style. This is evidenced by the fact that even after using the same instructional methods as my colleagues, I get totally different results. This realization propelled me to accept things that I cannot change: Some students will never like me. However, I will continue the journey and learn better ways of dealing with such situations. I will continue to document the positive interactions between students and myself and the learning that ensues.

Taking action on micro-aggression has positive effects, even though I may not be able to change students' perceptions about me. Nothing is gained by inaction or by fearing that students will complain about me to the department head or write negative comments in course evaluations. Documenting interactions, meetings, and conferences with students is a form of action (Deems, as cited in Bart, 2010). Action also entails preserving written communications with the students, so that if anything escalates or if we have to refer to some record for whatever reason, it will be available for reference. The positive psychological effect of this action is incredible: I no longer have to keep battling in my mind about what to do. It is one burden released, leaving me the energy to do something else. To think that for years I did not do anything about such issues is scary.

I have also learned to value collegial mentorship. I have learned to engage more than one mentor at a time. In a survey a colleague of mine and I conducted on the marginalization of racial minority women, most participants expressed the fact that having "access to experienced mentors helped them gauge the areas to focus on" (Odhiambo & Charoenpanitkul, 2011, p. 74) in teaching and scholarship. I have found this to be truly helpful over the years. There is nothing I can do about my skin color and birthplace. My accent is clean enough to have earned me a job in an institution of higher learning, and I am proud of that.

It is evident that for students to embrace diversity, it will be the responsibility of the entire university community, not mine alone nor that of a specific department. Of course, the department has its role to play by consistently supporting the individual faculty to avoid some of the issues expressed here (Odhiambo & Charoenpanitkul, 2011). Without such support, tenure and promotion for foreign-born professors may be difficult, if not impossible.

## CONCLUSION

Foreign-born professors have peculiar issues to navigate, including cultural, pedagogical, collegial, and student relationships. They often experience negative physical, psychological, and social effects, yet many of them continue to serve diligently and even excel professionally. Navigating the complexities of teaching in an American institution can be a slow and difficult journey, but with the appropriate support, they can weather the challenges. For their part, they need to be persistent, reflective, and resilient to achieve success.

## REFERENCES

Abelson, R. P., Dasgupta, N., Park, J., & Banaji, M. R. (1998). Perceptions of the collective other. *Personality and Social Psychology Review, 2*, 243–250.
Deems, S. (2010). Things my first unhappy student taught me. In M. Bart (Ed.), *Teaching mistakes from the college classroom. Faculty Focus: Special Report*

132 *Eucabeth Odhiambo*

(pp. 11–13). A Magna Publication. Retrieved July 1, 2014, from www.Faculty focus.com

Dyson, A. H., & Genishi, C. (Eds.). (1994). *The need for story: Cultural diversity in classroom and community*. Urbana, IL: National Council of Teachers of English.

Franklin, A. J. (2004). *From brotherhood to manhood: How black men rescue their relationships and dreams from the invisibility syndrome*. Hoboken, NJ: Wiley.

Jones, J. M. (1997). Prejudice and racism (2nd ed.). Washington, DC: McGraw-Hill.

Keltner, D., & Robinson, R. J. (1996). Extremism, power, and imagined basis of social conflict. *Current Directions in Psychological Science, 5*, 101–105.

Mayher, J. S. (1990). Foreword. In J. M. Newman (Ed.), *Finding our way: Teachers exploring their assumptions* (p. x). Portsmouth, NH: Heinemann.

Nieto, S. (1999). *The light in their eyes: Creating multicultural learning communities*. New York: Teachers College Press.

Nieto, S. (2000). Affirming Diversity: *The sociopolitical context of multicultural education* (3rd ed.). White Plains, NY: Longman.

Odhiambo, E., & Charoenpanitkul, C. (2011). Marginalization: A continuing problem in higher education. In V. Yenika-Agbaw & A. Hidalgo-de Jesus (Eds.), *Race, women of color, and the state university system: Critical reflections* (pp. 64–79). Maryland: University Press of America.

Reid, L. D., & Radhakrishnan, P. (2003). Race matters: The relations between race and general campus climate. *Cultural Diversity and Ethnic Minority Psychology, 9*, 263–275.

Rowe, M. P. (1990). Barriers to equality: The power of subtle discrimination to maintain unequal opportunity. *Employee Responsibilities and Rights Journal, 3*, 153–163.

Solorzano, D., Ceja, M., & Yosso, T. (2000). Critical race theory, racial micro-aggressions and campus racial climate: The experiences of African American college students. *The Journal of Negro Education, 69*(1/2), 6–73.

Spanierman, L. B., & Heppner, M. J. (2004). Psychosocial costs of racism to whites scale (PCRW): Construction and initial validation. *Journal of Counseling Psychology, 51*, 249–262.

Sue, D. W., Capodilupo, C. M., Torino, G. C., Bucceri, J. M., Aisha, M. B., Holder, K. N., & Esquilin, M. (2007). Racial micro-aggressions in everyday life: Implications for clinical practice. *American Psychologist, 62*(4), 271–286.

Thompson, C. E., & Neville, H. A. (1999). Racism, mental health, and mental health practice. *Counseling Psychologist, 27*, 155–223.

Weimer, M. (2013). How to get better feedback from students. *Faculty Focus*. Retrieved May 22, 2013, from http://www.facultyfocus.com

# 11 My Professional Teaching Experience in the United States, 1977–2014

## The Case of an African-Born Immigrant

*Peter F. B. Nayenga*

### INTRODUCTION

Using autobiographical and historical approaches, this chapter examines my U.S. professional teaching experience (from 1977–2014) in the context of the following related aspects: the challenges I encountered when looking for a job, the academic roadblocks I faced, the difficulties of settling in a new culture, and how I went about to alleviate some of these problems. Although it might be argued that native-born scholars face relatively similar challenges, what distinguishes the professional experience of African-born scholars from others is that they are confronted with somewhat unique problems, namely, "race, immigrant status, blackness, and gender" (Yewah & Togunde, 2010).

### THE PROCESS OF PROCURING A JOB IN THE UNITED STATES

My initial objective when I started graduate work at the University of Michigan in 1968 was to get an MA in European history. My professors, however, encouraged me to pursue a PhD in African and not European history. After serious soul searching, I switched from European to African history, although this was against my initial academic interest.

### Coming to the United States

In 1971, I returned to Uganda to conduct research for my PhD. The original plan was that I would return to Michigan in 1972 and complete my PhD in 1973. This did not happen because Idi Amin's military dictatorial rule (1971–1979) in Uganda pursued ruthless policies that made his regime notorious for massive human rights violations, economic decline, and social disintegration. To express their disapproval, the United States and Western European countries closed their embassies and encouraged their citizens to leave Uganda. To make up for the loss from the departure of foreign nationals, Amin's government restricted educated Ugandans from leaving

## 134 Peter F. B. Nayenga

the country. It was under these circumstances that I was hired to teach at Makerere University in 1972. Not able to work on my PhD dissertation, it was not until 1975 that I was allowed (without my family) to return to the United States to complete my PhD. When the opportunity arose, I moved to Kenya.

It was during my stay in Kenya (April–August, 1977) that I was simultaneously offered a tenure-track job at St. Cloud State University (SCSU, Minnesota) and a 1-year Fulbright fellowship at the University of North Florida (UNF) and Florida Junior College (FJC) at Jacksonville (UNF/FJC). Three weeks later, however, I got the chilling news from SCSU that it would take anywhere between 6 months to a year to process the paperwork that would permit me to work as a non-U.S. citizen. Rather than wait for a year in Kenya, I accepted the 1-year position at UNF/FJC.

## My Experience at UNF/FJC

Professionally, my stay at UNF/FJC (1977–1978) was a productive year involving teaching and giving public speeches. I used this period to experiment with a number of teaching methods and drafted a textbook that I later used for my classes.

Through the concerted efforts by Professors James Crooks, Robert Gentry, and Steven Wise, we were well received in Jacksonville, Florida. However, one of the immediate challenges we faced was how we could raise our children in a "foreign culture." For example, we wanted our children to maintain our Ugandan culture of respecting elders, working collaboratively, sharing whatever little they had, and obeying the authorities. Initially, this worked well until we ran into what I may call "American everyday racism" involving the use of racial slurs at school, work, shopping malls, and neighborhoods. The situation became so bad around the apartment where we lived that my children decided not to go out and play because of the daily harassment they faced.

Some of our neighbors who observed what was going on advised that we needed to do more than merely report these incidents to the apartment officials. One neighbor advised us that if any of our kids were beaten by another kid, rather than burst into tears, he or she should hit back even harder. As sad and unfortunate as this advice may appear, it was effective because word went around in the neighborhood that our kids could no longer be bullied without their fighting back. The apartment officials who previously refused to address the many complaints we had presented them became furious by my children's decision to defend themselves against the injustice being meted to them. So upset were the officials that they evicted us from our apartment on the grounds that we failed to comply with the terms of our lease. Several people in the community urged us to resist what they saw as a possible case of racial discrimination, but out of our desire not to publicize this negative event, we moved out of the apartment, although we

My Professional Teaching Experience in the United States  135

had about 4 months left on our lease. Our decision not to follow the legal route, out of fear of reprisals, is in keeping with what many other African immigrants do when faced with similar situations.

The other significant challenge I encountered came at the end of our stay at UNF/FJC in 1978, when I applied for a waiver from the J-I visa, which enabled me to enter the United States as a visitor. This visa required me to return to my country of origin for 2 years before I could apply for a permanent work visa. Frankly, I did not foresee this coming because when I applied for entry to the United States I clearly indicated to the Immigration and Nationalization Service (INS) that I was a refugee from Uganda. The INS position, however, was that I had to return to Kenya, where I received my visa. Part of my 1-year appointment at UNF/FJC in 1977–1978 required me to teach and give public speeches, many of which focused on Amin's brutality. With the help of my attorney, therefore, we eventually demonstrated that returning to Kenya would be a security risk for me and received a waiver, on the grounds of Amin's brutality.

## SUPPORT AND CHALLENGES FROM THE
## HISTORY DEPARTMENT AT SCSU

The waiver from my J-I visa obligations would have been meaningless if not for the unwavering support I received from SCSU. Not only did the university offer me the job, but the officials did whatever they could to help me procure a work visa. Aside from sending letters to the INS on my behalf, Dr. Charles Graham (SCSU president, 1971–1981) granted me a leave of absence when I accepted the 1-year (1977/78) appointment at UNF/FJC.

The history department I joined in 1978 was composed of "traditionalists," as opposed to liberal scholars. I reached this conclusion after a one-to-one visit I paid to various members of the department. Aside from building connections with my colleagues, I also received some general information about how everyone taught their courses. My visit with the chairperson summed up everything when he politely, but clearly, told me that teaching was central at SCSU and that for me to get tenure and promotion, I would need to "shine above the old-timers."

In addition to the frank but useful advice from the chair, I was lucky that two African students I did not know visited me at my office and gave me advice that helped me understand some of the "campus culture." The importance of these students' advice was critical, particularly because being one of the two first African professors to be appointed at SCSU in 1977, I did not have the luxury of seeking advice from other African-born colleagues.

Equipped with this advice, I made an early conscious decision that while I would serve on committees to which I was selected, I would avoid seeking sensitive positions in the department or at the university at large. Looking back, this served me very well because it helped me avoid the potential

## 136    Peter F. B. Nayenga

misfortune of crossing paths with some of the "troublemaking" administrators or faculty.

## Gaining Self-Confidence in Teaching

A fellow immigrant colleague once remarked that even after teaching for 16 years, he still was nervous before going to teach his classes. In my early years, I also felt this same challenge caused in part by my anxiety to teach students from a different cultural background than mine. The issue was not that I did not have a mastery of the subject matter in my field, but rather, I was initially disheartened to read some students' evaluations making remarks such as "I do not understand his accent," "he speaks too fast," or "the materials he teaches have no relationship to what I am used to."

Over the years, I gained self-confidence and devised solutions to address some of the issues that repeatedly appeared in my evaluations. As a graduate student at the University of Michigan (1968–1975), I taught some courses. I further developed self-confidence when I taught at Makerere University in Uganda. Because some of the courses I taught were required, I sometimes had as many students as 200 in one lecture hall. The fact that my classes were always both large and informed forced me to adopt a habit of being organized and well prepared whenever I have to address a group of people. Later on, as a Fulbright Scholar at UNF/FJC in 1977–1978, I strengthened my self-confidence in public speaking because I addressed several large civic groups. Additionally, I drafted a textbook that I used in the teaching of my courses. This somewhat lessened the issue of "I do not understand his accent" because students had something they could refer to.

To deal with the issue of having a "non-American accent," I devoted a segment at the beginning of each semester in which I discussed with students, what I call "misconceptions about Africa." We also discussed issues relating to different accents in the United States. Students learned that even in Britain, where English originates from, there are various accents. I also gave them examples of prominent Americans who came to the country as recent immigrants and have retained their accents. The example that students found interesting is when I told them that my children who were raised in "Central Minnesota" speak English with a "White accent," as opposed to an "African American accent." From this discussion students learned that accents ought to be respected because they are the embodiment of one's heritage and that the issue is not that one's accent is different but, rather, that one should listen and try to understand what the other party is communicating.

## Difficulties of Teaching African History in a Limited Time

One of the challenges I confronted was how one could meaningfully teach African history to students with a different cultural background and in a limited time. Given the brevity of teaching semesters, I made sure that irrelevant materials were kept out of the content of the course. Thus, while acknowledging the existence of different climatic zones, the enormous size of the African continent, and its huge population, I also emphasized that Africa has commonalities expressed in similarities of worldview, socioeconomic structures, and economic and political problems inherited from European colonial rule. Such an approach necessitated using a thematic method of teaching. To encourage students view African history from a balanced perspective, I made them read novels and watch films and videos.

Although tests were part of course requirements, I downplayed the significance of examinations and instead emphasized learning for its own sake. Initially, I only gave writing-based examinations because I felt this was probably the best way for students to learn. This was both time-consuming and frustrating. Some of the students were puzzled as to why an instructor with a "foreign accent" could detect English grammatical mistakes in their papers. Others could not understand why grammar should be taken into account when one is grading a history essay or paper. To address these challenges, I changed my grading systems from essay writing to piecemeal testing, consisting of true-and-false questions, multiple-choice questions, matching, identifications, short answers, long essay, and papers for higher level classes. To my surprise, many students preferred this grading approach since, as some of them noted in their evaluations, "this gave them the opportunity to learn and digest the material."

## Preparing for Tenure and Promotion

Over the years, the history department has encouraged its members to engage in research and teaching. I personally find this appealing on several fronts: I strongly believe that teaching and research complement one another; research lessens the boredom from teaching general education courses, and of course, it helps to uplift one's professional development and profile through publications.

It was hard to achieve this noble objective partly because of the heavy teaching load at a university where teaching, not research, was central to its mission. What further complicated the situation was the lack of primary and secondary sources. These challenges notwithstanding, I had no choice but to devise a way of conducting my research and publishing pieces that enabled me to receive tenure and promotion early in my career. Through research grants, I managed to publish articles in national and international journals.

## My Experience as Director of African Studies at SCSU

While I exerted most of my energy to teaching and research, I also was actively involved in "nonthreatening" administrative assignments. One such assignment was my involvement in the origins, operation, and directorship of the African Studies program (ASP) at SCSU since 2000. During the 1980s, a group of Africanists at SCSU met and agreed to form the ASP, whose main objective was to enhance awareness of African cultures, as well as provide a framework within which students could integrate the specific knowledge they gained about Africa from various courses they completed.

Realizing the noble goals put forward by the ASP was somewhat problematic. First, the university was undergoing severe budget cuts, which made it almost impossible to start new programs. Limited funds also had a negative impact on the hiring of Africanists who would teach courses on campus and help in the development of exchange programs with African universities. To its credit, SCSU hired many Africanists in the 1990s. The ASP became vibrant and enriched with the arrival of African-born scholars from many parts of the continent. At one point, there were close to 20 African-born professors on campus.

The arrival of other Africanists on campus also brought new issues that almost derailed the ASP. The bone of contention first centered on the ideological differences between Afrocentrists and Eurocentrists, with the former group contending that the membership of the ASP should not include Whites. Some in this group also believed that it was inappropriate for Whites to teach African-related courses.

Dealing with the foregoing situation was somewhat delicate in that I had to deal with racial issues, fellow African-born professors, and the SCSU administration. I successfully managed to resolve such issues by reaching out to all parties, including those who attacked me personally. I also closely worked with the SCSU administration to ensure that they did not become entangled in the conflicts.

As director of the program, I supported various members of the ASP to collaboratively work on projects, build bridges and partnerships with other academic units, and form linkages with public organizations. The concerted efforts by various members of the ASP benefitted SCSU and the St. Cloud community at large. We collaboratively worked with various institutional units to bring prominent, internationally well-known scholars such as Wole Soyinka (winner of the 1986 Nobel literature prize), Ali Mazrui (presenter of the famous PBS series titled *The Africans*), Wangari Maathai (winner of the 2004 Nobel Peace Prize), and Sulayman Nyang from Howard University. These scholars gave public lectures, visited classes on campus, and provided interviews to the mass media. Thus, aside from the unique international education students received, these events catapulted our program, and indeed SCSU, to national and international prominence.

## My Experience as Chair of the History Department, 2002–2011

Under unexpected circumstances, I was elected in 2002 to chair the history department. The task I took on as chair was enormous, because there were deep divisions in the department; we were understaffed; locally and

## My Professional Teaching Experience in the United States 139

nationally, the department's image had been tainted; and to crown all this, the leadership of the College of Social Sciences (COSS), which was our immediate supervisor, was unstable. Frankly, as a foreign-born scholar, I was somewhat apprehensive about taking on this task, partly because I was not certain if I fully understood the American culture enough to assume such a sensitive position and to resolve the challenges the department confronted.

To mitigate the stakes, I concluded that the only meaningful approach was to run the department collaboratively, where the chair was one among equals. With this in mind, every member of the department was called on to participate in this collaborative leadership by serving on various committees. I also made a conscious decision to limit the use of long, rambling e-mails as a form of communication and instead reached out to every member individually. Additionally, I invited and encouraged my colleagues to go out together on social activities such as lunch or dinner or to attend annual department social events. Time-consuming as this was, it enabled me to galvanize everyone into the mood to rebuild the department. Today, the history department is one of the more successful units at SCSU. I am thankful that this happened under my watch, and it is an illustration to show that foreign-born professors can use their broad cultural experience in helping to resolve conflicts.

### SETTLING DOWN IN A NEW CULTURE

There is a strong relationship between one's performance in one's job and the socioeconomic challenges one faces. These challenges become even more magnified when one is foreign born because one may not have such important support systems such as family ties in the USA or have the financial base to help them establish good credit. Partly for this reason, they may be subject to closer scrutiny in what they do. Besides, their lack of contacts with influential people in the community may exacerbate their ability to redress the problems they may be confronted with.

The foregoing challenges were more pronounced when I came to the United States as a worker in 1977 than during my days as a graduate student (1968–1975). As a recipient of a U.S.–Uganda scholarship, I was restricted by my visa from seeking employment outside the university. Consequently, I did not fully realize the major differences between living in the United States as a worker and as a student. The difference, however, became clear to me the moment I left Uganda in 1977 and joined thousands of refugees who were living in Kenya. I survived my stay in Kenya because of the loan I received from the Mennonite Central Committee (MCC) of the United States and the generosity of the Reverend and Mrs. Daniel Slabaugh, my host family at the University of Michigan.

My economic hardships at UNF/FJC during the 1977–1978 academic year were somewhat lessened because the MCC did not require me to start

## 140  *Peter F. B. Nayenga*

paying off their loan right away. Additionally, the Jacksonville community heartily welcomed me by donating several household items and getting me a cheap vehicle that enabled me to move around the spread-out city. I also was provided with excellent academic facilities that enabled me to carry out my academic work. In brief, my stay in Jacksonville laid the foundation for my future teaching and research agenda by easing my economic hardships.

I was also fortunate that the challenges I encountered that would have had a negative impact on my work at UNF/FJC came toward the end of my stay in 1978. The first of these problems, which I earlier referred to, occurred when we decided to leave our apartment in April 1978 rather than endure the publicity that would have come out if we had gone to court to challenge the eviction. The more serious challenge I confronted, however, was the financial instability resulting from having to support my immediate and extended family. This was partly due to my inability to save any money, in spite of being employed for a year. Part of the explanation is due to my respect for Ugandan culture, which emphasizes collectivism, as opposed to individualism. In collective societies the personal goal is subordinated to that of the group's (a family or an ethnic group). Without a stable retirement savings system in Uganda, people's social security becomes the responsibility of their children, who are supposed to look after their parents in their old age. Thus, in spite of the personal financial problems I faced, I remitted funds to my relatives in Uganda. Additionally, I sponsored several relatives to come and study in the United States. As noble as this cause was and still is, it came at a significant financial sacrifice to my immediate family.

Like Jacksonville, Florida, the St. Cloud community generally welcomed us. We, however, later learned that getting us a house to rent was problematic because of the reluctance by some landlords to rent to people of color. Despite this overall negative house hunting experience, we developed a special friendship with our landlord who rented his house to us for 8 years. Renting a house for 8 years is a good example to demonstrate the plight African immigrants face. For example, in our case, we had to pay expenses for the lawyer who helped us with the immigration problems, pay off the loan from MCC that I used to bring my family to the United States, and have funds for day-to-day family expenses. What further complicated our situation was our lack of contacts in the community, our lack of family support that could step in to help, and our lack of a credit history, which made it hard to borrow from financial institutions. This made it difficult for us to purchase a house right away.

To ease our economic hardships, my wife, Monica, after a rather painful experience of job seeking, was offered a job in October 1978 at a local corporation. Because of our continuing cash-flow problems and the fact that one of our children was ready to attend college, my wife took another job with the Inter Faculty Organization (IFO) at SCSU in 1985. Later on, friends introduced us to banks that loaned us funds to purchase household items. Others donated items to support us. These generous acts by several members of the St. Cloud community made our settlement easier than would have been the case. It is also important to note that without the help we received these personal financial challenges would have had a negative impact on our ability to function efficiently at our jobs.

Social-cultural challenges can be harmful to one's ability to function efficiently. This was the challenge we faced when we settled in St. Cloud, a city critics refer to as "White Cloud" (Dominick & Massmann, 2012). Until the recent arrival of Somalis, who transformed the St. Cloud landscape, this community has been monolithic. Although before our arrival we knew that most of the residents in St. Cloud were of European descent, it was just natural that the overall atmosphere to us was so intimidating as to make us somewhat nervous. Aside from the day-to-day racial encounters we experienced, my children faced racial issues at school. During our early years in St. Cloud, my children were teased because their last names were different from mine (Phillips, 1989). The usual question children were asked, "Are you adopted?" At one point the children were so frustrated that they requested if they could change their names.

Rather than accuse the school system of racism, we took it upon ourselves to educate people in the community to understand the naming system in Uganda. Additionally, my children were able to break away from the problem of having "strange names" by participating in sports. Aside from making many friends, my children's names appeared in the newspapers and thus became known to the public. One of the beneficial cultural things we did was to introduce the children to the Ugandan community in the region. Cumbersome as this was because St. Cloud is about 70 miles from the "Twin Cities" (Minneapolis–St. Paul), where most Ugandans live, the children found out that other people, and not only they, have different last names from their parents.

## LESSONS LEARNED

Without the support I received from various sources, I would not have attained the achievements I have referred to earlier.

### Family Support

I partly attribute my success to the overall family support I received in general and my wife's tenacious support in particular. Her critical support of my career, including her decision to allow me to leave her in Uganda and come to the United States for graduate work (two months after our wedding), her postponing her own educational pursuit to allow me to work on my PhD, and, subsequently, her supporting my professional life as an immigrant professor.

### Not Burning One's Bridges

My support system was further strengthened by the friends I have made in the United States. Even when I left the United States, I made it a point to

## 142   *Peter F. B. Nayenga*

keep in touch with them whenever the unstable political situation in Amin's Uganda (1971–1979) permitted me to do so. These friends were critical to alerting me to advertised jobs in the United States and assisted me with either straightening out my immigration papers or getting me funds I used to initially settle down in the United States.

## Networking

Aside from being in touch with close friends, I have always networked with many people with the objective of sharing information and resources, educating and increasing each other's awareness, and establishing emotional, moral, and social support. Through networking, I have learned a lot about the challenges other scholars in the same field faced and what they did to alleviate these problems. For example, I initially only sent my papers for publication consideration to the so-called prestigious journals until some of my colleagues cautioned me that publishing and job hunting may not necessarily depend on "what you know" but, rather, on "whom you know." Networking also enabled me to connect with two organizations that enabled my family to minimize our isolation from other Africans, in general, and Ugandans, in particular.

## Willingness to Adapt to Changing Conditions

Working on the premise that "we must borrow the best [aspects of a culture] and tailor it to our [Ugandans] needs" (Olweny, 1996), I have been guided by an open-minded philosophy in my dealings with other people. Consequently, over the years I have developed such general philosophical views as "there is no such thing as a perfect person or place." For this reason, I regard challenges not as impediments to one's progress but as inspiration to push further. I believe in the view that "you do your best and hope for the best," and rather than be guided by labels that may be misleading, I have instead dealt with individuals, one-on-one. In other words, while I have maintained my fundamentals (my identity and core beliefs as an African), I have at the same time avoided being labeled as a "one-dimensional person."

## Keeping a Low Profile

I am, by nature a "low-key person." Consequently, my approach to "conflict resolution" has been more inclined toward diplomacy than confrontation. Thus, rather than respond to a controversial challenge immediately, I would rather give myself a "cooling-off period" that enables me to review the issue at hand carefully. This diplomatic approach has helped me avoid the danger of making rushed, damaging responses that usually tarnish one's reputation.

## CONCLUDING REMARKS

Through the complexity of methods of approaches I referred to in this chapter, I have attained such important achievements as successfully completing my PhD despite the hurdles I had to overcome, getting a tenure-track job in the United States in the crowded liberal arts field, attaining a successful professional record with regard to teaching and research, and successfully chairing the history department and being the director of the African Studies program at St. Cloud State University, Minnesota. Additionally, I have successfully helped my children and several relatives I sponsored to graduate from U.S. colleges and have established friendships with several people in the United States and various countries.

I consider my experience as that of an African immigrant who overcame hardships in my transition to a successful life in the United States. This sentiment is echoed in the following observations of SCSU president, Earl H. Potter III (2013), in which he recognized me for my services to SCSU:

> Peter Nayenga . . . came to St. Cloud State . . . in 1978. . . . His scholarly journey had been one of overcoming barriers in his native Uganda where Idi Amin's oppressive policies threatened safety and freedom. . . . He arrived on a campus with only a few persons of color and went about creating . . . an African Studies Program, helping to launch the South African Study-abroad partnerships and chairing the History Department during turbulent times. . . . Nayenga met the challenges of teaching African history to students from very different cultural background with grace, determination and effectiveness. (Potter, 2013, p. 3)

## REFERENCES

Dominick, J. J., & Massmann, J. C. (2012). *St. Cloud: The triplet city* (p. 137). Sun Valley, CA: American Historical Press. ("White Cloud" is a reference indicating St. Cloud is 97% white does not welcome minorities and considers them to be outsiders).

Olweny, C. L. M., Dr. (1996). *Ugandans in the diaspora: Strategies for survival* (p. 6). Toronto: UNAA Convention.

Phillips, M. (1989). Ugandan family fled homeland. *St. Cloud (Minn) Times*, Sunday, August 6, p. 5C.

Potter, III, E. H. (2013, Summer). Exceptional faculty leave their mark. *Outlook: St. Cloud State University* (p. 3). Official university magazine.

Yewah, E., & Togunde D. (Eds.). (2010). *Across the Atlantic: African immigrants in the United States diaspora* (p. 62). Champaign, IL: Common Ground Publishing, LLC.

# 12 Negotiating the Trilogy of Blackness, "Africanness," and "Accentness"
## A "Native-Alien" Professor's Tale

*Obed Mfum-Mensah*

### SETTING THE STAGE

I am an African immigrant from Ghana who has lived in the United States and Canada for two decades. My long residence in the two countries makes me a native or indigenous of North America. I use the words *native* in this chapter to denote an unbroken residence and development of in-depth understanding of a particular place of residence (Dei, 2000). I also categorize myself as an "alien" because some people view me as an unfamiliar "guest" in both my professional domain and the broader society. In this chapter, I narrate my challenges as a "native-alien" professor in a predominantly White Christian college in the United States. I have organized the chapter around four themes: an African "guest" in a diasporized academy; a Black professor with new pedagogy, content, and accent; manifestations of "Africanness" in diasporized academic context; and concluding remarks for "alien" scholars seeking tenure positions. In this chapter, I argue that while underrepresented faculty in North America in general encounter multiple challenges (Stanley, 2006), Black African professors encounter immeasurable challenges relating to their trilogy identity of their *Blackness* (color), *Accentness* (how they sound), and *Africanness* (their native continent).

I deem storytelling as a useful tool and effective way to outlining my lived experiences teaching in a predominantly White, suburban, private Christian college in south-central Pennsylvania. Expressions in stories are metaphors that provide opportunities for reflections and guide the choices we make. Reflections on stories are mirrors for seeing things in particular ways and prisms that throw light on the concrete reality of lived experiences (Kanu, 2007). My insight in appropriating narrative here is also based on my recognition that humans are storytelling beings who individually and socially lead storied lives (Conle, 2000; Connelly & Clandinin, 1990). I also recognize that my "history and the story of [our] lives is always embedded in the story of communities from which we derive our identity" (Conle, 2000, p. 209).

## An African "Guest" in a Diasporized Academy

As a ritual for introducing myself at the beginning of each course, I wrote my name, Mfum-Mensah, on the board and invited students to pronounce my name—which they attempted with difficulty. Afterward, I mentioned that "I am an 'alien' from a distant planet called Ghana." The students wondered why I categorize myself an "alien." I am "Black" and "African" from the inside out. I have a surname that my students struggle to pronounce without muttering and twisting their tongue until I show them to swallow the *m* in front of my name. I also speak English with a Ghanaian accent, which is supposedly a baggage in this part of the world.

I began my expedition to academe in 1996, and after 19 years of this expedition, I have come to embrace myself as a "native-alien" and "guest within the majority culture's house," regardless of how long I take tenure in the academic domain (Cockrell, 2006, p. 129). I am constantly renegotiating my identity and values with each passing day, in a process that Homi Bhabha (1990, p. 109) discusses as being in the "third space of translation." Interestingly, I also crave a space to preserve my "alien-self," even if my colleagues and students deride me. My "foreignness" in academe stems from my trifold identity of being *Black*, coming from *Africa*, and having a different *accent*.

I did my undergraduate and graduate work in institutions in the United States and Canada. Prior to applying to take a tenure-track position in the academy, I had accrued teaching and research experience as a graduate student, as well as two years of productive postdoctoral work. With these credentials, I thought I had the profile to enter the academic space. Well, that kind of assumption was wrong for a candidate who was a minority seeking to enter the professorial ranks. My own experience and experiences shared by others confirm that faculty from the majority culture subtly and benignly question the ability of a candidate if she or he is a minority. They do this by overly scrutinizing minority candidates. Many of these colleagues are genuine people who demonstrate their desire to diversify their department but nonetheless fall into that trap. One frequently hears professors on search committees who remark something to the effect that if the institution is going to hire a minority, then it needs to hire somebody who is "qualified." Often, such people are themselves not outstanding by any measure. The refrain that "minorities are not qualified" is a subtle stereotype entertained by the majority culture, with the underlying belief that "difference is deficient"—a point that lies at the root of racism (Jaipal, 2006, p. 188).

The process for my hiring was long and arduous. I received several phone calls from the chair of the search committee. Every time I got the call from this individual to update me on the process, I sensed the lack of keenness about my candidature. The search committee decided to use videoconferencing to get to see the person at the other end. I was very much aware that my name and accent together made the committee tread cautiously. The

146 *Obed Mfum-Mensah*

committee then invited me for a campus visit and was subsequently offered the job after the interview.

Not long after I arrived on campus, I sensed some vibes that made me curious to know the nature of conversation the department had before recommending an African to be hired. For instance, one of the colleagues remarked that the "department needed somebody of your type, and so it did everything possible to recruit you; therefore, you should not allow the leadership to treat you as a token." To confirm the remarks made by the colleague, two semesters into my tenure, I had a disagreement with the department leadership who wanted to treat me like a graduate student in every sense. In the course of resolving the issue, this individual remarked that I "should be thankful to the department for getting you here." Such a remark is an example of the paternalistic elements that sometimes entangle minority hire. I believe that these kinds of remarks would not have come up if I were White. These experiences are examples of the ways minority faculty members become "guests in transition" who must play limited roles, have limited voice, and eventually leave some institutions.

## A Black Professor With New Pedagogy, Content, and Accent

During my campus visit for interview, I had some inkling that territorialism and provincialism was a part of the hidden curriculum of the disciplinary domain. I also sensed subtle, entrenched colonial forms of discourse in teaching and scholarship. I realized that if I accepted a job offer in the institution, I needed to find ways to interrogate the subtle monopolization of space and undemocratic frame (Perez, 2006) that I had witnessed. I sensed that my scholarship, teaching philosophy, and pedagogical approaches were going to be fugitive and viewed with suspicion in the disciplinary domain. From the onset, I determined not to succumb to the monopolized space and have my teaching and scholarship colonized. As an untenured faculty, I was not afraid to engage my colleagues in scholarly discourses, which I believed is an approach to inclusive excellence. Alas, this kind of thinking is sometimes viewed as suspicious and a threat to the status quo. Not long after I came to the department, my teaching approach and scholarship collided with that of a colleague who was at that time immortalized and idolized as the pedagogical "wonk" in my disciplinary domain.

My journey to achieving validation in scholarship and teaching in my disciplinary domain took efforts and skillful negotiations on my part. I was determined not to fall into the trap of being "a guest" in the majority culture's house to be pushed around and to the edge. To succumb to the monopolized space or make an early exit were options I was not ready to embrace. I know of two colleagues, immigrants from Africa, who entered academe just about the time I did and who have changed institutions three or four times. These kinds of transitions are not particularly helpful to someone like me who craves for professional stability.

Minorities hired into primarily homogenous spaces also tend to struggle with the issue of tokenization. Since my arrival in my current institution, I have entered into what I call a "transactional tolerance" with my colleagues.

### Students' Attitudes Toward "Diversity"

Teaching at a predominantly White suburban, private Christian college has its opportunities and challenges. Most white students who attend colleges of this kind tend to have limited experience with minorities of any type. Through my interactions with minority students on our campus, I have learned that their experiences of their White peers are not different from mine. My explanation for this phenomenon is that a majority of White American students live in a sheltered bubble, untouched by the gravity of diversity in the lived society or real life, until they come to college. Some of them are socialized into the stereotypes of their communities until they are confronted with the "unfamiliar" and then suddenly become overwhelmed.

I notice that many of our freshmen demonstrate initial discomfort when they come to my class or when they are assigned to me as advisees. Freshmen also tend to second-guess my teaching and scholarship and therefore provide lower teaching evaluations and comment on my accent in my course evaluations. It takes a while for these students to adjust to people like me who are different from them.

In terms of race issues, most of the students subscribe to the "color-blind" frame and prefer to shift discussions from race to their general tolerance as Christians, service trips, and missions abroad (Paris & Schoon, 2007). I have noticed that students who have had little experience with diversity tend to demonstrate vulnerability and feelings of guilt when diversity issues are being discussed. I suspect that my identity (as a minority) intensifies the students' feelings of vulnerability and guilt. Such feelings are a psychological experience supported in the literature (Nieto, 2004; Tatum, 2003). I admit that leading a discussion on diversity as a minority faculty is one of my uncomfortable moments. However, I am trapped in this uncomfortable situation because of the nature of my courses. One of the strategies I have developed to minimize the tensions is to clarify at the beginning of my courses that students respect each other's opinion (there are some students who, in all honesty, come to my class with interesting ideas). I also assure my students of my commitment to fostering a safe classroom environment for all discussions. Furthermore, I help students approach discussions on diversity from intellectual and scholarly perspectives. These approaches have helped to minimize students' feeling of guilt for past injustices.

One of my courses discusses the intersection of education and issues of poverty, colonialism, slavery, Christian missions abroad, and social justice. Students tend to struggle to make connections that help to foster the connections between the global and the local in educational discourse. A majority of the students entertain paternalistic, superior, and colonial

## 148 *Obed Mfum-Mensah*

attitudes and routinely point out that the U.S. educational system is the best, and therefore other societies (especially those on the African continent) must learn from the United States but not vice versa. There is the danger of becoming aggravated when one hears such attitudes expressed by students, but I nonetheless am patient with them because they are in a deep learning curve.

### Responding to the "Accent" Issue?

Language is embodied in a group's identity, history, and culture (Alleyne, 1993, as cited in Wassink, 1999; Ulibarri, 1972). Language is also linked to social status and therefore attitudes toward language can be markedly polarized and tightly held both institutionally and personally, overtly or covertly. Beyond this observation, there is the tendency for many to view the language and ways spoken by the dominant culture as more sophisticated than those of the dominated (Wassink, 1999).

Many faculty colleagues and students in North America tend to have an initial discomfort with a professor who speaks with a different accent. The level of discomfort is even greater when one speaks English with an African accent. In other words, in this part of the world, if you are Black, African, and one who speaks English with an African accent, then you must be aware that you create some level of discomfort for colleagues and students who are unfamiliar with people like you. I recall my astonishment when I received my first peer teaching evaluation. The evaluation included small comments on my teaching, and a tall list of comments about how I needed to speak to make students understand my accent (my accent is not so distinct by any stretch). When I read the comments, I discussed the memo with a senior colleague from another department (also a minority), who was stunned and livid about the comments and encouraged me to respond to those unwholesome comments—which I did. The irony faced by foreign-born professors who speak with different accent is that colleagues in our disciplinary domains in the same institutions know how we speak when they recommend us for hire. But once we come to the department, some of the same colleagues turn around and become "enablers" of students' complaints of our accents.

Students who realize that commenting on a professor's accent is politically incorrect hide behind comments such as "the professor does not explain things well" or "the professor's questions are not clear" to express their disdain for the professor's accent. The intended meaning behind these comments is that because the professor speaks with a different accent, she or he is incoherent, inarticulate, incomprehensible, and incapable. A Ghanaian friend of mine at another institution narrated a funny story to me on a related issue: A student came to her for advising, and she suggested two courses that the student could register for the upcoming school year. The student inquired about the instructor who taught those courses. The professor told the student that the courses are taught by one African professor in their institution. The student indicated that he would not take the courses because "the professor's accent interferes with the way he sets his exam questions." Along the same lines, 5 years ago, one of my advisees came to me to discuss her plan to study abroad in England. Because our program is a highly structured one, I advised her to plan strategically to ensure that when she returned from studying abroad, she could graduate with her matriculated group. Two days later, I received an e-mail from my chair indicating that my advisee's mother had called, complained, and requested the institution to assign a new advisor to her daughter because I "do not communicate clearly." I had a follow-up discussion with my chair and realized that the advisee had complained about my accent. Basically, the advisee doubted my capability to provide good advising because of the way I sounded. Fortunately, after I met with the advisee, I had followed up with two e-mails. After my conversation with the department chair, I e-mailed the advisee and copied my chair. To cut this long story short, the advisee did not follow the plan we worked out and left for England. I was maintained as her advisor. She came back 5 months later and realized how she had messed up her course-sequencing plan.

### Attempting to Resolve the Accent Issue

About 5 years ago, I decided to confront the accent issue head on, so I began to make it a routine practice to help students understand the benefits of learning from an African or other foreign-born professors who speak differently. As part of the conversation, students learned that I pronounce the letter *t* audibly and that they did not offend me by calling my attention to repeat a word or phrase if they did not comprehend what I said. This strategy has been an effective way for us to engage in issues on language, power, and status. I promise students, in a more humorous way, that by the end of the semester, they would come to clearly understand my ways and idiosyncrasies of communicating. Interestingly, a lot of students who take my course for the first time take more of my courses afterward. These students are my "missionaries" who use the "dormitory lore" as a medium to spread the news about the benefits of my classes.

## Manifestations of "Africanness" in a Diasporized Context

Two years ago, I received a letter that an internal scholarship grant application I submitted to enable me pursue a fieldwork in Ghana had been approved. The committee, however, inserted a clause in the letter indicating that I should look for external grant for my research and that "you should not expect the Development Office to award you any more grant in the future to pursue research in Africa." Interestingly, some faculty members have received the grant multiple times for their field study in Europe and Asia. So many questions crossed my mind when I received the letter. Was

## 150   *Obed Mfum-Mensah*

the clause a coded message that was meant to communicate a disdain for my research work? Was it an invalidation of studies focusing on sub-Saharan Africa? Did the committee have a problem with an African going back to Africa to pursue research? These questions bothered me for some time.

### Theorizing Africanness

Spronk (2009, p. 3) defines *Africanness* as the emic and innate sense of "being African" as a shared history, race, or culture. The concept of Africanness is also a state of being, shared identity, and a prism for understanding the lived experiences of Africans in the diaspora. It is spatial, conceptual, and contextual in the sense that it encompasses Africa as a space, a concept, an ideology, and a set of power relations (Dei, 2012; Ovens & Prinsloo, 2010). Africanness is about the multiple ways Africans and people of African descent negotiate their identity (race, culture, history, etc.).

In the academic context, Africanness is a framework of being, which enables the African academic and scholar to maintain his or her sense of identity, and use it to leverage and negotiate his or her views and ideas which some colleagues in the majority culture sometimes view as (in)valid, and radical (Dei, 2000). Africanness, is a process of power relations: It entails a baggage (stigma) and burden that people from Africa (and people of African descent) carry because of their connection to the African continent and a result of centuries of slavery, colonization, imperialism, and subjugation (Wainaina, 2005). Although Africans are varied in many ways, they nonetheless share collective identities and carry similar baggage (Dei, 2012). The negative images cast on Blacks go back to European explorations of Africa during which they systematically framed the continent as a "dark" primitive space ridden with poverty, diseases, and famine. At the same time Europeans were taking away Africa's wealth, they cultivated these negative images of Africans to justify the horrors of slavery (Wainaina, 2005).

The West's negative categorizations and stereotypes of the African continent and its people have unleashed prejudicial treatments, racism and discrimination, and disrespect of Africans in diasporized spaces. As an instructor at a Christian college that invests in global, development, missions, and service-learning programs, I commend many faculty and students at this Christian college campus for their passion for service in Africa. However, I am of the belief that an "empowered benevolence"—the kind that does not focus on a person's situation and limitations but elevates the peoples' humanness, potential, and capabilities—goes a long way to accord and reinforce respect for the beneficiaries.

Because a lot of the service learning programs that faculty and students are involved occur on the African continent, they take trips to different countries in sub-Saharan Africa. What one realizes is that reports from these mission-oriented and service-learning programs on Africa tend to focus on the same bleak and negative categorizations that have perpetuated and reinforced stereotypes and stigma on Africa and Africans in the first place. Many of the posters, billboards, pictures, and video clips on Africa highlight poverty, diseases, sicknesses, and wars. These depictions become a source of discomfort and a burden that African-born faculty and students on Christian college campuses shoulder. Some years ago when I served as the advisor to the African Students Association on our campus, I led the association to register our displeasure of the negative ways various entities on campus continue to portray and depict Africa and Africans.

### The Saga of "Rooted" Africanness

African-born professors in the diaspora have to constantly negotiate the challenges of being a rooted African by maintaining strong links and connections with their immediate and extended families back home. For immigrants and other minorities, such connections come with challenges. As an example, I was enjoying my early-morning sleep one day when a phone call abruptly woke me up. Before I could pick the call, the line got disconnected. I became confused and disoriented. I checked the time, and it was about 3 a.m., which even made me more annoyed and groggy. I lifted myself up and sat on the bed, wondering why I should be disturbed this early in the morning when I was to teach at 8 a.m. The phone rang again. I picked it up, and at the other end of the line I heard my brother's voice. I sensed from his voice that something was wrong. I hurriedly inquired about the reason for the early-morning call. In less than a minute, I posed a series of incoherent questions in an attempt to find out the reason(s) for the early morning call. Finally, my brother informed me that our father had a massive stroke and had been admitted to a hospital. My confusion intensified because of the responsibility that came with the call.

My parents live thousands of miles away. It is impossible to hop on the plane to attend to my aged parents when they needed me most. To embark on a journey to see my father at the time required about $5,000 and arrangements that could create a lot of inconveniences for my immediate family, students, and the department. As an immigrant professor who also supports his extended family back in Ghana, my embarking on a journey to Ghana to visit my father required financial planning because of the financial responsibility the situation placed on me. My father had retired only a few years prior to this incident; however, my parents' limited financial resources meant that, I (and my brothers) had to support my father's long-term health needs due to his stroke.

As people from collective cultures, most African-born professors cannot ignore remittances to families, friends and kinsmen back home because they are a necessary part of our rootedness in our families and communities (Ovens & Prinsloo, 2010). Many of our native-born colleagues may not have any idea about the nature of the challenges that many immigrant professors from developing nations in particular shoulder, in addition to those that are presented within the context of our host nations.

## 152   Obed Mfum-Mensah

## CONCLUDING REMARKS FOR "ALIEN" SCHOLARS
## SEEKING TENURE POSITIONS

I end this chapter by focusing on three issues I believe may provide insights for immigrant scholars (Africans in particular) who have the desire to enter the professoriate domain in North America. First, the professoriate space is a political domain. Therefore, most activities that occur in this domain are socially and politically constructed. Underneath those activities are coded messages. The space tends to be inhabited by individuals who are territorial in several ways. Minority faculty in particular are likely to confront a monopolization of sacred frame in your new department—especially when the department is not racially or ethnically diverse. Having good negotiation skills will empower you to carve a space for yourself and to avoid succumbing to all forms of professional colonization and domination.

Second, assertiveness is needed to carve a space and survive in the professoriate. Some are often tempted to entertain the mentality that people have to succumb to the dictates of their veteran colleagues in the department to succeed. My advice for individuals who entertain this ideology is that they should exercise caution and understand that this does not apply in every situation in the academic space—certainly not in racially homogeneous spaces. Unassertive African-born professors who give in to the dictates of veteran colleagues in their department who pretend to mentor them sometimes face the danger of compromising their scholarship, teaching, and sense of identity. I know of a promising African-born untenured professor who gave in to his department chair's requests to coteach with him because students complained that he spoke with an accent. The suggestion initially seemed a laudable one; however, as the complaints continued, the department chair did little to save the situation, and the individual was finally relieved of his position. My point here is that the untenured African-born professor must constantly remind his or her departmental colleagues and students regarding what he or she brings to the department and work to resolve petty challenges that have tangible solutions.

Third, minority faculty who teach in predominantly White institutions must maintain a positive personal identity and hold the same for their colleagues. A positive view of oneself and others is a powerful tool for maintaining positive attitudes and minimizing one's own prejudices and biases (Pate, 1982, as cited by Bennette, 2007). This approach requires hard work on our part but is nonetheless enriching. It often requires that we position ourselves in a vulnerable situation to achieve positive results. For example, the first time I taught Sociocultural Perspectives on Education course in my current institution, I had only four students enrolled. The course enrollment increased to 6, and then to 16. Currently, the course is among the most popular in our department, with a typical enrollment of between 32 and 37 (this is a large number for a small Christian liberal arts institution in Pennsylvania). What I do differently in this course is that I create a safe space for all of us (students and myself) to have honest conversations about all the sociocultural issues we deal with in our society on a daily basis. Another way I try to (re)position students' truths in favor of minority sensibilities is the nature of the texts I select for students to read. I deliberately select diverse voices and perspectives in my course as a way of fostering inclusive excellence.

African-born-and-raised professors enter the academic space with our trifold identities. Therefore, we need to constantly remind ourselves that our trifold identity mediates our teaching, scholarship, and perspectives. Furthermore, we need to constantly remind our colleagues about the different ways our unique identities and experiences inform our perspectives on issues and about how such perspectives are beneficial to our disciplinary domain. In this sense, reclaiming and reinventing our Africanness in a diasporized context is not an option but is necessary for survival and sanity.

## REFERENCES

Bennette, C. I. (2007). *Comprehensive multicultural education*. Boston: Allyn and Bacon.

Bhabha, H. (1990). Third space. Interview with Rutherford, Jonathan. In J. Rutherford (Ed.), *Identity, community, culture and difference* (pp. 301–307). London: Lawrence & Wishart. Quote is on p. 109.

Cockrell, K. S. (2006). Solitary sojourn: An American Indian faculty member's journey. In C. A. Stanley (Ed.), *Faculty of color: Teaching in predominantly white colleges and universities* (pp. 123–137). Bolton, MA: Anker Publishing Company.

Conle, C. (2000). Thesis as narrative or "what is the inquiry in narrative inquiry?" *Curriculum Inquiry, 30*(2), 189–214.

Connelly, F. M., & Clandinin, D. J. (1990). Studies of experience and narrative inquiry. *Educational Researcher, 19*(5), 2–14.

Dei, G. J. S. (2000). Rethinking the role of Indigenous knowledges the academy. *International Journal of Inclusive Education, 4*(2), 111–132.

Dei, G. J. S. (2012). Reclaiming our Africanness in the diasporized context: The challenge of asserting a critical African personality. *The Journal of Pan African Studies, 4*(10), 42–57.

Jaipal, R. (2006). Anatomy of difference: The meaning of diversity and the diversity of meaning. In C. A. Stanley (Ed.), *Faculty of color: Teaching in predominantly white colleges and universities* (pp. 182–195). Bolton, MA: Anker Publishing Company.

Kanu, Y. (2007). Tradition and educational reconstruction in Africa in postcolonial and global times: The case of Sierra Leone. *African Studies Quarterly, 10*(3), 65–84.

Nieto, S. (2004). *Affirming Diversity: The Sociopolitical Contexts of Multicultural Education*. New York: Longman Publishing Group.

Ovens, M., & Prinsloo, J. (2010). The significance of "Africanness" for the development of contemporary criminological propositions: A multidisciplinary approach. *Phronimon, 11*(2), 19–33.

Paris, J. W., & Schoon, K. (2007). Antiracism, pedagogy, and the development of affirmative white identities among evangelical college students. *Christian Scholar's Review, 36*(3), 285–301.

## 154  Obed Mfum-Mensah

Perez, M. (2006). Negotiating identity and learning from a native pacific perspective: Contradictions of higher learning in cultural diversity classes. In C. A. Stanley (Ed.), *Faculty of color: Teaching in predominantly white colleges and universities* (pp. 247–262). Bolton, MA: Anker Publishing Company.

Spronk, R. (2009). Sex, sexuality and negotiating Africanness in Nairobi. *Africa,* 79(4), 500–519.

Stanley, C. A. (2006). *Faculty of color: Teaching in predominantly white colleges and universities.* Bolton, MA: Anker Publishing Company.

Tatum, B. D. (2003). *Why are all the Black kids sitting together in the cafeteria?* New York: Basic Books.

Ulibarri, S. R. (1972). *El Alma de la Raza.* Albuquerque, NM: University of New Mexico College of Education.

Wainaina, B. (2005). How to write about Africa. *Granta,* 92. Retrieved from http://www.granta.com/Magazine/92/How-to-Write-about-Africa/Page-1

Wassink, A. B. (1999). Historic low prestige and seeds of change: Attitudes toward Jamaican Creole. *Language in Society,* 28(1), 57–92.


## BIOGRAPHICAL NOTES

Obed Mfum-Mensah teaches foundations of education at Messiah College in Grantham, Pennsylvania. His current research is in the areas of curriculum theorizing, complementary education programs in the developing world, education in sub-Saharan Africa, and education of marginalized groups. Obed completed his PhD in Comparative, International and Development Education at the Ontario Institute for the Studies in Education at University of Toronto.

# 13 From Essential and Central to Constructivist Trenches

## Navigating the Transnational Contexts of the Instructional Practice of a Foreign-Born Professor

*Fonkem Achankeng*

### INTRODUCTION

> *In my native university, Professor Adamu threatened a perceptively bad student with failure in a classroom full of students. He was also an influential dean of a college, in a largely authoritarian culture. From that point on, that student failed his examinations and was compelled to leave the university. In mainstream American culture in which individual rights and freedoms are a way of life, it would be an abomination for a professor to threaten a student with failure, for no good reason. In other words, a professor's behavior that may be normal in the home country may be far from normal in a new teaching culture.*

The phenomenon described by Bryceson and Vuorela (2002) as "persisting attachment" in the "multi-locational identities that bridge the geographical space" of immigrant experiences (p. 6) is very relevant for foreign-born professors. In this chapter, I use my personal experience to help illustrate the lives of foreign-born professors as they grapple with the problems of teaching in a transcultural context, where not only language and accents, but issues of power, authority, and relationships, as well, pose as challenges in instructional spaces and other spaces. Coming from a country where the professor was the center of practice to a host country where culturally the professor is increasingly called on to serve as a guide, I also explore in this chapter the tensions that arise in the minds of foreign-born professors when confronted with the acculturation processes and adaption to new instructional approaches. Although much research has focused on how teachers teach (Brookfield, 1995; Hooks, 1994; Tompkins, 1991) and on how students learn (Barr & Tagg, 1995; Barton, 1994; Fosnot, 1996; Weimar, 2002), the question remains as to how foreign-born professors navigate the cross-cultural context of teaching and learning.

The purpose of this chapter is to document my experiences of teaching and learning from a transnational and transcultural perspective. I use an autoethnographic methodology to highlight issues of power, authority, and

# 156    Fonkem Achankeng

relationships of professors and students in higher education classrooms in both the home and host societies. I argue that understanding the realities of migration and the related cultural difference foreign-born professors face, add to a deeper understanding of the complex experiences of foreign-born professors, with implications for instructional practice and career success. Besides, understanding the sociological and psychological realities of immigrant professors and the challenges of the two cultural universes in which they live and function is equally significant for supporting the global education and diversity objectives of higher institutions across the world. Based on constructivist theory, the chapter concludes with a discussion of the implications of the highlighted issues for cross-cultural teaching and learning.

## MY AMERICAN UNIVERSITY CLASSROOM EXPERIENCE

As a foreign-born professor, for me my experience of the American classroom has been the exact opposite of the situation I had in my home country. I was in my 40s when I arrived in the United States; I had been teaching at the university in Cameroon for some 12 years. I was hired at a small 2-year college that was part of a statewide system, and it was my first time teaching in a different university system. I was not paid by virtue of my qualifications and experience; rather, I was paid by what the adjunct teaching position offered and the time my services were needed.

In my country of origin, professors were paid by their qualifications rather than by what they actually did because they were part of the civil service of the country. In the United States, however, I learned that a professor was paid for what he or she was hired to do, especially when the professor was hired on an ad hoc basis. Back home, the university was a place where faculty members came together and worked together, learning from each other's experiences. Here, I was alone in my department, all to myself! In addition, I encountered so much new technology that was rather overwhelming.

The pay system and my loneliness were not all that frustrated me. There were also student behaviors and expectations. Unlike back home, students saw themselves as the employers of professors because professors' salaries partly depended on the tuition students paid to the university. And because students pay a lot of money for their education in the host country, they also almost always expect to get A grades irrespective of the quality of their work. In the host country, students often refer to professors by the professor's first name. Coming from a culture where the use of first names is considered disrespectful, it was shocking for students not only to call me by my first name but also to beckon me with their little finger to come to them.

Being an African immigrant professor also means that one carries all the perceptions that come with being a "person of color." This label is unfortunately associated with such prejudicial notions of underachievement, underclass, laziness, and unworthiness, among others. Some of these perceptions may explain why if a foreign-born professor arrives late for a faculty meeting, it may be perceived as a tradition among people of color who are not respectful of time. Immigrants in general, in my host country's culture, are also perceived as people who cannot speak proper English or who speak with "a thick accent." From this standpoint, my students probably must feel insulted that I correct their language after I grade their papers.

In spite of any frustrations I feel and the challenges that I must meet in my professional journey, I still consider myself fortunate. I know of two other friends—one a refugee and the other an immigrant like me—who, to this day, continue to teach on an ad hoc basis with no prospects of ever having full-time faculty contracts because of their advanced ages.

My major struggle is related to reducing the amount of control and balancing with structures that promote student growth. Inasmuch as my American students want to learn the instructional content, they want the professor to be less domineering. They do not seem to like professors who are at the center of the classroom lecturing them. Probably as part of the larger culture in which they are socialized to guard and protect their personal space and freedoms, American students also wish to be at the center of everything that goes on around them. As such, I have had to learn rather fast to "move aside" (Weimar, 2002, p. 74) while remaining relevant. My greatest challenge has been to navigate this shift from being essential and central to finding a location in the trenches of constructivism.

## FROM ESSENTIAL AND CENTRAL TO CONSTRUCTIVIST TRENCHES

The constructivist theory in education is about the relationship between learners and the learning content. "Constructivist approaches emphasize learners actively constructing their own knowledge rather than passively receiving information transmitted to them from teachers and textbooks. From a constructivist perspective, knowledge cannot simply be given to students: Students must construct their own meanings" (Stage, Muller, Kinzie, & Simmons, 1998, p. 35). This thinking has contributed to developments in the collaborative learning movement involving group work with the teacher functioning mainly as a master learner and resource. In this approach, according to Weimar (2002), by working in groups, students are required to function as a community. Weimar (2002) has also stated that when students work in groups they "jointly create their own unique solutions to problems" (p. 12). For constructivists, students discover more and are told less. In other words, students become very involved with content, with a goal to using it to develop unique and individual ways of understanding. Fosnot (1996, p. 29) also described this situation as requiring "intervention and self-organization on the part of the learner." In this teaching

158   *Fonkem Achankeng*

and learning approach, students need not wait until they have developed expertise before they interact with content. They are rather encouraged to explore it, handle it, relate it to their own experience, and challenge it whatever their level of expertise . . . the goal being to involve students in the process of acquiring and retaining information (Weimar, 2002, p. 13). This thinking is close to the teacher's role in Ayers's (1986, p. 50) analogy of teachers as midwives, a viewpoint in which "Good teachers, like midwives, empower. Good teachers find ways to activate students, for they know that learning requires active engagement between the subject and object matter."

The experiences analyzed in this chapter demonstrate that the foreign-born professor finds him or herself at the intersection of two worlds, struggling between the cultural expectations of their home and host countries. Recognizing the difficulty associated with being a foreign-born professor in the United States can contribute to understanding professor behaviors that may appear unfamiliar for host country's campus communities. From a behavioral standpoint, one can envision such themes in the narratives of power and authority in the classroom, as well as in relationships with students in the context of teaching and learning.

## POWER

The literature on teaching and learning emphasizes issues of power. Critical pedagogues like Paulo Freire (1993) articulate the locus of power as a central tenet of teaching and learning, stating that education can be a vehicle for social change. According to Stage, Muller, Kinze, and Simmons (1998), "education's role is to challenge inequality and dominant myths rather than socialize students into the status quo . . . [and] 'true' learning empowers students to challenge oppression in their lives" (p. 57). In illustrating the thinking of critical pedagogy, Tompkins (1991) noted that "the kind of classroom situation one creates is the acid test of what it is one really stands for" (p. 26). bell hooks (1994) described classrooms as "radical spaces of possibility" (p. 12). These images reflect more of the American instructional practices, in contrast to the situation back home, where professors had all the power to decide on content, approach, and issues of timing in instructional practice. In this teaching and learning situation, professors got students to obey them. By letting students obey them, the professors received the esteem and recognition that came with owning all the power in instructional practice. In such a grim and threatening condition, however, one wonders how much the students learned, considering they were not free to make the choices that determine the course of their lives.

Having been gone from my home country for over a decade and returned on occasion, I see that many things have changed. In the summer of 2013, I had a visiting professorship position at one of the local universities where I used many of my American instructional practices. Although the students

## From Essential and Central to Constructivist Trenches    159

insisted on referring to me as "the lecturer," as the tradition there dictates, probably because professors "lecture" all the time, I did the best I could in my planning and delivery to shift the locus of the learning process from myself to the students. I later learned from the chair of the program that some of the students stayed on in groups working until well past midnight. Whenever the small groups shared their learning with the larger class, it was evident from their faces that they were proud of what they had accomplished. From my teaching in the United States, I have come to learn that when students are empowered with their learning and when they take ownership of their own learning, they are much better off in the knowledge gained, in their self-esteem, and in the broader social scheme of things than when they are lectured to and expected to memorize the teaching/learning content. What struck the students I taught in the summer of 2013 is that, using my American classroom experience, I tried to dialogue with them rather than exert my power over them.

From my experience, students, like all people, want the freedom to choose how things are done. They also want learning to be fun and enjoyable—it gives them an incentive to assimilate content. Therefore, the power of the professor, in the context of the classroom (from the standpoints of a professor's tone of voice, language use, and the kind of nuanced perspectives), should be employed in ways that optimize learning, not stifle it.


## AUTHORITY

Closely related to power and its use in the classroom is the authority of professors to control students' acting, thinking, and feelings, which are components of behavior emanating from each individual's thoughts (Glasser, 1998). Learning is not imposed on students. Teachers can impose assignments on students, and such students may well "complete" the assignment and yet not learn. bell hooks (1994, p. 12) in her characterization of classrooms as "radical spaces of possibility" observed that for critical pedagogues, teacher authority figures do not dispense knowledge. In this conceptualization of teaching/learning, learning is expected to be more effective when the locus of the learning process is shifted from the teacher to the students.

My experiences of teaching in a transcultural context highlight the differences of teacher authority in classrooms in the two countries of my experience. I have grown in my perception of teaching and student learning to understand that students are likely to enjoy their learning when they co-own the process by sharing part of the authority in the classroom. When teaching is more student centered, for example, by involving students in the process of acquiring and retaining information, they are likely to feel included, and perceive themselves as having some authority, in the decisions that affect their learning. Considering student input on tests and examination dates, for example, gives them some authority and ownership of their

160 *Fonkem Achankeng*

own experiences—especially when they have other pending tests scheduled for the same dates.

Increasingly, there is more shared authority in my teaching in the host country than I ever experienced before, especially back in my home country, where professors appeared to be exclusively concerned about transferring their accumulated knowledge of their discipline to the minds of their students. The difference between students in my home and host countries may also be in their behaviors, as dictated by both societies: Students in my home country culture quietly took whatever was doled out to them; however, students in my host culture question the monopoly of authority by any professor.

## PROFESSOR–STUDENT RELATIONSHIPS

Fonkem (2012), writing about relationships in the classroom, emphasized the need to plan with the students in mind as an important component of instructional practice. She stated that "teachers can be as ready as they can be to teach, have the best differentiated lesson plans for varied learning styles, but if they do not meet the respective needs of the students, the students will not learn" (p. 180). Effective relationship building means discovering and incorporating students' interests into class goals, noticing individual accomplishments and events in students' lives, and interacting with each student as an individual (Marzano, Gaddy, Foseid, Foseid, & Marzano, 2005). In the classes I teach, I do not only respond to student messages routinely and wish them well when they are ill but also follow up on their conditions often. Many students continue to write to me after they have taken my classes. Some other things I do include getting to know every student's name in the first weeks of classes so that I can address them on a personal level, in spite of the large numbers of students I teach. Whether at the door, in or outside of class, I not only say, "Hello, Mark," for example, but start a conversation about the student's day and how things are going for him or her or ask about other classes the student may be taking. Many students return to my classes to visit, and I invite some of them to share their experiences about when they took the class. I also try to learn about each individual student to have an idea of his/her strengths and weaknesses. In addition, I make it a point of duty to compliment students on achievements in and outside of school and sometimes sing "Happy Birthday" to students in class. Whether working in small or large groups, we take turns asking or answering questions or sharing viewpoints. In these turn-taking exercises, I try as much as possible to be as equitable as I can.

When we explore any ideas in class, the policy is "no participant left behind." And referring to questions, not only is every question important to the student who may have posed the question, but more important, every question is also a contribution to the knowledge base of the class. Because

## From Essential and Central to Constructivist Trenches   161

students who come to the class come from a variety of experiences, backgrounds, and needs, the approach in my classes is that as a class we are made up of unique individuals. As a consequence, I am very aware of the needs of different students and try to accommodate the individual needs in the learning activities and processes. Referring to the place of relationships in the classroom in student learning, Marzano et al. (2005, p. 56) asserted that "the relationship between teacher and student is the starting place for a good classroom experience." Emphasizing the relationship component of the instructional practice, Fonkem (2012) noted that most often because of the need to meet the required curricula expectations, teachers find themselves engrossed in teaching students they do not know, not because they do not believe in building these relationships, but more because they do not have the time to artfully teach and socialize.

Relationships between professors and students as a way of enhancing student learning were not the case in my home country teaching experience. Relationship building in the host culture is important not only for student learning (Marzano et al., 2005) but also for the professor who needs students' feedback to retain his or her job and to gain promotion. In my home country, professors were never accountable to students as their promotions depended on a hierarchical relationship in and out of the university, and even with political connections in the ruling regime. In my host society, professor–student relationships are conditioned by the fact that professors exist because there are students to be taught. Students are consequently at the center of everything that happens in the classroom.

Part of my learning in the host country has been that to make progress in human relationships, we need to give up seeking to control others. In my teaching experience back home, I did not know that the only behavior we can control is our own and that no one can make us do anything we do not want to do. The desire to control student behaviors was hurtful to students because student behaviors were anchored more on fear than on respect and cordiality. Relationships with students were more between an all-knowing, powerful professor and little-knowing, powerless students.

This professor–student relationship theme in the narratives stands out in postindustrial American culture within a learner-centered context. In my home country context, where the professor was the center of learning, students had to adapt to the teaching styles of even the worst, eccentric professors. It did not matter whether an entire class failed. I remember proctoring a mathematics examination for a professor who did not care about the students and probably have had no productive relationships with them. This professor had set his exams from material that he had not even taught and knew that no student would understand the question; however, he was happy that no student would pass. At the same time he knew that his job was not in jeopardy whether anyone passed or not.

An interesting point related to relationships has to do with issues of personal space and social zones in American society. Issues of space and social

## 162   Fonkem Achankeng

zones can be problematic to foreign-born professors, especially those who come from home countries where spaces and zones are not a major sociocultural consideration. American students feel they are being invaded when strangers and people they are not emotionally close to get too close to them physically. Professors and public speakers in America are expected to use a distance of 12 to 18 feet from their audience (Zastrow & Kirst-Ashman, 2010, p. 482) and not too close during personal conversations. For foreign-born professors who are unaware of this sociocultural expectation, issues of personal space, personal and social zones have caused problems.

In all, relationships between faculty members are experienced differently in the two worlds of foreign-born professors. Being raised and socialized in a different culture, it is often a problem for the foreign-born professor to grasp the subtleties in relationships, some of which may have an impact in one's professional success. From my experience, immigrant professors can find themselves unconsciously functioning socially in the host country culture, as though they are still living back home. Immigrant professors therefore need to be aware of some of the behaviors that are considered acceptable in their native countries but are hurtful to others and their own success in the host culture.

## LESSONS LEARNED

I have learned some lessons as an immigrant professor. These lessons include some of the requirements for success in instructional practice as well as some not-so-obvious challenges or hidden obstacles to career success in the American university environment.

To succeed in a cross-cultural academic context, international professors need to focus on making plans for instructional practice with students in mind especially regarding issues power, authority, and relationships in the classroom. In mainstream American culture, where individual rights and freedoms are a way of life as earlier discussed, it is important to have students at the center of all planning and delivery. Foreign-born professors will learn to plan with students in mind at all times. Based on my experience, immigrant professors need to remember that learning is more effective when the locus of the learning process shifts from the teacher to the students, and shift very quickly to reflect that in their practice.

An area of great importance I raised in this chapter is the issue of the not-so-obvious challenges or hidden obstacles in the career advancement of foreign-born professors in the United States. In societies with corporate race-to-the-top culture that favors people "blowing their own trumpets" and stepping on others to rise to the top, foreign-born professors may have difficulties in the tenure-track system in corporate-style universities. This situation can be a major challenge to immigrant professors who, prior to immigration, were socialized to work quietly expecting career success as part of the civil service norms of the home country.

*From Essential and Central to Constructivist Trenches*   163

I must note in this chapter that, as a foreign-born professor, one could teach well, have a great record of scholarship, and serve the university community yet not get tenure and promotion. Being raised and socialized in a different culture, I faced this problem. I learned that renewal and career advancement in an American university milieu are not clear in relation to the professorial responsibility expectations for teaching, scholarship, and service. I had much success in my teaching considering my popularity with students and my student and peer evaluations. I also had an impressive record of disseminating research and knowledge through the many publications I authored and conference presentations at state, regional, national, and international levels. Equally, I had a good record of service in department, college, and university committees, including serving as chair of a major university-wide committee, volunteering my services beyond the university community, and serving my professional organizations as senior reviewer of conference proposals. Yet, at the end of my fourth year, I received a letter stating that I would not be renewed because I did "not meet expectations for teaching, scholarship and service." I had been renewed at the end of my first year for 3 years. During the 3 years, I worked even harder to improve my teaching and service record, and to publish even more. Everyone congratulated me, and I thought I met and even exceeded the expectations set out for teaching, research, and service. I was shocked when I received my nonrenewal letter and decided to fight the decision. I share this personal experience story to indicate that for the foreign-born professor, grasping the subtleties and issues of relationships involved in the tenure process can be very challenging.

## CONCLUSION

This chapter set out to capture the deep meaning of experience in the life of foreign-born professors in a host country's university classroom. Focusing mainly on my teaching experience in both the home and host countries and particularly on the central and domineering teaching role as a part of the defining issues in student learning, the reflection in the chapter was carried out on the basis of the dynamic implications of uprooting and resettlement, social and psychological adjustment, and the prospects for continued links to a migrant's home country cultures. It was argued that the realities of immigration and the attendant cultural diversity into which foreign-born professors plunge can not only be a cause for a difficult career but can also add to performance complexities in a postindustrialized culture where performance is a strict requirement for career success.

Among several different challenges, including accent problems, image, and cultural knowledge and adaptation, shifting from a central and dominating teacher role to teaching in which instructors act as "guides and facilitators of learning" means instructors "must move aside, often and regularly" (Weimar, 2002, p. 74). Back in my home country teaching was

## 164 Fonkem Achankeng

usually based on the assumption that "students are not capable of expanding their maturity," as Mallinger (1998, p. 473) pointed out in his critique of instructor-directed leadership.

The chapter demonstrated that the problems of cultural and professional adaptation experienced by migrant professors are real and can be a source of perceived failure of foreign-born professors when reflected in student evaluations. In the particular case of the stories of this immigrant professor, it was argued that continuing to function, at least psychologically, from the home country's society of origin in a host country, as is often the case with adult immigrants, is in itself very challenging. This happens because the hearts of many first-generation adult immigrants remain socially located mainly in the home country's culture, a situation that may account for a kind of slow adaptation and even career failures.

The central concern of the analysis was not only to uncover orientations to the behavior of foreign-born professors, but also to understand such behaviors as the primary site of cross-cultural lives. Because for immigrant professors, their experiences can be further compounded by psychological and acculturative difficulties, such difficulties play out within the university classroom and always have implications not only for instructional practice but also for career success. Understanding these situations is important for the scholarship on foreign-born professors.

## REFERENCES

Ayers, W. (1986). Thinking about teachers and the curriculum. *Harvard Educational Review, 56*(1), 49–51.

Barr, R. B., & Tagg, J. (1995, November–December). From teaching to learning–a new paradigm for undergraduate education. *Change*, 13–25.

Barton, L. O. (1994). Ten advantages of a student-centered test design. *Teaching Professor, 8*(1), 4.

Brookfield, S. D. (1995). *Becoming a critically reflective teacher.* San Francisco, CA: Jossey-Bass.

Bryceson, D., &Vuorela, U. (2002). Transnational families in the twenty-first century. In D. Bryceson & U. Vuorela (Eds.), *The transnational family: New European frontiers and global networks* (pp. 3–30). Oxford: Berg Publishers.

Fonkem, P. (2012). *High school experiences of students with chronic behavior problems.* Unpublished doctoral dissertation, Marian University, Fond du Lac, Wisconsin.

Fosnot, C. T. (Ed.). (1996). *Constructivism: Theory, perspectives and practice.* New York: College Teachers Press.

Friere, P. (1993). *Pedagogy of the oppressed.* New York: Continuum.

Glasser, W. (1998). *Choice theory: A new psychology of personal freedom.* New York: Harper Perennial.

Hooks, B. (1994). *Teaching to transgress: Education as the practice of freedom.* New York: Routledge.

Mallinger, M. (1998). Maintaining control in the classroom bygiving up control. *Journal of Management Education, 22*(4), 472–483.

## From Essential and Central to Constructivist Trenches 165

Marzano, R. J., Gaddy, B. B., Foseid, M. C., Foseid, M. P., & Marzano, J. S. (2005). *A handbook for classroom management that works*. Alexandria, VA: Association for supervision and Curriculum development.

Stage, F. K., Muller, P. A., Kinzie, J., & Simmons A. (1998). "Creating learning centered classrooms: What does learning theory have to say?" *ASHE-ERIC Higher Education Report* 26(4).

Tompkins, J. (1991). "Teaching like it matters." *Lingua Franca* 1(6), 24–27.

Weimar, M. (2002). *Learner-centered teaching: Five key changes to practice*. San Francisco, CA: Jossey-Bass.

Zastrow, C., & Kirst-Ashman, K. K. (2010). *Understanding human behavior and the social environment*. Belmont, CA: Brooks/Cole.

# 14 Unpacking the Invisible Knapsack of African-Born Professor's Identity in the U.S. Academe

*Michael Takafor Ndemanu*

## INTRODUCTION

In this chapter I employ autoethnographic inquiry to reveal my thoughts about my professional experiences as an academic in the United States. In addition to being ethnographic in nature, autoethnography uses the author's autobiographic information as primary data (Chang, 2007). Given the interpretive nature of an ethnographic study, the cultural lens through which I view the world will have an accentuating leverage in the way I interpret other people's attitudes, beliefs, and behaviors toward me and my professional competence and aptitude. Because reality is socially constructed (Merriam, 2009), the social location, time, and space must be taken into consideration in constructing meaning from autoethnographic data because one's cultural background, socioeconomic status (SES), gender, and early socialization experiences all influence how one constructs the meaning of data. My awareness of this social reality enabled me to contextualize the meaning I made from people's attitudes and behavior toward me.

This chapter explores the ways in which my ethnic and linguistic identities have shaped my professional experiences as a professor, in general, and as a professor of multicultural education (ME) courses, in particular, in the United States. ME courses deals with human diversity and equity issues in education. They cover topics on race, ethnicity, gender, class, language, religion, sexual orientation, immigration, and so on. They are one of the most difficult courses to teach in education because of the discomfort and the sense of guilt it elicits in students, especially those of the dominant racial group. Thus, the racial and ethnic identities of the instructors of the course affect students' judgment of the course readings, as well as their predisposition to listen to the instructor. According to Housee (2008), an instructor's racialized identity is a huge factor to students with respect to determining the receivability of the course content because while Black instructors may be prejudged by White preservice teachers (PSTs) for their "loyalties and sensibilities" with African Americans, doubts are cast by African American PSTs at White instructors' abilities to empathize with victims of racism. In one study, White PSTs were suspicious of an African American instructor

(Dixson & Dingus, 2007), just as in another study carried out by Housee (2008), some African American PSTs viewed their White instructors as being insensitive and insensible with regard to teaching race-related courses. Consequently, White students may prefer a White professor to a U.S-born professor of color teaching the ME course. On the other hand, members of historically oppressed group may prefer a professor of similar racial background teaching the course because they believe that he or she may relate to their experiences as co-victims of racism. Given the tendency for both groups to be suspicious of one another on matters of race, a foreign-born professor, especially one of color, is generally viewed as relatively neutral and is highly preferred in teaching race-related issues because his or her forebearers are not members of the historically oppressed group in the United States. For example, Shaun (a pseudonym is used here) a student of ME, echoed the importance of such neutrality when his opinion was sought about his African-born instructor as follows:

> I liked him, and I felt like he was very well qualified, and I appreciate that they had someone who wasn't just a White teacher coming in and teaching the class, which I'm sure they did on purpose. Yeah, I liked that for the most part. And I especially liked that he was someone who wasn't just the majority and wasn't the just the minority either, but was literally was from outside.
>
> (Ndemanu, 2012, p. 156)

In the preceding example, the foreign-born instructor positioned himself as an arbitrator in his class on issues of race and SES.

Although I have been relatively successful in teaching these sensitive issues than some racial minority faculty members, the students' limited knowledge about world Englishes and sociolinguistics has been a stumbling block to my professional experiences in the academia. Most of the students that I have taught so far had had little or no prior exposure to people who speak English differently from them—and the fact that I am fluent in five languages does not help. Unlike my colleagues of color teaching ME courses who are often accused of "reverse racism" in their anonymous course evaluation, the few negative evaluations that I often receive hover around my English accent, as well as those ensuing from dissimilar academic and pedagogic cultures.

## Comparing Classroom Settings and Resources

Classrooms in Cameroon, where I was born and raised, are arranged in a way that sets a stage for a professor to stand facing the students with a chalkboard behind him or her while all the students sit in unmovable chairs or benches facing the professor and the chalkboard. This class arrangement does not give much room for any other pedagogy apart from the teacher-centered. The students are sometimes divided into manageable groups and

## 168  Michael Takafor Ndemanu

assigned a graduate assistant to review some of the materials that had been covered in the course by the principal instructor of the course, in preparation for the final examinations. Thus, in addition to attending large lectures of a given course, the students attend small-group follow-up lectures taught by graduate assistants working with the course instructors. Unlike in the United States, college classrooms in Cameroon are always arranged in a way that any visitor to any of the classrooms can always easily distinguish the instructor from the students by nature of the elevated floor in front of the room on which the instructor stands and teaches like a pastor preaching from the pulpit. This physical elevation also projected a psychological power structure and a hierarchical gap between instructors and their students.

When I first started teaching in the U.S college classroom, I wrestled with how to organize my classroom in a democratic way that, I believe, gives room for robust discussions and critical thinking. Although I did immediately begin to engage my students in the course content, the discomfort that came with it was alarming because of cultural barriers. I needed to think of activities that would be of most impact to my students, and such activities needed to relate to their cultural experiences in order to harness their interests. However, given the challenges that foreign-born academics surmount in their countries of origin to be successful academically, it did not take long for me to adapt to the new pedagogic culture which entails shifting the contours of my reasoning from being the "all-knowing" instructor who possesses all the knowledge (Freire, 1970) to a facilitator of learning in the classroom. This happened through deliberate efforts that encompassed research on progressive pedagogic approaches as well as through observing other teacher educators who let me and other associate instructors into their classrooms, not because they thought we could not teach effectively but because they wanted us to be successful instructors of touchy issues. Students' feedback was pivotal to my new pedagogic acculturation and transformation. It took me little time to adjust to the new pedagogic culture, given that teacher-centered approach is first and foremost burdensome.

In my new capacity as an assistant professor, I also serve as an advisor to teacher candidates. No workshops are organized to prepare recently hired professors for advising responsibilities. Everyone has to learn it on the job, and there is no gainsaying that it is no easy task, given that because of immense pressure from state legislature, changes occur almost every year in our program. When that happens, we all have to go back to the drawing board every time, discarding what we had learned the previous year and embracing new programs and standards. It is worth recognizing the fact that colleagues in my department have been very supportive to me and other newly hired colleagues. In my first year of advising, some colleagues would come to my office and invite me to sit in their advising sessions to learn the process. Although I never had to sit in anyone's advising session, I was very grateful to colleagues for their willingness to support me in the advising immersion.

Instructional technology is one aspect of didactic resources that defines the extent to which the government cares about the education of its citizenry. It is something that I was not very familiar with until I started teaching a course as an associate instructor (during my doctoral studies). The course coordinator accompanied me to one of the rooms in which I was supposed to teach my first undergraduate class and showed me how to access the university's instructional website and its related tools. These included various classroom technology tools such as the projector, SMART Board, and the sound system. Although I had a home computer in Cameroon, none of the schools in which I taught had classrooms equipped with technological devices. Again, it took me no time to become familiar and proficient in integrating instructional technology in my pedagogy. Thanks to additional computer workshops offered in my doctoral program, I became very proficient in using instructional technology both in class and online. Although I initially attributed my limited technological skills to the shortcomings of my education in Cameroon, I realized that many of my colleagues born before 1970 in the United States were equally unfamiliar with the instructional technology.

## Struggle for Legitimacy and Acceptance in Academia

In less racially heterogeneous cities in the United States, people still tend to have a stereotypical imagery of the race and gender of a professor, just like many of us would of astronauts and pilots. They have the propensity to assume that professors are generally White males or, at the very least, White females. Any image of a professor other than White is still a culture shock to some. For example, toward the end of my multicultural education class in December 2012, one of my students shared with me and the rest of the class how shocking and unbelievable it was for him to have me as his first Black teacher since he was born. As the students walked into the class and took their seats that first day of class, this particular student said he sat quietly and impatiently waiting to see the instructor of the course. He looked around the room and could not find a White matured adult male to qualify as a professor; however, he found a White woman in her 40s who, judging by her outfit and age, closely resembled his stereotypical image of a professor. So, he concluded that this woman, unbeknown to him yet as his classmate, was his instructor who was just waiting to stand up and take over the class at the top of the hour. Few minutes before the class time, I walked in straight to the computer to set up my PowerPoint for the introduction to the course, and this particular student still did not believe that I was the instructor of the course. Although I had one of my best Western attire on that day, he still thought I was a handyman coming to do some repairs on the computer before the "professor" sitting in their midst takes over. Everyone giggled, including me, as he shared his first-day experience in my class.

170  *Michael Takafor Ndemanu*

It is worth noting that this student grew up in communities with little or no racial diversity, and the television programs he was accustomed to watching did not help either, because they were mired with stereotypical images of people of color doing menial jobs. The dual culture shock this student experienced that day was as a result of the fact that not only did his instructor turn out to be Black, but he also spoke "English with an accent." He blamed his cultural encapsulation to a complete lack of people of diverse racial backgrounds in his elementary and secondary schools. Americans in general have been erroneously socialized into believing that White is superior and Black is inferior. This explains why when it became apparent to him that his professor was Black and foreign born, he became even more doubtful about my professional competence. He did not know that he was out for a moment of reawakening. He left the class that first day in bewilderment because he was beginning to realize that his empire of cultural knowledge was collapsing in the face of direct exposure to reality: his perceptions were becoming misperceptions, and what he had long held as a truism was becoming nothing but stereotypes emanating from sheltered life experiences.

If a student can share this kind of troubling but refreshing experience with the entire class in his professor's presence, one can easily decipher the kind of safe and convivial atmosphere under which the students operate with their professor. Few students would be courageous enough to share their misperceptions, irrespective of the safety and friendliness of the environment in which the class operates. Nevertheless, I have successfully instilled a genial climate in my classes because I believe that it a precursor to a transactional pedagogic approach (Knight-Abowitz, 2000) which is revered by academics who teach controversial issues in college.

On a different occasion, during a class discussion on inequitable school funding in the United States, another student turned on her computer and googled up information about public school funding in Cameroon and began asking me questions about dilapidated school buildings there. Her peers found her approach not only disrespectful but also "delusional," as one termed it in a private e-mail sent to me after the class. Notwithstanding this behavior, however, I engaged the student about school funding in Cameroon. I helped her to understand that although the most underfunded school in the United States may still be better than an average public school in Cameroon, funding is distributed proportionately to the number of students per school and that funding was not based on the property taxes of the neighborhood in which a given school is located. I also made her to understand that in Cameroon, like in many African countries, one can enroll in any public school of one's choice regardless of one's family income and the neighborhood in which one lives. So parents choose schools for their children based on how they are performing in standardized tests and their proximity to the students' homes. Because my classes cover issues of race and class discrimination, our class topics often elicit discomfort in students. As alluded to earlier, my "outsider" status affords me a unique privilege to teach

*Unpacking the Invisible Knapsack* 171

ME courses without much backlash and resistance of students who tend to feel victimized when topics around institutional racism is covered in class.

The struggle for legitimacy for foreign-born scholars is not limited only to academic milieu; it extends to the larger community. During a basketball tournament for elementary schools in my city, my son's classmate, a fifth grader, asked me, "Joe [my son] told us that you are a professor at [University of X]; is that really true?" I could sense the embarrassment of the boy's mother at the question by the way she queried him as to why he asked the question. Although he did not respond to his mother, he still looked overwhelmed by my affirmative response, but I left that afternoon with the assumption that the boy might have thought that Joe's father was in a prestigious and classy profession. Nonetheless, the extent to which my being professor generates curiosity among the locals, gives me room to assume that this child might just have been doubtful of a Black man with a "thick accent" or "beautiful accent" teaching at a famous university in town.

The fact that people are quick to ask what I teach whenever I introduce myself as a professor has led me to the conclusion that it is my credentials and legitimacy that is being questioned. For instance, on introducing myself to one of our church members, she immediately asked what I teach and I responded, "I teach a course on language, literacy, and culture." "African language?" she retorted. I had deliberately avoided adding the ME course among the list of courses I teach because I have come to understand that there is an underlying, U.S. mainstream assumption that faculty of color can only teach ethnic studies and advocacy-related courses. However, the woman still managed to ask a follow-up question that, unbeknown to her, questioned my academic credentials. Similarly, a colleague of mine from India receives all sorts of questions and stares whenever she introduces herself as a professor of English. Foreign-born professors of color often interpret the question related to their professional expertise differently. So, the "*What do you teach*" question for me is almost tantamount to "What *can* you teach?" However, the context and the setting in which such a question is asked also matter. The racial, ethnic, and socioeconomic backgrounds of the questioner also influence my deconstruction of the hidden message veiled in that question. I used to respond to that kind of question by saying, "I teach multicultural education," until I realized that my response was fostering the stereotype that the dominant group had about professors of color. A friend of mine who is Native American told me that in her department, administrative assistants often make foregone conclusions about the course(s) she teaches in official documents: When they are in doubt of her specialty, they just put ME against her name. It boils down to the deficit thinking and subtractive beliefs the dominant and the dominated groups have been made to internalize about people of color. Here is how the reasoning goes: Because people of color are not very smart, they cannot possibility be professors, and if they are professors, they must be teaching an unsophisticated course or an

172  *Michael Takafor Ndemanu*

advocacy course that shuns different forms of "isms" and discriminations against minorities like themselves.

## Foreign-Born Professors as Assets to Academia

I am thrilled that the myth on the stereotypical identity of a "real" professor is waning as students and colleagues become more exposed to professional and scholarly accomplishments of foreign-born professors. A professor should be judged on his or her professional competence and not on his or her racial, ethnic, and linguistic identity. As stated earlier, the racialized identity and ethnicity of an instructor is a factor for students in deciding whether to take the course content seriously (Dixson & Dingus, 2007; Housee, 2008). There is an implicit conflict of interest from White students' perspectives for a member of a historically oppressed group to discuss past and current racial discrimination without appearing biased. On the other hand, Black students can be quick to find fault in the ways in which a White instructor teaches the course because of concerns of bias and superficiality (Cochran-Smith, 2000). It is within this backdrop that foreign-born professors play a pivotal role in helping American college students construct knowledge from a multiplicity of perspectives—a window curriculum (Style, 1996) that is still very lacking in elementary and secondary school settings.

The contributions of foreign-born professors in U.S. higher education in particular are significant. A study by Kim, Wolf-Wendel, and Twombly (2011) shows that foreign-born professors with a foreign bachelor's degree produce an average of 40% more peer-reviewed articles per year as compared to their U.S counterparts and other foreign-born colleagues who earned their bachelor's in the United States. The study collected data on 5,527 faculty members born in the United States, 424 faculty members born outside the United States who obtained their bachelor's degrees in the United States, as well as 987 foreign-born faculty members who completed their bachelor's degrees abroad. The study also reported that U.S.-born faculty members who work in campuses with more foreign-born professors were likely to be more scholarly productive than their colleagues working with less diverse, foreign-born faculty. In any major corporation with many workers, hard work can be as contagious as laziness. The more faculty members know about the impressive productivity of one of their colleagues, the more they would want to emulate their example. Paradoxically, the same study showed that these highly productive foreign-born professors were not satisfied with their jobs. I wonder whether their dissatisfaction with their jobs has to do with a lack of recognition from their institutional leadership. As Rath (2007, p. iv) intimates, "having a manager who ignores you is even more detrimental than having a manager who primarily focuses on your weaknesses."

Foreign-born immigrants (including foreign-born professors) are generally harder working in every economic sector because many of them grew up doing harder tasks with far less remuneration than what they are currently doing in their host countries. They are more likely to have been educated in a system in which grade retention was the order of the day, which means that if a student did not meet the targeted benchmark to be promoted to the next grade, he or she would be retained in the grade. So, those who eventually make it through college tend to be the more academically oriented students. They also derive from cultures that are very family-oriented and tend to have dependent families (both nuclear and extended) in the United States and back "home." Therefore, they are more likely to work hard and pursue economic activities that would help them support their families financially; they tend to see weekends as extensions of the 5-day workweek to get more work done.

According to Collins (2008), foreign-born faculty members are often stricter in their classroom management policies. Some of my students and colleagues have made similar observations about my syllabi which is very prescriptive and include the following:

- Your technological devices such as cell phones, iPods, iPads, games, laptops, etc. should remain turned off during class.
- Under no circumstances will more than two absences be excused since not more than two doctor's notes will be accepted.
- Justification of your absence must be made within six days following the absence after which no consideration will be given to any proof of absence, be it tangible or not.
- Any assignment that may be due on a day you miss a class must still be submitted in/on time.
- I expect you to arrive in class *on time* and to leave class only when it ends.

It is worth noting that the expectations for the courses I teach were very flexible at the beginning of my teaching career in the United States because I expected undergraduate students to take their school work seriously. Unfortunately, it was not the case with some of the students, so I tightened the policy over the years in response to the loopholes the students were trying to exploit to their advantage. Now, I rarely receive any end-of-semester query from students about their absences.

Another point of interest is that foreign-born professors tend to have experienced several forms of "isms," such as nepotism, homophobia, cronyism, ethnocentrism, and sexism, in their home countries from fellow compatriots, and such probably went unpunished. For this reason, they are more likely to shrug off insensitive remarks pertaining to racism and other isms, because their dual frame of reference affords them the opportunity to understand that as much as we must not condone any form of isms, there is no country that is completely immune from them. As a result, foreign-born professors tend to have good working relationship with their students and

174 *Michael Takafor Ndemanu*

colleagues, since their wide scope of understanding helps them to focus on bigger pictures of issues.

Further to the aforementioned, foreign-born faculty from developing countries in particular are more likely to be more productive in the U.S. academe because they tend to take advantage of the availability of physical and virtual libraries, modern technology on campuses, grants for research, and travel expenses, many of which were unavailable in their home countries. Native-born scholars can sometimes take the availability of these opportunities for granted until they visit colleagues in other parts of the world where they see fellow academics doing a lot with very little. Based on my experience, I believe that this may also explain why immigrant children who do very well upon enrollment in the U.S. public schools do not necessarily do well when they return to their native countries—although partly because of limited resources and the large class sizes in those countries.

In sum, the hard work of American-born faculty has laid the foundation for the body of academic knowledge on which foreign-born counterparts stand to make their contributions in their respective fields. However, in the context of this chapter, it must be noted that foreign-born professors can thrive in foreign academies, thanks to their sound comparative global knowledge about opportunities or the lack thereof—and the overrepresentation of foreign-born scholars in the U.S.-based Nobel Prize winners goes a long way to confirm their productivity (cf. Perri, 2007).

## LESSONS LEARNED

For the eight years I have spent in the U.S. higher education system as a graduate student and then as a professor, I have learned that most Americans have had very little exposure to world Englishes. For this reason, foreign-born professors should not assume that because they studied from kindergarten through college in English, people would automatically embrace their British English writing and speaking conventions. If you speak British English, understand that your pronunciation, spelling, and punctuation will be challenged in the classroom, as well as in the scholarly and nonscholarly communities. Do not despair, however; on the contrary, seize the opportunity to educate people about your home country's educational system and your own academic background. You will definitely become proficient in the local English, but make sure you do not lose your British English, because you may need it to publish in many international journals. It is preferable to be bi-dialectal than to be mono-dialectal, since you can always code-switch from one dialect to the other without losing the original dialect. I still remember a colleague who corrected me when I pronounced the word *herbs* with aspirated /h/. She told me that the *h* was silent. Prior to that incident, I had never heard someone utter that word with a silent *h*. I could not argue instantly because there was no third party present for me to feel utterly embarrassed, but I was still convinced

*Unpacking the Invisible Knapsack* 175

that I did not mispronounced the word. I went home later that afternoon and looked it up. I found that British English pronounces the *h* on *herbalist* while American English does not. I discovered that I was correct because I used the British version of the pronunciation and that she was equally correct because she used the American version of the correct. However, what was troubling to me was the hegemonic assumption that the British variety was still wrong and worth disallowing. It is hard to have a robust self-esteem in the environment where your prior knowledge is discounted and dishonored. This deficit perspective about your language should not hamper the full display of your innate and acquired competence. When you prove to colleagues and students that you are masterful at what you do, your presumed weaknesses could very soon be viewed as strengths; your despised accent could become the cherished accent. When you succeed in gaining the love and trust of your community, their deficit thinking about you would dissipate.

Besides the aforementioned, it is important to understand that as you choose to become a professor outside your native country, you are not only representing everyone of your skin color but also your continent, as well as your country and its educational system, be it weak or strong. If you fail to deliver the expected goals, your failure would have a future ripple effect on people of your racial and continental descent. I cannot count how many times I was asked in the graduate school to weigh in on the strength of an educational system of a specific African country of a candidate for admission. Inasmuch as it is important to challenge that kind of mentality, it is also important to be aware of the duality of racial and ethnic identities, which contributes tremendously to how subsequent generations of people of similar skin color are treated at their job sites. Minority faculty members are not supposed to represent their race or their ethnicity; unfortunately, it is the case; therefore, do play that role well. The pressure that comes with tokenistic hiring is immeasurable yet surmountable.

## REFERENCES

Chang, H. (2007). Autoethnography: Raising cultural awareness of self and others. In G. Walford (Ed.), *Methodolgoical developments in ethnography* (Studies in educational ethnography, Vol. 12, pp. 201–221). Boston: Elsevier.

Cochran-Smith, M. (2000). Blind vision: Unlearning racism in teacher education. *Harvard Educational Review, 70*(2), 157–190.

Collins, J. M. (2008). Coming to America: Challenges for Faculty Coming to United States' Universities. *Journal of Geography in Higher Education, 32*(2), 179–188.

Dixson, A. D., & Dingus, J. E. (2007). Tyranny of the majority: Re-enfranchisment of African-American teacher educators teaching for democracy. *International Journal of Qualitative Studies in Education, 20*(6), 639–654.

Freire, P. (1970). *Pedagogy of the oppressed.* New York, NY: The Continuum Publishing Company.

Housee, S. (2008). Should identity matter when teaching about 'race' and racism in classroom. *Race Ethnicity and Education, 4*, 415–428.

## 176 Michael Takafor Ndemanu

Kim, D., Wolf-Wendel, L., & Twombly, S. (2011). International faculty: Experiences of academic life and productivity in US universities. *Journal of Higher Education, 82*(6), 720–747.

Knight-Abowitz, K. (2000). A pragmatist revisioning of resistance theory. *American Educational Research Journal, 37*(4), 877–907.

Merriam, B. S. (2009). *Qualitative research: A guide to design and implementation.* San Francisco, CA: Jossey-Bass.

Ndemanu, M. (2012). Exploring preservice teachers' perspective about human diversity: Experience in multicultural education courses (doctoral dissertation). Retrieved from ProQuest Dissertations and Theses (open access).

Perri, G. (2007). *Immigrants' complementarities and native wages: Evidence from California* (NBER Working Paper No. W12956). Cambridge, MA: National Bureau of Economic Research.

Rath, T. (2007). *Strengths finder.* New York, NY: Gallup Press.

Style, E. (1996). Curriculum as a window and mirror: The SEED Project on inclusive curriculum. Retreived June 26, 2013, from www.wcwonline.org/seed/curriculum.html.

# 15 Not an Easy Road
## Journey of a Jamaican Academic
*Leonie J. Brooks*

### JAMAICAN BEGINNINGS AND TRANSITIONS TO AMERICA

When I think about my formative years as a primary and secondary school student in Jamaica, what stands out most is how structured, culturally diverse, and safe the environment felt and how much I loved my school experience. Expectations from my teachers, principals, parents, and extended family were clear and high: I would work hard and earn good grades. Of course, I would respect my teachers who were devoted to helping me succeed. My critical years spent in both private and public schools in the British-based Jamaican educational system, which included high expectations, respect for all, and knowledgeable-but-strict and devoted instructors formed the basis for my worldview surrounding the educational process.

As a high school student, I attended a U.S. Catholic school (selected by my immigrant parents for its discipline and strong academics), and it was a classic culture shock experience. Watching the freedom my American peers experienced in school was dizzying, frightening, and overwhelming. I tried hard to avoid the relentless teasing and ridicule "You sound funny; why don't you speak real English?" and uninformed, sometimes insulting questions such as "Do you have roads in Jamaica?" and "Do you live in trees?" I quickly realized that my own brand of uniqueness as a Black Jamaican immigrant was a liability, not an asset. The day this was made unquestionably clear to me was when my homeroom teacher, whom I both adored and feared, used a red marker to make a huge red X across my paper, because I continued to spell words like *colour* and *neighbour* with an *ou*, instead of the standard American *o*, and ripped my paper in half in front of the entire classroom. As noted by Hutchison, Quach, and Wiggan (2006), regardless of how well one communicates in English, if there are differences in spelling, meaning of words, expressions, or accents, there is likely to be a devaluing of the immigrant's communication and experience. The humiliation I felt was more than I could bear so I decided to "become American." I quickly learned to speak with an American accent and adopted a "cool" posture, while still preserving my respect for teachers and love of learning.

178   *Leonie J. Brooks*

## INSIDE THE ACADEMY: BALANCING JAMAICAN ROOTS AND AMERICAN STRATEGIES

My journey into academia was a gradual one. After earning my PhD in psychology I worked as a staff psychologist at a college counseling center. I created a course to support struggling, mostly minority students at another institution as an adjunct professor. I became increasingly enamored with being in the classroom and eventually obtained a tenure-track faculty position. Interestingly, I still carried the formal, hierarchical student–teacher relationship schema in my mind when I pictured a classroom setting (cf. Hutchison, Quach and Wiggan, 2006). Consistent with my Jamaican heritage, I challenged my students to express themselves well and evaluated student knowledge and performance in the same way I was assessed in my formative years in Jamaica. I rarely gave multiple-choice exams, preferring instead to use case studies, essay questions, digitally recorded counseling sessions with clients and integrated theoretical, analysis, and practice papers to evaluate their knowledge and counseling competence. I still believe that having students provide in-depth, critically thought-out answers to essay or short-answer questions and case studies is the best way to assess their knowledge and ability to apply what has been learned. I do, however, see the benefit of using multiple-choice questions as part of an overall assessment process.

I assumed that since I had worked as a student development professional in a college setting for years, completed higher education in the United States, and had accumulated a few years of teaching college students in the United States, my transition into becoming a full-time academic would be a breeze. I soon learned, however, to be careful about my assumptions.

## My Challenges: An Overview

As a foreign-born Caribbean- and U.S.-educated scholar, I have experienced a number of interesting challenges as an academic. I have grappled with an internal struggle that manifests as an "impostor syndrome," and I have felt guilty for having an opportunity others did not have to complete higher education and work as a professional in the social sciences here in the United States. Other adversities have been interpersonal and are reflected in interactions with students and colleagues who may contest my professional legitimacy through questions about my credentials or qualifications. There are also systemic challenges related to migration status, institutional support, tokenism, and overutilization as "the representative of diversity."

### Internal Struggles: Impostor and Guilt Syndromes

Feeling like an impostor when one is a foreign-born faculty member is not an unusual experience. Although faculty members in higher education have become increasingly diverse, the majority of professors in the academy remain White and male (Jayakumar, Howard, Allen & Han, 2009). There are occasional moments when in a committee or faculty department meeting, while presenting at a conference, or standing in front of the classroom, when I wonder, "Do I really belong here, when I am so different from the norm?" Because one often is so different from what is expected as a professor, the burden of having to prove oneself and one's worth can be exhausting, insidiously internalized and can become self-doubt.

Vargas (2002) writes about her struggle with sharing her academic achievements and introducing herself to her students: "Doing this is not easy, because as a Mexican, lower-middle-class girl, I was not only taught, but disciplined, to be humble. Underneath, sometimes I feel like an impostor. . . . Like other stigmatized individuals, I have even occasionally questioned my legitimacy" (p. 44). Vargas found this theme of doubting one's own self-worth, typically an expression of internalized oppression, a common experience shared by many other foreign-born academics in her own research. In the same vein, Manrique (2002) also revealed that she experienced "nagging doubts about who I was, where I was from and why I was here? Was it just me? Was I just imagining things . . . ?" (p. 150). These doubts have surfaced frequently in my conversations with foreign-born junior and senior faculty colleagues at a variety of institutions. I have seen this phenomenon occur across gender, disciplines, academic rank, countries of origin, and even length of time in the United States. These doubts can be accompanied by the sense that you have to go above and beyond normal expectations and performance to prove that you measure up and have earned your right to be legitimately included as part of the professoriate (cf. Manrique & Manrique, 1999; Stanley, 2006).

### Interpersonal Struggles: Communication, Cultural Expectations, and Social Interactions

Although the "impostor syndrome" highlights mostly internal struggles, challenges regarding one's qualifications and credibility from American students because one is from a foreign country can be just as disheartening (Luthura, 2002; Thomas, 1999). There is evidence that people who speak with an accent are more likely to be challenged (Braine, 1999), receive poorer student evaluations (Rubin & Smith, 1990), and are viewed as less knowledgeable or qualified by American-born students (Rong, 2002, Vargas, 2002). Although there has been an emphasis on English proficiency, communication styles, and language barriers and their impact on teaching effectiveness (Fortuijn, 2002; Hutchison, Butler, & Fuller, 2005), other scholars contend that students' overall attitudes towards foreign-born professors (rather than the instructor's English skills per se) should be examined when investigating the quality of success in classroom interactions and teacher effectiveness (Collins, 2008; Rubin, 1992). Other research has shown that American students have rated their foreign-born teachers positively and value learning from an instructor who exposed them to a different international (non-U.S.) perspective (Alberts, 2008). From my own experience

180  *Leonie J. Brooks*

and that of my Caribbean-born peers, the vast majority of students appreciate hearing about our diverse cultural perspectives when it is placed in the proper context during class discussions. Presenting our personal stories and explaining the worldviews and cultural contexts from which we operate as one of many ways in which to view and experience the world can be an eye-opening and enriching experience for students (Kubota, 2002). This often leads to self-examination of students' own cultural identities and experiences and increases their ability to see things from multiple points of view. Student reactions to having a faculty member with a distinct accent vary from being negative and rejecting to curious and appreciative. I often point out that everyone has an "accent" that reflects the region they were raised in, something that students find illuminating and amusing.

Cultural differences in expectations of classroom interactions between faculty and students due to socialization can sometimes result in difficult encounters (Collins, 2008). In countries outside of the United States, teachers may be treated with a greater amount of respect and deference than in the United States (Manrique & Manrique, 1999; Thomas & Johnson, 2004). Han (2012) suggests that in Confucian-heritage collectivistic societies, such as China, Korea, and Japan, where education is prized and viewed as an important means of honoring one's family lineage, teachers and professors are held in high regard. To this list of countries—mostly group-oriented Asian civilizations (including India and Southeast Asia)—many other collectivistic societies are represented, including the Middle East; the African continent; Central, South, and Latin America; and the Caribbean. All these cultures practice obedience to authority, group harmony, and loyalty to teachers, and deference inside and outside of the classroom is expected. This contrasts with individualistic societies such as the United States, where free speech, rugged individualism, individual drive, and merit are valued. American students are socialized to think independently, "initiate communication and interrupt the professor, challenge and criticize authority figures and seek equal status with their professors through casual relationships including calling their professors by their first name" (Han, 2012, p. 27).

Many foreign-born professors often perceive their American students as lacking discipline, being much more verbally interactive, challenging of teachers' authority, and being less respectful and more argumentative (than students in their homelands; Skachkova, 2007; Thomas & Johnson, 2004). Besides, they felt challenged by American students' lack of knowledge and apathy about events occurring outside of the United States, the perception of students feeling entitled to receive a good grade, and the aggressiveness and persistence with which students attempt to have their grades adjusted and expect extra credit assignments (Alberts, 2008). Despite my own educational training in the United States, I still sometimes struggle with the divergent expectations of classroom conduct and interpersonal relations between myself and my students. I recall an incident early in my teaching career when a White female student consistently addressed me as "Ms. Brooks" while addressing my White male colleague who taught her in another class as "Dr. X." I pointed this out to her and encouraged her to examine why she made this distinction and what underlying assumptions she might have held. Christine Stanley, another Jamaican-born professor, describes a similar encounter and suggests that developing successful faculty–student relationships when one is a Black immigrant faculty member "takes a lot of mental and physical energy" (Stanley, 2006, p. 336). My friendly, laid-back, nurturing personality is reflected in my interactions with students, and I feel genuinely liked by and successfully engaged with most of them. Yet, I am still formal, maintain clear boundaries, and insist now on being addressed as Dr. or Professor (and not by my first name). Like many of my international colleagues, I am viewed as a tough-but-fair professor. I have made adjustments to become more flexible, offer extra-credit opportunities, and have reduced the quantity of required work while maintaining lofty benchmarks for excellence. This adaptation is consistent with what is found in the literature on international teachers' experiences (Hutchison, 2005) and is advised as a part of being a "reflective practitioner" (Schon, 1983). I acknowledge the cultural differences in educational experiences we bring to class and make my expectations for classroom decorum explicit in my syllabi. We have discussions about our shared expectations of respect, civility, and quality of participation and about how this contributes to a safe and mutually beneficial learning environment. Sharing about my cultural background on the first day and inviting students to do the same has been beneficial in fostering rapport.

Research on institutional climate and social interactions with colleagues reveal that some immigrant faculty and American-born faculty of color describe feeling alienated and marginalized in the "chilly" social atmosphere in their departments (Turner & Myers, 2000; Skachkova, 2007). Interactions with White American-born colleagues who have limited experiences with cultural and international diversity can result in exchanges with foreign-born faculty fraught with stumbling blocks. Foreign-born faculty have described these encounters as ranging from welcoming, courteous, polite, and tinged with curiosity, to awkward, hostile, tiresome, and alienating experiences. My own interactions with colleagues have also run the gamut, although the majority has been positive. I have had interesting experiences learning about both positive and negative perceptions of immigrants during these exchanges. I have had some rare occasions when the not-so-subtle demand to prove myself through the questioning of my credentials have occurred. Being a member of a cultural group that is outside of the norm can create additional pressure to be collegial and make others comfortable with you.

Intraracial interactions between foreign- and native-born faculty of color can also be complex. I have benefitted tremendously from the warmth, collegiality, support, and research collaborations with my African American faculty counterparts. Some native-born minority faculty might perceive

182　*Leonie J. Brooks*

their foreign-born counterparts as being given preferential treatment and may resent them for taking jobs away from deserving U.S.-born minority faculty; however, the suspicion and biases can be prevalent on both sides (Ngwainmbi, 2006). Stanley (2006) describes dealing with the presumption from African Americans that she "could not understand the various systems of oppression in the United States" because she was a "cultural outsider—an immigrant minority" (pp. 330–331). Skachkova (2007) notes that immigrant women faculty of color can feel alienated from U.S.-born faculty of color and that both can perceive themselves as being in competition (even when they are not). This is part of the terrain that one has to learn to understand and navigate to become successful in U.S. academia.

### Systemic and Institutional Barriers

The "publish or perish" climate that exists at most colleges and universities and the prevailing sentiment that individual work and solo-authored scholarship are superior to collaborative work can lead to isolation and alienation (Stanley, 2006). Jayakumar and colleagues (2009) note that faculty of color are more likely to engage in scholarship related to issues of social justice, race, and gender inequality, in contrast with their White counterparts, who tend to generate research on topics typically sought by top-tier, mainstream journals that reach a broader audience. Stanley (2006) and Skachkova (2007) state that many foreign-born faculty, female faculty, and faculty of color often pursue research on such topics as institutional climate, diversity and student outcomes, affirmative action, culture, nationality, and ethnicity. Although such topics benefit higher education systems, they are not always rewarded in the tenure and promotion process. Such lines of research are often dismissed as lacking legitimacy (Turner & Myers, 2000), perceived as fringe, "minor or self-serving . . . topics that do not constitute academic scholarship . . . inappropriate and narrow in scope" (Reyes & Halcon, 1988, p. 307).

Many faculty of color experience the pull between conducting research that naturally fit their personal interests, and fulfilling standards required for tenure that do not necessarily reflect their primary interests. I have experienced this challenge personally as a scholar, struggling with feelings of isolation, and occasionally adjusting my research focus away from my primary interests to collaborate on projects with colleagues that resulted in publications in more mainstream journals. Additional barriers associated with scholarship include a lack of mentoring and familiarity with the publication process, exclusion from networks of well-published academic peers, fewer opportunities for research collaboration, and cultural differences in writing style (Skachkova, 2007). Torres (2002) highlighted writing style differences, explaining "the 'American way' of writing grant proposals requires a language that is 'direct, very concise and formal' . . . this American way contrasts with the kind of rhetorical type of discourse that is very common in Latin America" (p. 80).

Diversity initiatives and policies enacted by academic institutions can result in the strategic recruitment of foreign-born faculty but can have paradoxical effects. Foreign-born faculty who have been recruited and hired to fulfill intentional diversity goals can be viewed with suspicion and perceived as less qualified, undeserving, and hired only to fill an affirmative action quota. This can be particularly challenging if one is the only foreign-born faculty or person of color in the department, a circumstance that can lead to perceptions of tokenism (Stanley, 2006; Turner & Reyes, 2000). Tokenism can be connected to implicit or explicit expectations that the foreign-born faculty member is to represent his or her cultural background and be the "spokesperson" for all issues related to diversity and multiculturalism, particularly on faculty search and university-wide committees and diversity initiatives—a potentially risky burden (Manrique & Manrique, 1999). This creates the sense that you have been hired or selected for committee membership for your mere presence rather than for your ability to make substantial contributions. Faculty can be overutilized as representatives of diversity in service-oriented activities that detract from other primary responsibilities. This becomes a disadvantage because it does not count in tenure and promotion processes. I have had the distasteful experience of being informed by disgruntled colleagues at different institutions that the only reason I was hired was because of my race or nationality. Although painful, these encounters did not dissuade me from remaining at the institution but, rather, made me more determined to succeed.

One might assume that obtaining tenure would improve the likelihood of retaining racial minority faculty and mitigate the negative effects of a chilly university climate. While having tenure has been shown to increase the probability of retaining faculty of color in general (including foreign-born faculty of color), they tend to remain at an institution because they are more likely to have developed strategies for coping with, and feel less vulnerable to, a hostile work climate and not due to the fact that the impact of the negative climate has disappeared (Jayakumar et. al., 2009).

## Faculty Resilience, Coping Strategies, and Contributions: Critical Lessons Learned

Foreign-born professors are very resourceful, resilient, and employ a variety of coping strategies to facilitate their accomplishments. These include seeking mentors within and outside of their home institutions, developing bicultural competence, and creating support networks consisting of other foreign-born peers and faculty of color with vital shared resources (i.e., information about how to successfully traverse the promotion and tenure process). In addition, they initiate mutually beneficial scholarly collaborations, learn to compartmentalize and not internalize negative discriminatory or oppressive experiences, and establish connections with communities and organizations that reflect their national origin. Many work twice as hard

## 184   Leonie J. Brooks

to disprove negative preconceptions, proactively challenge discrimination and institutional barriers, and use their national origin and experiences as strengths in the classroom (Alberts, 2008; Ford, 2011; Gregory, 2006; Vargas, 2002).

For new foreign-born faculty, I highly recommend seeking out mentors and support networks early on in your career (both within and outside of your institution) who can help you to learn and navigate the unique culture of your institution. These peers can also assist you with the important task of gauging your perceptions of campus climate, student and peer interactions, and institutional politics. It is important to adopt and maintain a long-term view when faced with challenges and to choose your battles carefully. Although it is not always easy, it is absolutely essential to remain true to who you are and your core values. I have stood by my principles even when it was unpopular because I need to look myself in the mirror without hesitation. It is also wise to keep detailed documentation, including e-mails and notes, of problematic encounters that you have, and to seek guidance from your peer-support system and mentors to assist you when responding to difficult situations. Learning to say "no" gracefully and without burning bridges is essential. Maintaining a sense of humor; incorporating things one finds enjoyable in teaching, scholarship, and service; and taking strategic breaks to replenish and restore oneself have also been a key part of my survival in academia.

Despite the myriad of challenges faced by foreign-born faculty, they make significant contributions to the academy and are tremendous assets to their institutions. Students who are taught by international faculty garner important benefits, including transnational competence (Hawkins & Cummings, 2000), development of sophisticated intellectual processes (i.e., multiplistic or relativistic thinking; Lee & Janda, 2006), and global literacy (Biddle, 2002). These benefits enable students to be more competitive in an increasingly diverse and global job market. Skachkova (2007) suggests that foreign-born faculty should consider ways in which we can effectively use our foreignness. She recommends sharing our specific experiences as foreigners with our students to provide them with perspectives of additional ways of seeing the world, thereby increasing appreciation of diversity and international perspectives and fostering inclusion of difference. Collins (2008) notes that some students view learning from faculty members who speak accented English as beneficial because it obliged them to listen more carefully and to pay attention in class. Students also benefitted from having their stereotypes about other people and places challenged, thus expanding their cultural lens and reducing their levels of ethnocentrism. My presence and shared experiences as a Black immigrant in the classroom has shattered my students' perceptions of the homogeneity of the Black experience in the United States, as well as stereotypes about immigrants and illegal immigration. As immigrant faculty members who have navigated the culture shock and acculturation process, we are able to empathize with and serve as resources for a variety of students who are struggling themselves with

*Not an Easy Road* 185

adjustment challenges on campus (i.e., international, nontraditional, racial/ethnic minority, and first-generation students). Immigrant faculty also serve as important resources for campuses that are pursuing cultural diversity and global awareness goals (Manrique & Manrique, 1999). Skachkova (2007) contends that immigrant women scholars are more active in their communities, engaging in community service that integrate global and local concerns. They also develop "international networks of knowledge and experience that contributed to the internationalization of American academia" (p. 729).

## Recommendations: Strategies for Success

A welcoming departmental and campus climate can ease the transition for foreign-born scholars, and assist institutions with "walking the walk" of diversity and inclusion that promotes success and satisfaction for all stakeholders. Direct institutional support from international offices for faculty managing visa and immigration concerns is critical (Collins, 2008). A sincere, proactive institutional commitment to diversity, equity, and inclusion that prizes internationalization on the campus is essential. This should include support for recruitment, retention and promotion of diverse faculty (Ford, 2011) and adequate education of faculty search committees (Ponjuan, 2011). Additionally, regular assessment of campus climate to identify factors that enhance or inhibit faculty collegiality, satisfaction, and productivity is important. Diversity training for administrators and faculty at all levels with accompanying incentives for participation and avenues for accountability (Stanley, 2006), and the establishment of a diversity committee or council in each department on campus to promote regular intergroup diversity dialogue, improve diversity and address conflicts (Lee & Janda, 2006) are highly recommended. The establishment of mentoring programs for junior and mid-career foreign-born faculty to provide direct professional guidance and to share resources and helpful information about the promotion and tenure process can also be useful (Han, 2012). Mentors can assist with identifying systemic knowledge gaps and provide direct feedback to faculty regarding how to adjust their expectations that might not fit within the American context (Hutchinson, 2005). The tenure and promotion reward structure should be reexamined, including the value placed on mainstream publications and traditional forms of research, as well as the devaluing of service activities (mentoring and advising of international students, engagement in community service) in which foreign-born faculty are often engaged (Jayakumar et al., 2009). There should also an increased support for research and publication (Turner & Myers, 2000).

At the department level, direct, ongoing conversations between foreign-born faculty and department chairpersons should occur about how the transition process is going, inquiring about any assistance that might be needed, and providing contact information for new faculty about on campus, and professional resources, including formal orientation programs designed to

186  *Leonie J. Brooks*

facilitate the adjustment of new foreign-born professors (Thomas & Johnson, 2004). Sensitivity to the fact that new and junior faculty might be reluctant to express their concerns with chairpersons and colleagues who are also in an evaluative position is important and highlights the necessity for a safe climate for honest dialogue, as well as other avenues outside of the department where faculty can gain instrumental and emotional support (Collins, 2008). Hosting a reception when new faculty join the department and facilitating networking with colleagues within and outside of the discipline (including other foreign-born scholars) can reduce feelings of isolation and facilitate effective rapport-building within a department (Collins, 2008; Turner & Myers, 2000).

In summary, foreign-born professors should take proactive steps to learn about their departmental and institutional culture, including working to gain knowledge of the practices, norms, and written and unwritten rules associated with the promotion and tenure process (Stanley, 2006). We bring a substantial amount of skills to the table and need to value our unique identities and experiences that add to the rich cultural mosaic of the academy and the broader society.

## REFERENCES

Alberts, H. C. (2008). The challenges and opportunities of foreign-born instructors in the classroom. *Journal of Geography in Higher Education, 32*(2), 189–203.

Biddle, S. (2002). *Internationalization: Rhetoric or reality?* New York: American Council of Learned Societies.

Braine, G. (1999). *Non-native educators in English-language teaching.* Mawah, NJ: Lawrence Erlbaum Associates.

Collins, J. M. (2008). Coming to America: Challenges for faculty coming to United States' universities. *Journal of Geography in Higher Education, 32*(2), 179–188.

Ford, K. A. (2011). Race, gender and bodily (mis)recognitions: Women of color faculty experiences with white students in the college classroom. *The Journal of Higher Education, 82*(4), 444–478.

Fortuijn, J. D. (2002). Internationalizing learning and teaching: A European experience. *Journal of Geography, 26*(3), 263–273.

Gregory, S. T. (2006). The cultural constructs of race gender and class: A study of how Afro-Caribbean women academics negotiate their careers. *International Journal of Qualitative Studies in Education, 19*(3), 347–366.

Han, K. T. (2012). Experiences of faculty of color teaching in a predominantly white university: Fostering interracial relationships among faculty of color and white preservice teachers. *International Journal of Progressive Education, 2*, 25–48.

Hawkins, J. N., & Cummings, W. K. (Eds.). (2000). *Transnational competence: Rethinking the US-Japan educational relationship.* Albany: State University of New York Press.

Hutchison, C. B. (2005). *Teaching in America. A cross-cultural guide for international Teachers and their employers.* The Netherlands: Springer.

Hutchison, C. B., Butler, M. B., & Fuller, S. M. (2005). Pedagogical communication issues arising during international migrations to teach science in America. *Electronic Journal of Science Education, 9*(3). Retrieved from http://wolfweb.unr.edu/homepage/crowther/ejse/ejsev9n3.html

Hutchison, C. B., Quach, L., & Wiggan, (2006, Fall). The interface of global migrations, ESL teaching and learning, and academic cosmopolitan identity development. *Forum on Public Policy Online*. 2006 Edition. Retrieved from http://www.forumonpublicpolicy.com/archive06/hutchison.pdf

Jayakumar, U. M., Howard, T. C., Walter, W. R., & Han, J. C. (2009). Racial privilege in the Professoriate: An exploration of campus climate, retention, and satisfaction. *The Journal Higher Education, 80*(5), 539–563.

Kubota, R. (2002). Marginality as an asset. In L. Vargas (Ed.), *Women faculty of color in the white classroom*. New York: Peter Lang.

Lee, G.-L., & Janda, L. (2006). Successful multicultural campus: Free from prejudice toward minority professors. *Multicultural Education, 14*, 27–30.

Luthura, R. (2002). Negotiating a minefield: Practicing transformative pedagogy as a teacher of color in a classroom climate of suspicion. In L. Vargas (Ed.), *Women faculty of color in the white classroom* (pp. 109–124). New York: Peter Lang.

Manrique, C. G. (2002). A foreign woman faculty's multiple whammies. In L. Vargas (Ed.), *Women faculty of color in the white classroom* (pp. 145–162). New York: Peter Lang.

Manrique, C. G., & Manrique, G. G. (Eds.). (1999). *The multicultural or immigrant faculty in American society*. New York: Edwin Mellen Press.

Ngwainmbi, E. K. (2006). The struggles of Foreign-born faculty. *Diverse Issues in Higher Education, 23*(10), 28.

Ponjuan, L. (2011, Fall). Recruiting and retaining Latino faculty members: The missing piece to Latino student success. *Thought & Action: The NEA Higher Education Journal, 27*, 99–110.

Reyes, M., & Halcon, J. (1988). Racism in academia: The old wolf revisited. *Harvard Educational Review, 58*(3), 299–314.

Rong, X. L. (2002). Teaching with differences and for differences: Reflections of a Chinese American educator. In L. Vargas (Ed.), *Women faculty of color in the white classroom* (pp. 125–144). New York: Peter Lang.

Rubin, D. (1992). Nonlanguage factors affecting undergraduates' judgments of non-native English speaking teaching assistants. *Research in Higher Education, 33*(4), 511–531.

Rubin, D., & Smith, K. (1990). Effect of accent, ethnicity and lecture topic on undergraduates' Perceptions of nonnative English-speaking teaching assistants. *International Journal of Intercultural Relations, 14*, 337–353.

Schon, D. A. (1983). *The reflective practitioner: How professionals think in action*. New York: Basic Books.

Skachkova, P. (2007). Academic careers of immigrant women professors in the U.S. *Higher Education, 53*, 697–738.

Stanley, C. (2006). Coloring the academic landscape: Faculty of color breaking the silence at predominantly white colleges and universities. *American Educational Research Journal, 43*(4), 701–736.

Thomas, J. (1999). Voices from the periphery: Non-native teachers and issues of credibility. In G. Braine (Ed.), *Non-native Educators in English Language Teaching* (pp. 5–13). Mahwah, NJ: Lawrence Erlbaum Associates.

Thomas, J. M., & Johnson, B. J. (2004). Perspectives of international faculty members: Their experiences and stories. *Education and Society, 22*(3), 47–62.

Torres, M. (2002). Reflecting on the games in academia: A view from "the porch". In L. Jacobs, J. Cintron, & C. Canon (Eds.), *The politics of survival in academia: Narratives of inequality, resilience, and success* (pp. 77–94). Lanham: Rowman & Littlefield Publishers.

Turner, C. S. V., & Myers, S. L. (2000). *Faculty of color in academe: Bittersweet success*. Needham Heights, MA: Allyn and Bacon.

Vargas, L. (Ed.). (2002). *Women faculty of color in the white classroom*. New York: Peter Lang.

# 16 "Almost American"

## The Challenges of a Canadian Professor Working in the United States

*Scott Kissau*

When attempting to share the challenges faced by a foreign-born professors living and working in the United States, there is, of course, the risk of appearing ungrateful and coming across as a disgruntled employee who is dissatisfied with his work. Neither description would be accurate in my case. Truth be told, I could not be happier in my current position as associate professor and acting department chair at a large American university. I have also been fortunate to have enjoyed considerable success.

The professional success that I have experienced in the United States may, in part, be due to my privileged position among foreign-born professors: In addition to being a young White man who speaks fluent English, I was very familiar with both the United States and American culture. Growing up in the shadows of the Detroit skyline in a mid-sized Canadian city, cross-border shopping, American television shows, and vacations in Florida were part of my childhood. In many ways I was almost American and was definitely not the kind of person one might expect to encounter the hardships commonly associated with international faculty members working in foreign lands. My American students had no difficulty understanding my Canadian accent. I was well accustomed to the assessment system and student-centered teaching approaches used in American schools. I was able to develop a good rapport with the graduate students in my classes and encountered none of the classroom management challenges commonly faced by foreign instructors. To many onlookers, my transition to life and work as a postsecondary instructor in the United States must have appeared seamless.

Unfortunately, appearances can be deceiving. I have encountered numerous, unexpected difficulties. Although these obstacles did not derail my career trajectory, they were at the very least annoying, occasionally harmful, and often could have been avoided. Offering a unique perspective on the plight of the foreign-born professor, the goals of this chapter are to draw attention to the hidden challenges faced by international faculty and to offer suggestions for how these challenges can be prevented or overcome.

## MY STORY

In May 2006 I decided to sell my house, quit my job, and leave my home, my country, my family, and my friends to pursue a career at a university in the United States. Not only did my new job offer a more hospitable climate, but it was also much more accessible and closer to my home in Ontario than any of the remote Canadian universities that had also offered me a position. Although I loved my job, in my early years of working in the United States, I experienced a number of personal, immigration, and career advancement challenges that are described in this chapter.

### Personal Challenges

Coming from Canada, I had the unique opportunity among foreign-born professors in the United States to enter the country using my own vehicle. While this facilitated the transportation of many of my immediate necessities and valued possessions, I quickly learned that bringing a Canadian automobile into the United States can be a complicated, expensive, and time-consuming proposition. To obtain a state license plate and vehicle registration card I had to first "import" my car into the United States. This required that I provide the original bill of sale, proof that my car met state emissions and safety standards, the current estimated value of the car, and evidence of where the car was made. After making multiple long-distance phone calls to the dealership where it was purchased and spending several hours searching for the required paperwork, I then had to locate the nearest U.S. Customs Office, make an appointment, and submit the documentation. Fortunately, although I purchased the car in Canada, it was actually assembled in the United States, which spared me the expense of paying duty on its value.

Driving a foreign-purchased car while residing in the United States has continued to cost me time and money over the years. As a somewhat comical example, it took me a couple of years and multiple trips to the mechanic to realize that my routine maintenance appointments were being scheduled according to the number of miles on my odometer. My odometer was, however, in kilometers. As a result, instead of scheduling maintenance checks for every 5,000 miles, my appointments were scheduled for every 5,000 kilometers, which translates to 60% more of my time and money being spent on automobile maintenance than was necessary. The issue of having an odometer and speedometer in kilometers also came back to haunt me more recently when I attempted to trade in my car while purchasing a new one. After being offered $3,000 for my Canadian vehicle, the dealership planned to charge me an additional $1,100 to convert the speedometer and odometer from kilometers to miles.

Another costly mishap that some may find humorous involved a trip to the hospital. One night during my first year in the United States I woke up very ill with the flu. Following routine procedures established while living in Canada, I got up and went to the local emergency room (ER) to receive treatment. Although not seriously ill, I decided to be cautious and requested tests that involved lab work. While relieved when all tests came back clear, several weeks later I once again felt ill when I received multiple bills in the mail that were not covered by my health care provider and that totaled more than $1,000. Had I known that a trip to the ER is not free in the United States, like it is in Canada, I would have waited until the morning to go to my family doctor.

There were yet other financial ramifications associated with being a foreign-born worker in the United States. A couple of months before moving to my new city I came for a visit to look for a new home. After finding the ideal house, close to campus, and within my budget I made an offer that was accepted. Only a few weeks before I was set to move, however, the deal fell through because my lack of American Social Security Number (SSN) prevented me from qualifying for a mortgage. Not only did this mean that my house-hunting trip was a waste of time and money; it also meant that I had to frantically find new accommodations from 800 miles away.

My financial woes did not end there. Once I had obtained an SSN and was able to purchase a home, a lack of credit history caused me to receive a less than favorable mortgage rate. As I attempted to furnish my new home, my poor credit rating in the United States added further financial strain. Take for instance my experience at a large home improvement store where I purchased my new appliances, along with several other home necessities. At the time of this purchase the store was offering a 15% discount for customers who applied for a store credit card and used the card to pay for their purchases. Considering that the total value of the merchandise I was intending to buy was more than $4,000, a 15% savings amounted to greater than $600. Needless to say, I was disappointed, angry, and embarrassed when my credit card application was denied because of a lack of credit history in this country. In the following months, my lack of credit history continued to be a financial burden. Each time I set up a new account, whether it was for water, gas, or cable service, I had to pay an additional security deposit, ranging from $50 to $150, because of my lack of history paying bills on time in the United States.

## Immigration Status Challenges

Although some of my personal struggles may seem trivial, the immigration challenges I experienced were not. Issues related to my legal right to reside in the United States actually began before I even entered the country to work. Months before my employment began I received an H1-B visa in the mail from my host institution. In the accompanying letter I was informed that this document provided me legal permission to enter the country to begin my employment. What was not made clear, however, was that I would not be allowed entry into the United States more than 10 days prior to my start date of August 15, 2006. This stipulation was, unfortunately, drawn to my attention as I attempted to cross the border on August 1 with a moving truck containing all of my worldly possessions. Unable to get through U.S. customs I had to turn around, scramble to find somewhere to store all of my belongings, unload the truck, find somewhere to stay, and then load the truck again 5 days later when I had the right to enter the country on August 6.

After my successful initial entry into the United States, the next couple of years were uneventful regarding my immigration status. This time was equally quiet with respect to any communication I had with the International Student/Scholar Office (ISSO) that oversees the employment of international faculty at my host institution. The only time I heard from anyone in the ISSO during my first three years of employment was when it was time to renew my visa, and I was asked to pay the $325 renewal fee. The successful renewal of my visa was followed by another 2-year period of silence from the ISSO. During this time I mistakenly assumed that my immigration status was being monitored by university officials. By the time December 2011 arrived I began to wonder about the next step in my immigration process. I could see on my visa that it expired in 8 months, so I decided to be proactive and contact the ISSO to verify if anything needed to be done on my part to advance my employment status from H1-B to permanent resident. The response that I received from the ISSO initiated what became, without a doubt, the most difficult period of my time working in the United States.

In a meeting with the director, I learned that I had missed the deadline to submit an Application for Certification from the Department of Labor and was now required to submit an Immigrant Petition for Alien Worker under the category of Outstanding Professor or Researcher. Only after this petition was approved, could I then apply for permanent residency. In other words, because I failed to submit paperwork on time, to maintain my right to work in this country I would have to provide proof to the U.S. Citizenship and Immigration Services (USCIS) that I was an internationally recognized, outstanding researcher or professor in my field. As I quickly ran through a list of my professional accomplishments with the Director to determine what criteria I could successfully meet, I could feel my anxiety rising. I was dumbfounded when the director mentioned the Nobel Prize as an example of a major prize or award for outstanding achievement. My blood pressure surely continued to escalate when she asked if anyone had written a book or article about me. I was a young man in the beginning stages of my career. Just a few short years earlier I was teaching fourth grade in Canada, and now I was expected by USCIS to have books written about me and to be the recipient of prestigious and international awards. Suddenly, my college of education awards for excellence in teaching and research, my exemplary course evaluations, and numerous publications in academic journals seemed insignificant. To make matters worse, I was informed by the director that

192   *Scott Kissau*

I was already late in getting this process started. My visa was to expire in less than 8 months, and the review process for my petition and application for permanent residency can take up to a year to complete. In essence, to maintain my employment and residence in the United States I was being asked to meet standards that far exceeded those necessary to be promoted to associate professor with tenure, and I was being given weeks to prepare the documentation. If I did not meet these expectations, I would lose my job and be forced to leave the country.

Needless to say, the following several weeks, which spanned the Christmas holidays, were spent frantically collecting necessary documentation. To demonstrate that I authored articles with an international circulation, I compiled a list of hundreds of libraries around the world that had journals containing my work. To prove that I was internationally recognized as an expert in my field beyond the United States, I contacted top researchers in countries such as Belgium, Australia, Germany, and Poland and asked that they provide me with a letter attesting to my international recognition. I then included these letters as part of my petition. To further speak to the high caliber, rigor, and international recognition of my work, I had to provide not only copies of my publications, but also evidence of the international nature and prestige of the journals that published my work. This task required hours of searching for information relating to journal acceptance rates, impact factors, circulation, and international composition of the journals' editorial boards. I also had to provide evidence to USCIS that my area of research was of value in the United States. This involved combing research articles, searching for comments that acknowledged the importance of my field of work for the U.S. economy, education system, and national security. To provide evidence of my participation as a judge evaluating the work of others in my field, I tracked down e-mail messages from editors confirming receipt of manuscript reviews I completed for their journals, as well as the feedback I provided the authors of these manuscripts. I provided letters attesting to my participation in hiring committees, doctoral dissertation committees, and grant application committees, and reports documenting my involvement reviewing teacher preparation programs for professional associations at both the state and national levels. The final document that I produced in a period of about 2 months was more than 400 pages in length, significantly longer and more impressive than my tenure dossier. While all of this was going on, I was also required by USCIS to complete a number of time-consuming tasks, such as getting three rounds of inoculations, having my fingerprints taken, completing multiple forms, and providing a long form copy of my birth certificate and copies of all pages in both my current and expired passports.

Once all of the documentation was submitted to USCIS the review process began, which as I mentioned earlier, could take up to a year to complete. During this time I was advised not to travel outside of the United States. It was explained to me that if I wanted to live permanently in the

United States, USCIS may question why I am voluntarily leaving the country. This unexpected challenge was complicated by the fact that I had a terminally ill sister in Canada whom I wanted to visit. This temporary ban on international travel was further complicated by my area of expertise. Researching topics in my discipline frequently involves international travel.

A few months later, I received an employment authorization document, often referred to as an EAD card. This card allowed me to continue working legally in the United States while my application for permanent residency was under review. Obtaining this EAD card was critical given that the review of my application took several months longer than the anticipated wait time, as advertised on the USCIS website, and my H1-B visa had expired. Finally, more than 9 months after submitting my application, I received an e-mail message from the ISSO informing me that my application for permanent residency had been approved and that I would shortly be receiving my "green card" in the mail.

## Career Advancement Challenges

To get a clear picture of the career advancement challenges that may be faced by foreign-born professors working in the United States, it is first necessary to have a general understanding of the common roles and responsibilities of university professors. There are three broad responsibilities of post-secondary faculty holding tenure-track positions. These responsibilities relate to research, teaching, and service. The expectations with regard to each of these professorial responsibilities are typically found in a document published by the university describing the guidelines and procedures for research, promotion, and tenure (RPT).

*Visa restrictions and international travel.* Having a better understanding of professorial responsibilities helps to see how a ban on international travel, even a temporary one, has the potential to have negative consequences on the career advancement of foreign-born professors. At my research-intensive university, an emphasis is placed on faculty research. This emphasis is reflected in the university's RPT document. According to this document, faculty members who wish to be promoted to associate professor are expected to present a record of disseminating research and knowledge at multiple levels including international conferences. This expectation would seem particularly critical for a professor like me whose research focuses on foreign language instruction and international education. Given that tenure-track faculty only have 5 years to demonstrate that they have met this expectation, a 6-month to 1-year ban on international travel has the potential to seriously impede one's ability to meet this standard.

Service to the profession is another important expectation of tenure-track faculty. As faculty members progress through the ranks, there is the increasing expectation that their outreach and involvement be felt beyond the local level. The RPT document at my host university states that faculty seeking promotion to Associate Professor must be involved in professional organizations and associations in one's field at the international level. An inability to travel abroad for a time could potentially make it more challenging for foreign-born faculty to meet this expectation. This challenge becomes more daunting and high stakes for foreign-born professors who are required to demonstrate to USCIS that they are internationally recognized researchers. Traveling abroad to present research to an international audience of colleagues is one way of developing and demonstrating international recognition of one's work. In fact, the immigration lawyer for my host university felt that my multiple conference presentations in different countries around the world significantly strengthened my petition. Given the important role international travel could play in a foreign-born faculty member's ability to meet tenure requirements and federal government requirements to be issued permanent residency, it is ironic that it be banned for such faculty, even for a short period.

*Visa limitations and outside work.* Another stipulation imposed on international employees with work visas that could adversely affect the career trajectory of foreign professors working in the United States is that they are forbidden to accept payment from any agency other than their employee sponsor (i.e., their host university). This was another hidden obstacle that I unfortunately uncovered several years into my employment. While awaiting a decision on my petition to USCIS, I was presented with two options that would allow me to continue to legally work in the United States should a decision not be made before my H1-B visa expired. I could apply for an EAD card or a short-term extension to my H1-B visa. While deliberating I was informed by the ISSO that my host university would prefer I opt for the H1-B extension. It was explained that having an EAD card allowed me to be employed outside of the university, whereas with an H1-B visa I was only allowed to work for the host university. Naturally, my host university would prefer me to focus my efforts on my university position and not be seeking other sources of income. I found this to be puzzling, given that administrators in my own college had arranged for me to do consulting and supervision work for which I was paid by outside agencies. For example, it was arranged for me to supervise a student teacher from another university who was completing his internship in our area. The administrator at my host university arranged for my payment to come directly from the other university. This is in direct opposition to the rules governing H1-B visas. When I mentioned this to the ISSO I was scolded, informed that this could jeopardize my legal right to work in the United States, and told that my supervisors would be informed of my transgressions. I found it odd that the supervisors who were going to be told of my infractions were the same people who arranged for them to occur.

The consequences of being unable to accept payment for services rendered to outside agencies could also potentially have an impact on the ability of foreign-born professors to meet professorial expectations and hence be promoted. My host university's RPT document mentioned that faculty members are expected to make substantial contributions to practitioners that draw upon their professional expertise. To meet this career expectation I frequently provided workshops to practitioners in the field. Ignorant of work visa restrictions, for this work I was occasionally paid a small stipend. Was I expected to spend countless hours doing this work, in some cases driving significant distances, for free? Another expectation of faculty seeking promotion at my host university is that they provide service to professional organizations. To effectively address this requirement I occasionally provided consultation services to the state Department of Public Instruction (DPI). Here again, this work occupied many hours of my time and required that I occasionally drive hundreds of miles. Was this work to be done on a volunteer basis? On the other hand, had I not done any of this work, would I have been promoted?

**Treatment of foreign credentials.** Another unexpected challenge that threatened my career advancement in the United States was the treatment of my credentials. Given that the education systems and teaching methodologies in the United States and Canada are very similar, that I had multiple graduate degrees from prestigious Canadian universities, and that my Canadian transcripts were all written in English and had been analyzed by my host university during the hiring process, I assumed that there would be no issue with my foreign education. I was mistaken. As an instructor of methodology courses at my host university, I was required by the National Council for Accreditation of Teachers (NCATE) to be licensed by the state in my content area. Despite having four degrees, including a PhD, and 11 years of teaching experience, all in my field, my Canadian credentials were not accepted by the DPI. Unfortunately, this failure to meet NCATE requirements was brought to my attention the very year in which we were to undergo an NCATE review. My failure to meet this standard could have potentially had a negative impact on the review of the college, particularly because faculty qualifications had been identified in our report as our strongest characteristic. To rectify this problem I contacted the office at my host university that handled teacher license applications. Much to my dismay, the officials were unsure how to proceed and directed me to the website of World Education Services (WES), an agency that evaluates foreign transcripts. After navigating the website and contacting the agency, I learned that to have my Canadian academic credentials determined to be equivalent to American credentials, I would have to have a course by course evaluation conducted by WES of all of my transcripts. This required transcripts from all the Canadian universities I attended, copies of all my diplomas, a letter from each of the universities I attended indicating conferral of my degrees, and a $212 fee. To complicate matters further, my undergraduate diploma was written in Latin, and WES requires all diplomas be in English. This required an additional translation fee. In addition to the WES evaluation, DPI required a copy of my Canadian teaching license, and a letter from the school district in Canada where I worked verifying my experience.

196  *Scott Kissau*

*Time.* Not to be overlooked among all of the challenges I have faced that could have potentially adversely affected my career advancement is the exorbitant amount of time I have spent trying to overcome them. To overcome many of the personal challenges mentioned earlier, I spent countless hours attempting to get an SSN, a state driver's license, a tag, registration, and insurance. I also had to find a home, purchase it, furnish it, insure it, and equip it with all the necessary services. To combat challenges related to immigration status, the months of December 2011 and January 2012, I did little else but prepare my petition. I also spent the better part of a week tracking down the documentation needed for my state teaching license. The hours I spent trying to overcome these challenges could have been spent conducting research, writing articles, planning lessons, and providing service. All this time could have been spent doing things to benefit my career, my employer, and the community.

## LESSONS LEARNED

In retrospect, I feel that lessons can be learned from the challenges that I experienced. One obvious lesson that can be taken from my experiences is that cultural similarity and geographical proximity do not necessarily shield foreign-born professors from encountering difficulties in their transition to life and work in the host country. Although I spoke English, looked like many Americans, and was familiar with the American lifestyle, my transition to life in the United States was not easy. Despite my privileged status, I encountered many obstacles.

More specific lessons can also be learned from my experiences as an international postsecondary instructor in the United States. These lessons relate to what can be done in the future to prevent other foreign-born professors from experiencing many of the same difficulties, or at least to help alleviate them. Whereas some of these lessons fall under the category of what I could have done, others pertain to what my host university could have done to support me.

### Personal Responsibility

I must assume some responsibility for the challenges I encountered. It was, after all, my decision to accept the offer of employment and move to this country. I was naïve to think that living and working in the United States would involve little more work and documentation than what was necessary on any one of my many cross-border shopping trips as a child. When moving to another country, ignorance of the rules and regulations surrounding immigration is not an acceptable excuse. I should have been more pro-active in looking into the matter of living and working in the United States. If I could go back and do it again, I would do a number of things differently.

*Ask lots of questions.* When first considering a potential move to another country, foreign-born faculty should contact an immigration lawyer to learn. I wish I had asked about restrictions placed on immigrant workers in possession of an H1-B visa. Had I done so, I might have known that I could only accept payment from my host university and that I would not be able to travel while my application for permanent residency was being reviewed. I may have been more informed with respect to deadlines and what needed to be done to extend my employment once my visa expired. I may also have learned of all associated fees.

In advance of my initial attempt to entry the United States on my H1-B visa, I should have made an appointment to speak with a U.S. customs officer. I should have asked what documentation was needed, what issues I might encounter bringing my vehicle, when I would be able to enter the country on my visa, and if I would have any later difficulty exiting and reentering the United States. Had I asked these questions in advance, I would not have made the costly and time-consuming error of trying to enter the country more than ten days prior to the official start date of my employment. I would have known what documentation I needed to leave and reenter the country. I also would have had more information about the requirements for importing a vehicle.

During my job interview and initial campus visit, it would have been wise to ask for a meeting with the office that oversees the employment of international faculty. While such a meeting could involve many of the same questions asked during meetings with an immigration lawyer or customs officer, it should not replace them. In my experience, such offices can be reluctant to provide answers to questions that involve legal matters. They can, however, address questions that relate to the type of support they provide international faculty: Do they provide legal advice? Do they offer any training geared toward international faculty? Do they provide information to facilitate the relocation process? Do they help with establishing permanent residency? What fees do they and do they not cover during this process? Do they organize social events for international faculty? Will they inform supervisors in the faculty member's department of policies regarding the employment of international professors? Will they help to establish mentoring relationships between new and more experienced international faculty?

*Compile documentation.* Many of the recommendations presented in this section are contingent upon the recommendations made above. For example, had I asked about the procedure involved with importing my vehicle, I would have known to go the dealership where it was purchased to compile the necessary documentation. This would have spared me the time trying to track down the paperwork and the expense of making multiple long-distance phone calls. Foreigners who wish to import their vehicle into the United States would be wise to bring with them a copy of the bill of sale, an estimate of its current value, evidence of where it was assembled, and proof that it meets safety standards in the United States. The documentation that I collected prior to moving to the United States should also have included official copies of my university transcripts, a letter from my previous employer attesting to my teaching experience, and copies in English of all of my diplomas. Having this documentation would have expedited the process of obtaining my state license to teach, and once again, would have spared me the time and expense of making multiple phone calls to Canada. If I had asked the ISSO about challenges I may encounter in becoming a permanent resident, I would have known to begin collecting documentation that could potentially support my petition to be considered by USCIS an internationally recognized outstanding researcher or professor in my field. For example, each time I presented at an international conference, I should have collected the names and contact information of people who attended my sessions and expressed interest in my work. This would have greatly facilitated the process of trying to find researchers in my field from other countries who could attest to the quality and international recognition of my research. Furthermore, had I known that I may have to prove to USCIS that I have judged the work of others in my field, I would have been systematically collecting all documentation of my participation in manuscript reviews and dissertation, hiring, and grant award committees instead of scrambling to track it down after the fact. Compilation of important documentation could even be extended to credit history. Because of my proximity to the United States while living in Canada, on one of my many trips across the border I could have applied for a credit card and begun using that card during future trips to the United States. This could have helped to boost my credit rating and may have saved me thousands of dollars.

***Legally circumvent USCIS restrictions.*** As I have learned throughout this experience, there are ways of legally getting around some of the USCIS restrictions imposed on foreign-born workers. For example, to allow for international travel while their petition for permanent residency is being reviewed by USCIS foreign-born faculty could apply for advanced parole. Advanced parole is often granted to individuals on compassionate grounds and to those whose work requires international travel. Although advanced parole does not guarantee reentry into the United States after traveling abroad, it does make international travel possible for nonpermanent residents without violating USCIS policies. Another reason to apply for advanced parole if international travel may be necessary is that there is no charge associated with the application.

There are also steps that could be taken that would permit foreign professors to be paid by outside agencies for services rendered without defying USCIS rules. In extreme cases in which service provided involves a significant amount of work and travel, and thus could not feasibly be done for free, the outside agency could potentially write a check to the university employer. The host university could then reimburse the faculty member for this service. The faculty member is, thus, being paid by the host university and not defying USCIS rules.

## University Support

While I accept personal responsibility for many of the challenges I experienced, so too should my host university, and more specifically the ISSO. While these two entities did nothing to directly cause my challenges, they could have done much more to prevent them. In my opinion, there should be a pipeline of communication whereby the hiring department informs the ISSO about a foreign hire and initiates a predetermined set of processes. These processes should then be monitored and the relevant supports, including mentoring, offered. While such communication and support would be beneficial to foreign-born professors throughout their transition to life in the United States, in my experience there were three distinct phases in which additional university support would have been greatly appreciated.

*Initial acceptance of a position.* Well in advance of my official employment, an initial relocation package provided by my host university and sent to my home in Canada could have been very informative. This package may have included critical information, such as the date on which I would first be allowed to enter the country. It could also have provided a list of recommended documentation that I compile to facilitate my transition to life in the United States, such as all university transcripts and diplomas, letters of employment, and documentation related to my Canadian vehicle. Other pertinent information that could have eased my move to the United States might have included contact numbers for a variety of services that I would need on my arrival, such as telephone, cable, and utilities.

*Job orientation.* Greater university support would have been further beneficial once my employment began. A welcoming orientation for international faculty could have potentially helped to ease nerves associated with living and working in a foreign country and could have helped me to connect with more experienced foreign-born professors who could have subsequently played a mentoring role. Had I been linked with a fellow Canadian professor who had already gone through the immigration process, it is possible that I could have been alerted to many of the hidden challenges I referenced earlier. A welcoming orientation would have also provided an ideal opportunity to share with foreign-born professors many of the rules and regulations associated with employment on a work visa. At such a venue, I could have been informed of the rules regarding payment from other agencies. Additional information to be shared during an orientation for international faculty should include a list of important dates and deadlines for extending work visas and for beginning the process to apply for permanent residency. It is worth reiterating that the monumental task of petitioning USCIS to be considered an internationally recognized outstanding professor or researcher could have been avoided had I not missed the deadline to submit an Application for Certification from the Department of Labor. Over the past 8 years I have authored numerous publications. I have presented at conferences all over the world, generated hundreds of thousands of dollars in grants, volunteered my time on multiple university committees, and served as interim department chair. It is inexcusable that I can do all of these things for and under the name of my host university, but it cannot provide me with a list of important dates. Furthermore, one would think that allowing its foreign-born faculty to be in this unfortunate position would not be in the university's best interest. Not only does it risk losing talented employees, but the faculty member's time and effort invested in the petition could also be put to better use.

In addition to inviting international faculty to such an orientation, supervisors, faculty, and staff that will be directly working with the international professors should also be invited. Had my department chair, for example, been invited to attend, he would have been more informed about the immigration process and could have provided additional support, guidance, and reminders over the years. Had my supervisor in the department that oversees student teacher supervision been invited, she may have known that arranging for me to be paid by another university to supervise one of its student teachers was in opposition to the rules governing workers on H1-B visas. Had someone from the office that is responsible for teacher license applications been invited to attend the orientation, perhaps there would have been less confusion when it came time for me to apply for a state teaching license. In short, an orientation for foreign-born professors could be highly informative for more than just the international faculty.

***Petition for Alien Worker.*** Having not received a list of important dates by ISSO, and subsequently missing the deadline to submit the necessary paperwork, I was required to prepare and submit a Petition for Alien Worker under the category of outstanding professor or researcher. In this onerous process, more support from the ISSO was desperately needed. I was told I needed to produce a significant document, with multiple sections, high expectations, and in a short time. Yet the only direction I received regarding this high stakes task was a brief e-mail message outlining the six USCIS criteria and stating that I needed to address at least two of them. To reduce my anxiety, clarify the task, and expedite the amount of time it took to complete, the ISSO should have provided me with a template to follow or examples of previous submissions. Despite my pleas for help, the office was unable or unwilling to provide me with either. When it came time to compile six to eight letters from researchers in my field outside of the United States that attested to the quality of my work, I once again sought support from the ISSO and was again disappointed. I wanted to know exactly what the researchers were to include in these letters, but was only told that they should speak to my status as an outstanding and internationally recognized researcher and that they are perhaps the most important component of the petition. Despite giving me very little in the form of guidance, when several of the completed letters were presented to the ISSO, I was told they lacked pivotal information, contained inaccurate wording, and had to be revised. As a result, I had to again contact these international professors and ask them to revise what they had already written. This embarrassing and frustrating endeavor could have been avoided if the ISSO had provided me with a sample letter. This sample could have been written for a fictitious foreign-born faculty member and included the type of information and phrasing that the ISSO wanted to see. While I recognize that the ISSO's intention in rejecting the letters was to help me produce and submit the strongest petition possible, the process could have been expedited and less painful had examples been provided.

## CONCLUSION

Foreign professors should to be grateful for being given the right to live and work in the host country. I am truly fortunate to be presented with the many opportunities that have been made available to me in this great country. While this is important to acknowledge, it must also be recognized that in many ways host countries are fortunate to have us. International professors contribute greatly not only to postsecondary education in the host country but also to society in general. We conduct valuable research, offer unique perspectives and insights into other cultures, and help to address the critical shortage of qualified teachers in high-need areas. Furthermore, international faculty often provide native skills in diverse, underrepresented, and often critical languages for the security and economic well-being of the host country.

## REFERENCE

United States Citizenship and Immigration Services. (2013). *Employment-based immigration: First preference EB-1*. Retrieved October 12, 2014, from http://www.uscis.gov/portal/site/uscis/menuitem.eb1d4c2a3e5b9ac89243c6a7543f6d1a/?vgnextoid=17b983453d4a3210VgnVCM100000b92ca60aRCRD&vgnextchannel=17b983453d4a3210VgnVCM100000b92ca60aRCRD

# 17 Drained Brains
## Canadian Professors in the United States

*Dave Eaton*

## INTRODUCTION

A great deal of writing exists on foreign-born professors, particularly visible minorities, and the struggles they face adapting to departments controlled by the dominant culture. In many cases, staying true to their cultural heritage and activist research are major goals (Jacobs, Cintron, & Canton, 2002). However, little has been written on one of the largest groups of foreign-born professors in the United States—Canadians. The "brain drain" from Canada to the United States has been well documented (Zhao, Drew, & Murray 2000), but micro-narratives of this movement have not been widely published. This chapter is the personal narrative of one Canadian moving to the United States to become a professor, and it will make three main arguments: first, institutional support for migrants is extremely important to successful adaptation; second, the variety of universities in the United States makes teaching more challenging for those educated elsewhere; and, third, socialization within both the university and the local community is vital for any newly arrived foreign-born professor.

## GAINING STATUS

I am a Canadian immigrant living in the United States who studies African history. During the first 25 years of my life I lived in a variety of small Ontario farm towns and viewed the United States from the position of an outsider. When my family visited the United States as tourists, I can vividly remember being instructed to lock the car doors while we were driving. I remember the terror on my father's face when a wrong turn took us off the New York Turnpike and into the city of Albany. I remember the only major political protest in which I have ever participated: a protest against Canadian involvement in the American war on terror. Like many of my friends, I had nothing but contempt for American health care, American consumerism, and American beer. When the band called Sloan sang "One thing I know about the rest of my life, I know that I'll be livin' it in Canada!" I sang right along with them. To this Canadian, the United States served as a

*Drained Brains* 203

foil—a cautionary example of what could go wrong if Canada became more corporate, more belligerent, and more religious.

As fate would have it, I soon found myself having to contemplate a move south of the 49th parallel. In my chosen subfield of African history, many of the original professors had been hired during the 1960s and 1970s and were retiring in the early 2000s. This meant they were being replaced just as I was starting my PhD, and I realized I might have to wait decades for a Canadian Africanist position to open up. Any position that did appear would be unusually competitive because Canadians who had taken jobs in the United States earlier in their careers were often willing to accept a demotion to return home. Thus, I grudgingly began to consider positions in the United States, and during the final year of my PhD program, I applied to more than 30 American jobs. Despite not hearing back from anyone until very late in the process, I was able to get a 1-year African history position at a small liberal arts college in the Midwest.

Thankfully, Canadians enjoyed certain privileges as migrants to the United States, including access to a work permit that required no advance application. Created in 1988 and recognized as a part of North American Free Trade Agreement in 1994, the so-called TN status is granted at the American border for Canadian job candidates holding a university degree, a letter offering employment, and who do not intend to settle permanently in the United States. Because the TN status is adjudicated at the border, there is no centralized oversight, and decisions are made entirely at the individual discretion of the U.S. Customs and Border Protection (CBP) agent. As a result, it is hard to predict how a given application will be received.

Having been detained at the Congolese border a few years earlier, I was not wholly at ease when I applied for my TN status. This must have been apparent to the young agent who was assigned to my application. Displeased that my letter offering employment was not addressed to the CBP, he decided to deny my application, and I experienced the humiliation of being rejected by my reluctantly chosen new home. I had my biometric details taken and then suffered the indignity of the agent yelling a warning to his colleagues before leading me across the main processing area. I felt thoroughly drained of energy by the time I was curtly sent back to the Canadian side of the border. It was not a happy moment, but my department chair quickly resolved the situation. A new letter was sent to my hotel in Sarnia, and the next day my application was processed in less than an hour. As I pulled out of the post and onto the highway, I felt a surge of elation. With the open road in front of me and a job waiting for me, my life as an American worker had begun!

## TRANSITION CHALLENGES

A private, liberal arts college in the Midwest proved to be a wonderful first stop on an academic career, with eager students and talented faculty. As an immigrant, however, I had little time to prepare for my classroom

## 204   Dave Eaton

responsibilities; instead, my time was occupied with the mundane, but painstaking, tasks involved in changing countries. It took weeks to get a social security number (SSN) and a bank account, and I found it impossible to get a credit card of any sort because I had no American credit history. I began to view my passport, driver's license, and SSN as fetishes—symbols of my new transnational life. Except for a couple of other Canadian faculty members, I had few friends and no car, and my girlfriend was in Ottawa. I was experiencing something I had not felt since my time in Africa: culture shock. The college was located in a small, Rust Belt town with a population in rapid decline, a condition that had led to the closing of its hospital, an elementary school, and eventually its secondary school as well. The historically black labor force that had worked at the now-shuttered foundry had suffered the most, and racial tensions were sharp. The campus remained an enclave of affluence in the midst of general poverty. This isolation was reflected in the absence of a coffee shop, usually a staple business in any college town. In fact, few businesses remained open with the exception of party stores and fast-food chains. Students rarely ventured into the dilapidated downtown area. Without a car, I had to make the best of the place, but because there was not a coffee shop, I did most of my work in my office. My main hobby, long-distance running, was not helpful either: unleashed dogs roamed the streets, and the colleges' small nature reserve was full of hunters regardless of the season. I began to question my decision to move to the United States: Could I really ask my girlfriend to move here with me? Did I even want a tenure-track job if it meant living like this?

It was fortunate that I had no time for reflection because a new set of job applications and course preparations were due. One of the available tenure-track positions was at my liberal arts college, and I applied without much enthusiasm. However, the financial crisis hit with sufficient force they had to cancel that search, and fortuitously the department offered its full support toward my other applications. In the end, I completed more than 50 applications, and thanks to my publications, having my PhD in hand, and my American job experience, I was much more successful than the year before. From November to February I was busy interviewing, and one of the questions I made sure to ask was whether the university would support me if I applied for permanent residency (better known as the "green card"). Applying for a green card through an employer requires a series of steps taken at the institutional level before the individual application, and these steps can be expensive. Responses varied dramatically. Thankfully, by the end of February 2009, I had committed my future to my current university.

When my contract at the private liberal arts college ended that May, however, so did my TN status, and I returned to Canada to live with my fiancée until my new position began in August. I could finally promise her some stability in the future, and the tantalizing prospect of a green card meant she would be free to pursue her own career as a curator. As for me, I was excited to end the scrutiny I received as a TN status holder. Because a TN status can be withdrawn anytime a CBP agent suspects you intend to migrate permanently to the United States, they hold your future in their hands whenever you cross the border. For several months in early 2009, I was selected for extra screening every time I tried to enter the United States. Eventually, a sympathetic agent explained that this was happening because a new policy made special scrutiny mandatory for anyone with a rejected entry on record. It was disconcerting to realize just how well the CBP could "see" me. My girlfriend faced similar challenges when she crossed the border to visit me. In one instance, it took her several hours to convince the CBP agent that the "boyfriend" she was visiting in the United States was actually Canadian and that she had no intention of marrying an American and staying permanently. Anxiety and nerves replaced confidence whenever we approached border crossings, and my passport was often dripping with sweat by the time I reached an agent. My liminal immigration status was not very pleasant.

Thankfully, my new institution quickly resolved these problems. The first step was transitioning me from TN to H1-B status. This took place only a month after I arrived, and meant that I could no longer be turned away for "immigrant intent." My fiancée and I had in the meantime married, and together we decided to apply for green cards. This set off a whirlwind of activity. Because my wife was still working at a major museum back in Canada and we lacked the resources to hire an immigration lawyer, I had to complete the dozens of forms and compile all the necessary documents for our green card application. It was exhausting work, and I became consumed by the acronyms that suddenly determined our fate—G325A, I-140, I-765, I-131, I-485, and I-693. My wife traveled constantly to be present for the medical exam, the submission of the forms, and the gathering of our biometric data. Once we submitted our applications I embarked on a long-awaited research trip to East Africa, and I was in Rwanda when we received a dreaded Request for Evidence (RFE). Because a response is required within 30 days, I flew back to the Midwest and sent the U.S. Citizenship and Immigration Services (CIS) our long-form birth certificates, as well as proof that our marriage was real. Given the surprisingly few pictures we had of each other, this evidence included Facebook message threads. Thankfully, this proved acceptable!

Because I was juggling my writing, three new course preparations, and a 5-day-a-week teaching schedule on top of all the immigration paperwork, my first year was a blur. I met a newly arrived Canadian couple working at the university and a few people in my department who were about my age and happy enough to chat over beer at a brew pub—but this was a pale imitation of my social life back in Canada. In the discipline of African studies, most researchers place great emphasis on meeting members of the local community, and I had made every effort to do so while conducting my research. But after 1 year in the Midwest, I only knew a handful of people from the region. Despite coming from a racially and culturally similar part of Canada, I was having less success socializing in America than in Africa.

## 206  *Dave Eaton*

## TEACHER–STUDENT RELATIONS

I did not anticipate any great difficulties acclimating to the American classroom, and I expected Canadian and American students would have much in common. The level of formality is similar, and schools on both sides of the border have struggled with grade inflation, rising tuition costs, and student disengagement (Cote & Allahar, 2007). These were issues when I taught in Canada, and I faced similar issues when teaching in the Midwest; however, there were a number of important differences I did not anticipate, and which made my adjustment to the U.S. more difficult.

Many foreign-born professors face discrimination because of their accent. According to Skachkova (2007), this is one of the most difficult challenges faced by an immigrant professor and one that is most likely to manifest itself in negative student evaluations. She notes that some instructors feel this is a class issue, with working-class students more likely to object to foreign accents in the classroom. At my institution, which enrolls a large number of first-generation college students, this is certainly an important concern for foreign-born professors. In my case, I did not believe that I had a distinctive accent, but I was quickly proved wrong! My students identified my origins immediately because they were familiar with the words such as *roof* and *house*, which I pronounce differently. Likewise, I could easily spot the nasal vowels so common in this part of the Midwest. Although I am a native English speaker and my accent was not as distinct as that of many other foreign-born professors, my students were fully aware that I was not American born.

Although my accent served to differentiate me from my students, it has not been a major concern. Americans seem to view Canadians as cute, but rustic cousins, and in the classroom it is more a source of amusement than anything else. The Olympic hockey competition in 2010 was followed closely by many of my male students, and before class we often bantered about the successes and failures of our respective national teams. As a passionate fan of the Toronto Maple Leafs, a struggling ice hockey team, I could commiserate with many of my students who supported a similarly unsuccessful football franchise. My accent and origins were rarely mentioned on student evaluations, with the exception of a handful of positive comments such as "Great Canadian Accent" and "I loved his Canadian stories, lol." The classroom is one place where my foreign origins seem to be trumped by the cultural similarities linking the United States and Canada. I suspect this classroom experience differs from that of many other foreign-born instructors.

Notwithstanding the preceding, I did encounter a different academic culture at my master's level institution in the Midwest than I was familiar with in Canada. This was true in terms of both the students and the professors. I was told (informally) by several colleagues to expect students who were nonconfrontational but also unusually sensitive to criticism, and this was quite helpful. My students were very respectful of my authority, and even though I looked young and wore jeans, they were generally focused, polite, and extremely pleasant to teach. However, this seemed to be part of a broader aversion to conflict that made the classroom dynamic very distinct from what I had experienced in Canada. Professors who picked students at random during discussions often received negative evaluations at the end of the term, as did those who released class early if no one had completed the assigned reading. Planned discussions around controversial topics such as natural selection or racism often elicited only brief, banal comments.

My Midwestern students seemed reluctant to inadvertently offend anyone by saying something wrong but, on the other hand, did not seem open to changing their minds about their core beliefs. For example, a week into my first semester, I received an e-mail from a student, informing me that he did not believe in the theory of evolution; however, understanding that it is an important theory in today's society, he was willing to learn about this topic and use this "to test his faith"—and that he would still work hard and learn the facts. This e-mail represents a larger subsection of my students who go to university primarily for a degree. They want to "learn the facts" but compartmentalize these as academic, necessary to get the desired credential but of no consequence to their day-to-day life.

As mentioned earlier, my students also seemed very sensitive even to constructive criticism. This became a significant problem during one of my group projects when one group submitted a lesson plan that had been hastily assembled at the last minute and was so poorly written as to be incomprehensible. I gathered the group together after the class and told them they had failed their proposal because it did not include much specific material from the book, did not engage with the author's main argument, and did not provide a clear outline of what would be presented. I told them that they could still do well but would have to make these very significant changes. My hope was that by challenging them on the proposal they would work harder on the presentation. In this I think I was successful, and the presentation went quite well, but I also faced severe criticism from the group members on my student evaluations: They described me as "rude," "not fair in any way," and having "ridiculous expectations." My sense was the criticism I had leveled at the proposal had been internalized by the students to an extent I had rarely seen while teaching in Canada.

One last change has been pedagogical. As an undergraduate in Canada, my classes were designed to utilize the Socratic method of learning. My professors eschewed technology in the classroom and focused instead on lengthy readings that would be discussed by about 15 to 20 students. This is not necessarily the case at my American institutions. Students seem less interested in these discussions, especially because classes of 30 to 45 make it difficult to engage with everyone. They also seemed to have shorter attention spans, although this is as likely to be a generational, as well as a cultural, issue. With this in mind, I have changed the way I approach the

208  *Dave Eaton*

classroom: I have abandoned 75- or even 50-minute lectures. To maintain student engagement, I incorporate shorter discussions, lecture less, and use a variety of images, videos, or exercises to keep the students constantly on their toes. This has been fairly successful, although it does require more effort in class preparation. With lecture and discussion now integrated into the same class, I have been able to hold student interest more effectively but at the expense of the sophisticated knowledge that can be conveyed through in-depth seminars.

## ADAPTING TO AMERICAN UNIVERSITIES

### Teaching Expectations

The quality of teaching also differs considerably from Canada. At my PhD-granting institution, I taught two courses that were very well received, and my student evaluations were consistently among the best in the department. At the midwestern schools where I worked, however, classes were smaller (usually 15–45 students), but the expectation was that instructors would take advantage of this to experiment with their pedagogy and create a more engaging student experience. Because I had no pedagogical training, I soon found myself struggling. Although my teaching has not been so poor as to jeopardize my prospects for tenure, it has been fascinating to discover how much more thought is put into teaching in the Midwest. Thanks to generous colleagues and constructive criticism from my students, I have gradually begun to improve. I now read far more on teaching methods, have experimented with new learning strategies, and even hosted a teaching circle on world history surveys in 2013 (see Zevin & Gerwin, 2011).

My university was deeply committed to helping professors adjust to institutional norms, particularly through peer mentoring. I found the monthly, university-wide meetings for first-year faculty most helpful. These were moderated by a more senior colleague, and although nominally these mentoring sessions involved reading a book on how to become a great college teacher, they were also a "safe" site to voice our frustrations with our students. This formal mentoring was coupled with informal gatherings that also proved very helpful. After my first year, I began to organize Friday get-togethers at nearby restaurants and pubs in the hopes of better getting to know both my colleagues and the city. Over beer, I learned a great deal about how other professors handled certain challenges in the classroom and was able to the relate some of my own successes and failures. In fact, the Friday beer get-togethers were extremely helpful in this regard, and I discovered a great deal about the department as others opened up about earlier controversies. I found it fascinating that I had a say in how the department proceeded on personnel decisions and took advantage of this to encourage some additional changes to the system.

*Drained Brains* 209

Overall culturally, Canada is similar to the Midwest, but university-level teaching is handled quite differently. This proved a major challenge for me as I adjusted to life at an American university.

### Research Expectations

My new institutions' research expectations also differed significantly from those in Canada. I sensed that large public research institutions in the United States most closely matched the Canadian school where I completed my PhD. My new institution was certainly a large public university, and at the job interview, it was made clear that research was secondary to teaching performance. Other faculty members were clear and consistent when they described the research requirements for tenure, which involved publishing peer-reviewed articles or book chapters. Although no similarly quantifiable measure of teaching performance existed, at the job interview I was told that student evaluations were one of several metrics that would be taken seriously. Peer evaluations, professional development, and our integrative statement (which should include reflections on our teaching performance) would also be considered.

I witnessed my first tenure review soon after my arrival. In my department, all tenure-track professors participated in personnel decisions, and one of the eligible candidates faced a difficult vote. The candidate was an excellent teacher and had served the department well in a variety of capacities but lacked the obligatory peer-reviewed articles. The candidate's defenders argued that this person's other contributions outweighed this deficiency and noted that at the time of hiring the candidate was instructed only to maintain an active scholarly agenda rather than produce a set number of publications. However, those who felt the candidate had not met the department and college research guidelines argued that the chair had given a warning during the 4-year review that additional publications were required for tenure, but nothing had been done. I studied the candidate's portfolio intently, trying to determine which specific aspects of this file were most important. In the end, the candidate received tenure from the department, and I, as a new professor, had a chance to see the personnel process in action.

## COMMUNITY SOCIALIZATION

When I moved to the United States, I wanted my social networks to extend beyond the "ivory tower," and although my wife and I struggled with this at first, we gradually built relationships and became settled. Having lived there for 5 years, we both now call the Midwest home.

During the whirlwind of my first year as an assistant professor, there was little time to worry about social life. Once my wife arrived and we received our green cards, however, she was able to find work at a local museum, and we began to consider settling permanently. In these discussions, the

## 210  Dave Eaton

issue of "community socialization" loomed large. I had introduced my wife to several of my colleagues, but with a few exceptions they were in very different places in their lives. Age was a critical factor: I was in my early 30s and the youngest of the tenure-track faculty in my department. My wife was used to a lively social life and was distraught over our lack of close friends. Deep down I knew she was right: I had become friends with a few of my colleagues, but they either had children or were extremely busy with their career obligations. I was worried that her unhappiness would lead to pressure to return to Canada, in effect forcing me to choose between my wife and my career. The more I thought about it, the more I was led to the same conclusion: We needed to make some friends outside the academy.

In the Midwest, my wife and I were starting from scratch. Despite more than 6 months in the city, the only locals we had met were our housemates and landlords. Having reached this breaking point, we decided to take action—by joining a dodgeball league! Run by the local sport and social club, it had no link to the university, required limited athletic skill, and was focused more on drinking together after the game than testing our athletic acumen. Mostly composed of 20-somethings who had moved to the area on business, it also included a number of people from the area looking to meet new friends or have fun with coworkers. Our team was a collection of people who had signed up independently, and although we were not particularly adept at dodgeball, we certainly held our own at the bar. Tuesday evenings became an escape for my wife and me, and we formed close friendships with several people, including sales representatives, teachers, nurses, genetic counselors, a graduate student, a marriage counselor, and an engineer. This crowd was a little younger than our work friends and provided us with a very different social circle. We now had people we could call if we wanted to go dancing, camping, or just watch sports together. And most important, they were all planning to stay.

Four years later, we are still close with many of our dodgeball friends. They introduced us to tailgating at college football games, tubing down winding rivers, and a variety of board games. They accompanied us to Friday-night hockey games that make this part of the Midwest feel so culturally similar to Canada. But most important, our dodgeball friends offered vital support to my wife when her mother became ill, and they volunteered for an ovarian cancer awareness walk we helped organize after her mother passed away. By developing relationships beyond the university, we became a part of a community. In my experience, these friendships were every bit as important to adjusting to the Midwest as my adjustment to the departmental culture within the university. When my wife and I returned from her mother's funeral, she turned to me and said, "This feels like home now."

Foreign-born professors often face social isolation, but most are primarily concerned with isolation from colleagues within the department. My experiences led me to believe that isolation from the local community is also an important problem. Academics do not always make good friends—their ambition, long hours, and frequent travel that come with being dynamic professors also make it unlikely they will be able to offer meaningful social support in times of need. From my perspective, foreign-born professors would be better served by meeting people outside the university. These local relationships may well be more valuable in the long-term.

In conclusion, I was extremely fortunate to join a department that has been clear about its expectations as well as amenable to contributions from new faculty. This allowed me to both absorb aspects of the institutional culture as well as try to transform it through my own ideas about appropriate levels of service, research, and teaching. If I had not had confidence in my colleagues, I would not have been able to direct so much energy to the logistical and social challenges I faced in the United States. For this I am very grateful.

## LESSONS LEARNED

My experience as a migrant professor taught me a number of lessons that might be relevant to others going through a similar process. First, any academic considering a move should do everything they can to find a supportive institution. There are a multitude of logistical challenges when moving to the United States, and these are far more daunting if faced alone. An on-campus job interview is an ideal situation to determine just how helpful they will be. Second, it is important to prepare for greater teaching responsibilities. While most publications on foreign-born professors are understandably focused on those employed at research-oriented institutions, numerous migrants will find themselves working for schools that place greater emphasis on teaching. There are advantages to this, including a less adversarial tenure process, but the teaching environment will be very different from that experienced before migrating to the United States. And last but certainly not least, migrant professors should consider socializing outside their university. I think that some of the isolation we face is a result of our efforts to establish personal friendships exclusively within the university. My impression is that the nature of academic work means professors do not always make good friends and that establishing social circles outside the university (and beyond our ethnic kin!) is critical to successfully adapting to our new home.

## REFERENCES

Cote, J. E., & Allahar, A. L. (2007). *Ivory tower blues: A university system in crisis.* Toronto: University of Toronto Press.

Jacobs, L., Cintron, J., & Canton, C. E. (Eds.). (2002). *The politics of survival in academia.* Oxford: Rowman and Littlefield.

## 212  *Dave Eaton*

Skachkova, P. (2007). Academic careers of immigrant women professors in the US. *Higher Education, 53*, 697–738.

Zevin, J., & Gerwin, D. (2011). *Teaching world history as mystery*. New York: Routledge.

Zhao, J., Drew, D., & Murray, T. S. (2000). Brain drain and brain gain: The migration of knowledge workers from and to Canada. *Education Quarterly Review, 6*(3), 8–35.

# 18 Identity Construction of a Second-Language Educator

*Tanita Saenkhum*

## INTRODUCTION

This chapter examines language and identity construction of a foreign-born, third year, tenure-track assistant professor of English from Thailand with a specialization in second-language writing at an American university, where I also direct an English as a Second Language program. My goal is to provide insights into my professional life, and in so doing, illustrate some of the "complexities" (Kamhi-Stein, 2004, p. 6) involved in being a nonnative English professional in the United States.

Through a personal narrative, I explore how I construct my identity, position myself, and am positioned by others, particularly students, in different academic settings. My goal in explicating this is twofold: to illustrate how my identity is socially and historically constructed (e.g., Norton, 1997; Norton & McKinney, 2011) and to share with the readers how I have overcome linguistic and cross-cultural challenges as an international graduate student and teaching assistant and how I continue to grapple with these issues as a professor in the context of U.S. higher education. I conclude the chapter with some lessons I have learned and discuss some implications for administrators and employing institutions as they work with professors from various linguistic, cultural, and experiential backgrounds.

## AN ENGLISH AS A SECOND-LANGUAGE LEARNER IN MULTIPLE CONTEXTS

I grew up in Thailand, but I got my initial exposure to the English language from private tutors before my formal exposure to the language in the classroom when I was in Grade 5. I also worked as a journalist for an English newspaper in Thailand for five years. Such experiences made me believe that I had a good command of English.

To my surprise, however, I may have overestimated myself. My very first American academic experience did not go as smoothly as I expected. When I began working on my master's degree, the first day of classes was terribly disappointing. I was able to understand only about 50% of what my professors said in their lectures. I could not participate in any class discussions because I had to form sentences in my head before expressing my ideas, which took a lot of time. When I was ready to speak out, the class discussion had already moved on to a new topic. My experiences during these lectures were similar to other second-language learners' who spend a lot of their classroom time to monitor how they express themselves in their second language. As Krashen's monitor hypothesis explains, while monitoring can contribute to language learners' accuracy of utterances, it can act as a barrier that slows down learning because learners focus more on accuracy, as opposed to fluency (Krashen, 1982). In my case, my speech overmonitoring held up my participation in class discussions.

After the first day of classes, I went home disappointed and started losing confidence in my English skills. I began questioning my English-language abilities. My confidence in my English skills was tremendously reduced when I could not grasp concepts and arguments in textbooks I was assigned to read. I had to go over those textbooks and other course materials three to four times to make sure that I understood what was discussed. This kept recurring for the first few months. Thanks to my personality, I did not give up easily. I accepted my weaknesses and gradually worked on them. When I could not understand what the professors said, I raised my hand and asked for clarification. At the same time, I was able to take part in class discussions, expressing my points of view on issues discussed in classes. It took a lot of courage to speak up because I was not sure whether what I said would make sense to my professors and classmates. However, I kept telling myself that if I never tried, I would never know. This worked out, and I gradually gained my confidence back and began to feel that I was part of this learning community. In sum, my first semester as an international graduate student was essentially devoted to adjusting myself to the American educational system, classroom participation and interactions, and intercultural communication.

Being an English learner in one context is totally different from being an English learner in other contexts. What I learned from this challenging transition could be summarized into three concepts: patience, acceptance, and persistence. First and foremost, an individual should be patient with him- or herself, accept his or her weaknesses, and work on them, and never ever give up easily. I should also mention that one main factor that helped ease my transition was my program of study, TESOL. Given the nature of the field, it taught me how languages are learned (Lightbown & Spada, 2006), how learners acquire and learn additional languages other than their mother tongue, and what difficulties and challenges second-language learners encounter (Ortega, 2009). Equipped with such knowledge, I was able to develop a better understanding of myself as a second-language learner and came to realize that second-language acquisition processes take a long time.

Language-related issues were not my primary concerns when I worked on a PhD. Through scholarly training and professional development

## Identity Construction of a Second-Language Educator  215

opportunities, I learned to construct my identity as a second-language educator. I regularly presented at regional, national, and international conferences related to second language writing. In addition to conference presentations, I had the opportunity to cultivate my leadership skills by serving as an associate chair for the Symposium on Second Language Writing in which I worked closely with several established professionals in the field. Such experiences allowed me to develop professional insights for my later career. In short, my identity as a second-language educator had been gradually shaped partly through my participation in these communities of practice (Lave & Wenger, 1991).

## AN ENGLISH AS A SECOND-LANGUAGE INSTRUCTOR IN U.S. HIGHER EDUCATION

When I began teaching, I faced other kinds of challenges. During my 7 years in graduate school, I taught first-year composition and professional writing to both native and nonnative English speakers and was thankful for the valuable learning opportunities it offered me. In what follows, I describe the challenges I faced as a second-language educator teaching in the United States, which represents the Inner Circle countries, in which English is used as a primary language, as opposed to the Outer Circle and the Expanding Circle, where English is used as a medium of international communication (Kachru, 1982). I divide my discussion into two parts: First, I reflect on my teaching experience as a teaching assistant at Southern Illinois University, Carbondale (SIUC), and Arizona State University (ASU), where I was assigned to teach composition to both native and nonnative speakers of English, respectively. Second, I share my current teaching experience as a tenure-track assistant professor at my current institution. In discussing my teaching experiences in these contexts, I attempt to demonstrate the ways I perceive myself as a second-language educator and how they have an impact on the ways I construct my identity as a second-language educator. As Braine (2010) points out, while nonnative English speakers' self-perceptions are important, "the way in which students perceive them is also vital to these NNS [non-native speaking] teachers" (p. xi). Thus, for each teaching context, I also describe how my students perceive me as their instructor, and I illustrate their perceptions by showing some comments from my past and most recent teaching evaluations.

### First-Time English as a Second Language Writing Instructor

My first teaching experience in a U.S. university took place at SIUC, where I was assigned to teach a first-year writing course to international students. Being a nonnative speaker of English teaching English in a U.S. university, I was prepared for all kinds of reactions from my students. I was not surprised when my students gave me a strange look when I stepped into the classroom and introduced myself to them, letting them know that I would be teaching them writing. The students presumed that their English teacher would be a native English speaker; this was something predictable and understandable. I did not blame them. On the contrary, I accepted this reality and tried to do my best as a writing teacher. I was aware that the way I spoke English was different from that of native speakers and that these students came to the United States with the hope of studying English from native speakers. With these in mind, I told my students up front that they were welcome to stop me at any time when they needed clarification and that I did not feel offended if they told me that they could not understand what I said. Establishing rapport with students at the beginning of the semester helped my teaching enormously.

One of the main challenges I faced was that I had to overcome students' perceptions of me as a writing teacher who was also a nonnative speaker *like them*. I realized that I could not change my accent. I could not change the way I spoke English, and I would never be a native English speaker; however, I did not consider these as disadvantages. On the contrary, I used them as my motivation in teaching; I had a strong determination to be a good writing teacher. I was a writer before; therefore, I believed that I should be able to share things about writing with my students.

At the end of the semester, students were asked to complete course evaluations. I shared some students' comments about my teaching. The comments were anonymous and original. The following two students (in their own words) appreciated the way I taught, and of interest is the fact that the second student mentioned the advantage of having a teacher who was also a nonnative speaker of English, like him:

- For what I liked about this class I would say the way the instructor teaches. The instructor was very helpful and she wanted us to learn, she worked very hard for this class and I respect that. (Student 1)
- I think when the instructor for this class is international like us. She will be able to communicate with the students more easy and they would feel much better. Because I think the instructor has been through the same process. So, she will be able to solve these problem[s] from the experience she has been through. (Student 2)

Other students commented on areas of teaching where they thought I could improve, two of which are as follows:

- I don't wish to be offensive, but it seems to be that you've been feeling a little bit nervous when giving instructions. Perhaps you could try to take it easy because you totally are qualified to handle this job. Just go for it, Tanita! (Student 3)
- I think the only thing you need to do to improve your teaching skill will be relax! Sometimes we can feel that you are very nervous, it also

*Identity Construction of a Second-Language Educator* 217

makes us feel nervous too actually . . .\ Haha, but we know this is your first time, so it's fine, but just relax!! (Student 4)

## A (More) Experienced English as a Second Language Writing Instructor

When I taught at ASU, my teaching assignments included first-year composition courses for native and nonnative speakers of English and professional writing for advanced native and nonnative English speaking undergraduate students. Working with these diverse groups of students, I received both positive and negative comments on and reactions to my teaching abilities (positive) and to how I sounded (negative). I discuss them in the next sections.

### *Praise From Native English-Speaking Students*
Working with students in mainstream composition classrooms was extremely challenging. I felt I had to prove myself that I was qualified to teach writing to native speakers of English. I felt that I had to do more than my fellow native English-speaking teaching assistants. I worked hard and was overprepared for every class, and it paid off. My students accepted who I was, and the way I taught. Some comments from my native English-speaking students in my English 101 and 102 were as follows:

- I love Tanita! She's an excellent teacher with a lot of enthusiasm. (Student 5)
- I felt that she was a very good instructor who truly cared about her students. (Student 6)
- Tanita is great. I am taking ENG 102 next semester with her because I enjoyed her class so much. (Student 7)
- Tanita was enthusiastic and knowledgeable about the course. (Student 12)

Based on their comments, native English-speaking students did not seem to care about where I came from or my accent. My situation is similar to that of Liu (2004), whose students came to understand that being a fine language teacher had nothing to do with nativeness or nonnativeness. Liu stated, "It is true that I am not a native speaker of English and never will be. But the quality of language teaching is not merely determined by native or nonnative speaker status, and I believe my students came to recognize this" (2004, p. 32).

### *Challenges From Nonnative English-Speaking Students*
Not all things last forever, and I was not able to enjoy those positive student comments indefinitely. In my third year at ASU, I chose to teach English 108, a second-semester writing course designed for students whose first or

218   *Tanita Saenkhum*

strongest language is not English. It looked like the majority of students appreciated my teaching approaches; however, a few students overlooked the ways I taught and raised some communication-related issues. Three of 25 students from two sections of this course commented on my English speaking skills and accent. Their comments were as follows:

- She needs to improve on her speaking skill. (Student 13)
- The strong accent is the one that [the] instructor has to overcome for better understanding the lectures for the students. (Student 14)
- Cannot understand her English. (Student 15)

As I read those comments, my heart sank. I felt that the students criticized me because they wondered how I could possibly teach the language if I still had a foreign accent. Honestly, such comments hurt. I felt bad because the students judged me because I sounded foreign to them. It would not have hurt if their comments were about my teaching abilities. As Thomas (1999) suggests, nonnative English-speaking teachers face challenges that "stem not only from professionals in the field or from the organization as a whole but also from *their non-native students*" (p. 8, emphasis added). Thomas continues that "this trickle-down effect is inevitable" (p. 8).

In retrospect, I should have taken it as a teaching moment to discuss with my students the notion of varieties of English in the world. In so doing, students would have been able to develop a better understanding of world English, to learn to embrace differences, and to consider these differences as valuable learning resources.

## An English as a Second Language Professor at an American University

At my current institution, I teach graduate and undergraduate courses in second-language writing, TESOL, and second-language acquisition. My main job is to train prospective teachers who will be working with English as a Second Language students in various contexts and settings, including the United States and other countries. In what follows, I discuss how being a nonnative speaker of English can be helpful to my students' learning. I end this section with some classroom challenges that I still continue to grapple with.

### The Privilege of Being a Nonnative Speaker of English

The majority of my students are native speakers of English. Being a second-language writer myself, I am able to share with my students some insightful information about the difficulties second-language learners encounter. I also share with them my experiences of learning English as a second language. These real-life experiences facilitate my students' learning and develop their understanding of English language learning and teaching. I consider this to be, as Kramsch points out, "the privilege of the nonnative speaker" (1997,

*Identity Construction of a Second-Language Educator* 219

p. 359). I am aware that I am different from my students, yet I see my difference as a learning resource for them. I am aware that I am not a native English speaker and never will be. Thus, I always strive to improve my teaching. As Liu (2004) puts it, "to make up for my lack of nativeness is by being aware of it. This keeps me constantly striving for a high goal, since I recognize that a journey of self-cultivation and refinement usually ends when one no longer feels the need for improvement" (p. 32).

In general, my current students appreciate my instruction, and that is a reflection on what a nonnative speaker of English can bring to the classroom. As Thomas (1999) suggests, it is a unique perspective that

> we [non-native English-speaking teachers] not only recognize but have experienced how high the stakes are when an individual struggles to acquire, not just language, but a language of immense power. Having been there, we can not only emphasize with our students' struggles but also share our stories as well. (p. 12)

### Pedagogical Challenges

Teaching in the context of U.S. higher education for 9 years (6 years as a teaching assistant and 3 years as a tenure-track assistant professor), I feel that one aspect of teaching that I have to fine-tune is related to class discussion and lectures. I am from an educational system in which teachers lead class discussions and students act as passive learners. Students listen to what teachers have to say through lecture and take notes, and they barely participate in class discussion or ask questions. For this reason, as a cross-cultural teacher in a country with a different pedagogical approach with an emphasis on student-centeredness, I am learning to handle these pedagogical differences and challenges. I take comments from students seriously because I want to develop more effective teaching approaches that address the needs of my students. As is common in the academia, my need for such a personal, professional development goal is partly reflected in comments from my graduate students. In one seminar course, the following comments we noted:

- It would be great if the class time format was different. Maybe direct questions for discussion or activities. (Student 19)
- More in-class activities! I enjoy discussion, but I felt I learned the most when we did activities on the board and in pairs. (Student 20)

As these comments suggest, for this course, I spent a lot of class time lecturing and leading class discussions. The students, however, believed that group activities and class discussion contributed most to their learning. Although I still include some instructor-led lectures, I minimize it and allow ample time for class discussion with guiding questions. In sum, by listening to what students have to say about my teaching, I have come to a better understanding of what works best for their learning.

## LESSONS LEARNED

In this section, building on the preceding discussion, I consider three lessons that I have learned from the process of my identity construction as a second language educator. First, I look at how my transition from an English as a second language learner from Thailand to an English as a second language learner in the United States taught me. Second, I discuss how I made up for my lack of nativeness in my teaching as a graduate teaching assistant. Finally, I describe the privilege of being a nonnative speaker of English and how it strengthens my teaching and professional career.

### Lessons Learned From My Transition From an English as a Second Language Learner From Thailand to an English as a Second Language Learner in the United States Taught Me: Never Give Up

My transition from an English language learner from one context to another was challenging. Through this process, I learned to be patient with myself, to accept my weaknesses and work on them, and to never give up on anything. As I discussed earlier, the process of second language acquisition takes a long time. English-language learners have to be patient with how they learn and acquire the target language. It is common that

> users of tongues other than their own can reveal unexpected ways of dealing with the cross-cultural crashes they encounter as they migrate between languages. Their appropriation of foreign languages enables them to construct linguistic and cultural identities in the interstices of national languages and on the margins of monolingual speakers' territories. (Kramsch, 1997, p. 368)

English-language learners should embrace and accept this process. At the same time, English-language learners should also be aware of their weaknesses and work on them so that they can improve on those weak areas. Finally, it is important to set a goal for oneself so that one has a target toward which to work. As migrant professionals, we likely have difficulties and obstacles that await us. The only way to overcome these struggles is to never give up. It does not hurt to try.

### Lessons Learned From My Lack of Nativeness in My Teaching as a Graduate Teaching Assistant: The Ways I Teach Mattered More Than My Accent

As a foreign worker in the United States, I also learned, while working as a teaching assistant, that in order to make up for my lack of nativeness, I had to strive for teaching methods and strategies that facilitated students' learning. I became aware that American students are taught differently from

## Identity Construction of a Second-Language Educator 221

what I experienced back in Thailand, and I needed to adapt to the new teaching environment. This awareness encouraged me to over-prepare for my classes. I always made sure that I was prepared to help my students to develop their critical and analytical skills. I could tell that students came to realize that the quality of teaching has nothing to do with where I am from and how I speak English. The ways I teach mattered more than my accent.

### Lessons Learned From Being a Nonnative Speaker of English: Be a More Insightful Instructor and Professional

A second language writer myself, I consider my personal experiences and insights to be among my professional strengths. Because of my personal experiences on the subject I teach, I can share with my students some challenges and difficulties that second language students face as they work toward their English proficiency. This real-life experience is a great learning resource for students, especially for those who are monolingual and are not familiar with learning additional languages. Medgyes (1999) calls this "the bright side" (p. 178) of being a nonnative-speaking English teacher.

As an educator who is a nonnative speaker of English, I feel empowered every time I walk into my classrooms. My secret is that I am aware that I am different, I accept who I am, and I am proud to be a nonnative speaker of English teaching English in the context of U.S. higher education, and I have a lot to say on the subject from a real-life, authentic perspective.

### CONCLUSION

Here is the surprising fact: About 80% of English teachers worldwide are nonnative speakers of English (Braine, 2010). As shown in this edited collection, foreign-born professionals bring with them diverse linguistic, cultural, and experiential backgrounds to employing institutions. These professionals "have . . . become more vocal and visible" (Kamhi-Stein, 2004, p. 6) in various teaching contexts across the globe. Therefore, it is crucial that administrators and employing institutions develop an understanding of challenges and difficulties that foreign-born professors encounter, as well as strengths that they bring to classroom teaching.

To address issues related to foreign-born professors more effectively, communication between employing institutions and these scholars should be encouraged and increased. This communication can be in various forms, including informal meetings and social gatherings. It is also worth examining the challenges these professors face while working in their institutions and living in the American culture. This can be done in the forms of surveys, interviews, or focus groups. Obtaining this information will help administrators and employing institutions to address concerns of foreign-born professors more effectively.

## REFERENCES

Briane, G. (2010). *Nonnative speaker English teachers: Research, pedagogy, and professional growth*. New York: Routledge.

Kachru, B. B. (Ed.). (1982). *The other tongue: English across cultures*. Urbana, IL: University of Illinois Press.

Kamhi-Stein, L. D. (Ed.). (2004). *Learning and teaching from experience: Perspectives on nonnative English-speaking professionals*. Ann Arbor: University of Michigan Press.

Kramsch, C. (1997). Guest column: The privilege of the nonnative speaker. *PMLA: Publications of the Modern Language Association, 112*(3), 359–369.

Krashen, S. D. (1982). *Principles and practice in second language acquisition*. Oxford: Pergamon.

Lave, J., & Wenger, E. (1991). *Situated learning: Legitimate peripheral participation*. Cambridge, UK: Cambridge University Press.

Lightbown, P. M., & Spada, N. (2006). *How languages are learned* (3rd ed.). New York: Oxford University Press.

Liu, J. (2004). Confessions of a nonnative English-speaking professional. In L. D. Kamhi-Stein (Ed.), *Learning and teaching from experience: Perspectives on nonnative English-speaking professionals* (pp. 25–39). Ann Arbor: University of Michigan Press.

Medgyes, P. (1999). Language training: A neglected area in teacher education. In G. Braine (Ed.), *Non-native educators in English language teaching* (pp. 177–195). Mahwah, NJ: Lawrence Erlbaum Associates.

Norton, B. (1997). Language, identity, and the ownership of English. *TESOL Quarterly, 31*(3), 409–429.

Norton, B., & McKinney, C. (2011). An identity approach to second language acquisition. In D. Atkinson (Ed.), *Alternative approaches to second language acquisition* (pp. 73–94). New York: Routledge.

Ortega, L. (2009). *Understanding second language acquisition*. London: Hodder Education.

Thomas, J. (1999). Voices from the periphery: Non-native teachers and issues of credibility. In G. Braine (Ed.), *Non-native educators in English language teaching* (pp. 5–13). Mahwah, NJ: Lawrence Erlbaum Associates.

# 19 My American Academia
## At Home and Abroad

*Mohanalakshmi Rajakumar*

## INTRODUCTION

The category of "immigrant" has many connotations, many of which revolve around a person's voluntary exile from his or her country for a brighter professional and personal future abroad. Within the context of this essay, I use the term *foreign-born faculty*, which is more neutral than immigrant or foreigner, yet the term still alludes to the outsider status. The *foreign* in foreign-born faculty is an important distinction and one I discuss, alongside notions of migration and immigration, as central to the way in which faculty, and especially I, constructed notions of *self* in relation to students and native faculty at various American academic institutions.

The foreign-born faculty member's experience of marginalization resonates with those of other minority faculty at academic institutions. Both groups "experience the academy differently than their White counterparts" (Johnsrud & Sadao, 1998, p. 324). Even at a research university in the diverse state of Hawai'i, which has no ethnic majority, Johnsrud and Sadao's study found that issues of difference persisted in keeping with minority faculty experiences elsewhere, including "ethnocentrism . . . on the part of White administrators and faculty . . . [and] the discriminatory behavior they experience as minorities" (p. 324). In this sense, Penka Skachkova's (2000, p. 15) suggestion that understanding the experiences of a foreign-born professor in American academia is a microcosm of "the politics of ethnicities" can help further define the position of female ethnic faculty in American universities. Academia, she explained, for the foreign-born professor, is much like an immigrant's experience in America at large.

The rules for professional success are often the same as those for the personal development of immigrant identity: assimilate and get along. Foreign-born faculty are more likely to blend in if they can decrease their "foreignness," be it in dressing, speech, or action. The irony of this expectation is that the idea of assimilation is contrary to the core principles of the academy—a place of learning that would appear to promote difference and differentiation, rather than eliminate or decrease them. Colleges and universities are gendered and racialized and are constructed around dominant knowledge systems. These include systems such as canonical literature,

224    *Mohanalakshmi Rajakumar*

which by default privilege Eurocentric and predominantly White world-views (Mayuzumi, 2011). In such a system, non-White scholars consistently report the marginalization of their work. Their research is often published in specialized journals or funded through special interest groups, which means their work is seen as being niche, rather than mainstream. Such categorization is a form of essentialism. The exception to such marginalization is the work of foreign-born faculty in the sciences, which has a much higher representation of foreign-born faculty working in research-related roles, as high as 54% for engineering, as compared to the 32% teaching in the social sciences (Lin, Pearce, & Weirong, 2009). While the sciences may have a greater representation of foreign-born faculty, the rate at which they are promoted or given tenure still lags behind that of White faculty (Lin, Pearce, & Weirong, 2009).

## Look and Sound the Part: Accent and Dress in the Classroom

The impossibility of the task for foreign-born professors to mainstream echoes the challenges faced by all immigrants in their everyday lives. Expectations to eliminate differences in accent, dress, or food preference are commonplace for those wishing to blend into the way their peers socialize or present themselves. Even if they manage to surmount these challenges, other faculty or students may still perceive them as different because of physical factors. Hutchison, Quach, and Wiggan (2009) describe the self that emerges from this constant negotiation as the "academic cosmopolite identity," and note that in this process, the linguistic and social characteristics of foreign-born faculty evolve towards the mainstream dominant identity, which includes American speech, dress, and social activities. In essence, the pressure is on the minority faculty members to adapt or conform. Even in an overseas setting, such as branch campuses of American universities in the Middle East, for example, students who learn English as a second language still complained about the accents of professors who were outside the expected American or British pronunciations. Research shows that a professor's accent often comes up in formal teaching assessments (Hutchison, Quach, & Wiggan, 2006).

The academy is a microcosm for understanding inequality and marginalized perspectives, whereby faculty and students become disoriented outside their home settings, as is the case with American branch campuses abroad. In such spaces, everyone in the classroom has to grapple with differences in teaching and learning styles, as well as curriculum and assessment" (Hutchison & Wiggan, 2009).

## LESSONS FROM MY FATHER

Because I immigrated to the United States at a young age with my parents, the lines between identities, communities, and self-perceptions have always been unclear for me. My father's journey in academia as a scholar in the sciences, however, fulfilled many of the research findings for foreign-born faculty as reported in the research across this book. As a postdoctoral research colleague, he experienced the range of challenges including differential treatment, questions about credibility, ethnocentrism, and a sterile social environment. Through his experiences, we as a family also underwent the identity crisis of having left India with a nationality but arriving in America as ethnic minorities. So imprinted in my father's mind was our Indianness that it took 15 years before any of us applied for American citizenship, living instead as foreigners in our adopted home. This disconnection between one's primary identity and new surrounding is not uncommon among immigrants because insular communities of some ethnic groups demonstrate the extreme response of clinging to one's heritage (Skachkova, 2007).

Unable to navigate the pitfalls of American academia, my father considered entering industry instead. This meant his moving away from teaching and into conducting clinical trials and research. In his twilight years, despite having a PhD from an Indian institution, he enrolled in a master's program. The completion of an American graduate degree from a well-known private university may have afforded him more opportunities in the time before his retirement than the previous 30 years as a foreign-born PhD.

## MY TURN IN THE AMERICAN ACADEMIA

Being an Indian-born scholar in the United States, and then an American-educated academic working abroad, has led to much introspection on my part in the ways in which identity politics shape faculty and student experiences in the classroom. The idea of being a "person of color" is not something I was born with in India but, rather, is conferred on me by society. Other South Asian faculty members have noted a similar trend in the American racial landscape, where much of race relations are defined through Blackness and Whiteness. Being Brown, or in between the dominant threads of Black and White, means others are confused about where to position you. As Nina Asher (2005, p. 166) explained, "in the United States, based only on my appearance, I may be variously construed as a Latina, an immigrant, a non–English speaker . . . I began identifying myself as a 'person of color' and a 'South Asian woman,' identities I had not needed in India."

The notion of subject making, and understanding Otherness, became central to my experience within the academy, as I understood the influence of others' perceptions of me, as compared to how I viewed myself. I struggled to establish myself as a legitimate academic citizen, frequently dealing with questions about my ability that rose because of my race and gender.

## Questions of Origin

"Where are you from?" is a constant refrain for foreign-born faculty, and in my case, the question was complicated with a history of more than 10 years of living in the United States, many of these during my adolescent years. If I chose to respond with "Florida," for example, the inquirer, usually someone of Anglo-Saxon background would smile and say, "No, where are you *really* from?" The constant reference to racial or ethnic category is a reminder of one's position as an outsider in an otherwise homogeneous, hegemonic space. Despite being from a so-called model minority group—that of South Asian heritage—this label does more to reinforce an Asian faculty member's minority status than create space for more diversity. Recognizing and singling out Asians with a positive stereotype for being a high-functioning minority group assumes that minorities in general are not naturally achievers—it carries the implicit assumption that the other minority groups, including Blacks and Latinos, as homogenous, and that underperforming is the group standard (Mayuzumi, 2011). By comparison, Asian Americans are the well-behaved minority who are "good, uncomplaining, hardworking and therefore successful" (Asher, 2005, p. 169). In their ability to be compliant, produce, and go along with the mainstream, the stereotype actually undermines the Asian American scholar's ability to challenge either the academy or the dominant narrative of immigration: their voices are limited "as critics of such oppressive forces as racism and ethnocentrism and their participation as agents of transformation in the larger social context" (Asher, 2005, p. 169).

## Gender and Foreignness for Female Asian Faculty

Based on my personal experience, foreign-born female professors constitute another important subgroup because of the constraints unique to their position as minorities and women. They are often junior faculty and paid less than their male counterparts because they teach in the humanities. They are typically not full professors, and often unlikely to get tenure. When compared to foreign-born male faculty, foreign-born female faculty report feeling the brunt of classroom politics. Their credibility is questioned more than men's is. Their respective positions within the academy and the White, Eurocentric nation-state, however, are often mirrors for each other.

International faculty may face similar challenges in being silenced or sidelined in favor of more mainstream genres in their disciplines. For female faculty of Asian descent, in particular, the stereotype is that of a youngish persona—one that other faculty find difficult to grant academic authority. Partly for this reason, they experience specific challenges related to gender stereotypes about Asian culture. Their small physical size often means that they are mistaken as students by other their own students as well as faculty, and their physical appearance is often glamorized and sexualized by both peers and students (Mayuzumi, 2011). I myself have often been mistaken for a student, not only by undergraduate students but by faculty as well. Once, while holding a senior administrative position at a well-respected university, a guest speaker at an event thought a student was flirting with me. "No, she's my dean," the embarrassed student explained. "When I went to school, our deans didn't look like that," the much older gentleman said with a chuckle. Comments about dress, appearance, and femininity are very common in relation to Asian women faculty, along with labels that assess these aspects such as "adorable," "cute," or "exotic" (Hune, 2011, p. 321). Many faculty report being called inappropriate endearments such as "dear" or "honey" by male students while handing back assignments (Skachkova, 2007). Although these direct phrases were never said to me, I do remember arriving at a class on a Florida campus, in the flush of spring when temperatures were already skyrocketing. "I'm hot," I explained, fanning myself with whatever object was nearby. "She's hot," a male student in the front row snickered under his breath. Naively, not catching his double entendre, I repeated, "I'm hot. He doesn't believe me." Only on repeating his phrase aloud did I realize that it could be interpreted as being a sexual innuendo. Embarrassed by being so obtuse, I turned back to the board and got on with class. This was an early and memorable instance when I became aware of my gendered and sexual status in the classroom.

I had another encounter that touched on my femininity and gendered position as a female instructor during mediation with a student, my department chair, and a student affairs administrator. We tried to explain to him why interrupting and challenging me during class was disruptive. "On the first day, the girls said you hated me," he said. "But I told them no, she loves me. I knew we had something special." His comments alarmed and yet informed me because I now understood that for him, as a nontraditional student in his late 20s, class was more than a learning opportunity. Our interactions were a chance for him to exert his masculinity in the presence of a similar-aged female. I had been wracking my brain for the difference between the all-female literature section I had in the morning that semester and the mostly male technical writing session I taught in the late afternoon. For me, having never encountered such a blatant reference to gender before in the classroom, the discussion turned on a lightbulb for me.

## Foreignness in the Humanities

Foreign-born faculty in the humanities report feeling that their nationality and subject interests are twinned by their peers and students. They occupy the space of the informant, which means that they are expected to be experts on their countries in a particular area of study, be it language, literature, or culture. Their situation is one of a double stigma in which they report feeling discrimination because of both their gender and their discipline. Their academic interests are often considered "not legitimate" or that their publications are marginal. In an effort to recognize the scholarship of these faculty, the advent of Area Studies has in many ways set nonmainstream interests to one side (Mayuzumi, 2011). Ethnic literature, women's studies, and Black studies are seen as separate from the curriculum and optional, and often serve as elective courses rather than as core elements of the curriculum.

228 *Mohanalakshmi Rajakumar*

The other major stereotype female faculty face, and which is not particular to foreign-born faculty, is the expectation that they will embody the more feminine aspects of faculty roles. Female faculty are expected to be more nurturing advisors and to offer sympathy and empathy to undergraduate students. Female faculty members are also seen as mentors and role models for other underrepresented groups in their departments. The contradiction many report is often between the official evaluations of their work by the institution and the perception-based evaluations by students. As a foreign-born female reared in American academia, I have been long conscious of my having to straddle this double divide. I am confronted by the gap between how I see myself and how others perceive me every time I step into the classroom.

Another early and memorable instance of being confronted by a dual identity was when I was teaching a section of American literature as a graduate student and posed a question, using myself up as an example. I was not prepared, however, for what I would learn: "For example," I asked the twenty or so students, "How would you classify me? American or Indian?" "You're really extroverted," a blonde girl in the front row said. "So I would say you're American. Because Asians don't talk as much." The comment took me aback. I never thought of my personality as an indication of nationality. The student was revealing her assumptions about Asians, especially Asian women. Shirley Hune (2011, p. 307) explained that this is understood as "appropriate behavior for an Asian American female, namely, being passive or "accommodating and demure"—behaviors she terms a "lotus blossom" stereotype. Coming as it did in my very first course as a graduate teaching assistant, this comment was a sign of student perceptions that would be reinforced during my later years in the academy.

## Race, Gender, and Teaching

I have also experienced both anger and pride when confronting students' racial notions of professorship when I became an adjunct faculty member at various American branch campuses in the Middle East. As a PhD holder, I found myself filling in for extra sections of core curriculum requirements for institutions that had larger than expected enrollments. My status as visiting professor or lecturer meant that I was on uneven ground in comparison with the other mostly Caucasian American faculty of the branch campuses. This overseas teaching, however, became my third cycle of coming to grips with the disconnection between the public and private perceptions of my scholarly identity. In a region where most people from the Indian subcontinent were cooks, maids, nannies, or drivers, every time I walked into a classroom with my American accent and Western clothing, to students, I was a monkey in a suit who reacted similarly to the White male students resisting or challenging the authority of non-White faculty in America. Only on this campus, these students were mostly of Arab and South Asian heritage—something I thought we shared in common and would help us establish a greater rapport. I never gave thought to my heritage as being problematic when moving to the Middle East; after all, I was closer to my birthplace than ever before and in a society that held gender roles and food preferences that were very similar to those of my family. What I did not know at the time, however, was that the migratory patterns of labor in the Arabian Gulf, in particular, had not changed with the rest of the world; it certainly did not mimic the transition from working class to intellectuals for Asians as seen in the United States. Most of the unskilled migrant labor putting up the skyscrapers, universities, hospitals, malls, and stadiums across the Arabian Gulf have been, and continue to be, from South Asia. Additionally, the drivers, cooks, and nannies, which most households, expatriate or national, rely on for day-to-day services, such as transportation, errands, child care, or meals, are from Sri Lanka, Pakistan, or India. By being a South Asian woman, it was assumed that I was either a maid or a cook, or possibly spouse to an Indian man because of the prevalence of those roles for Indian women. For many of my students who grew up with an Indian nanny, I was the first professional Indian woman they met. So, there I was again, for the second time in my life and, unbeknownst to me, defying a particular category as someone born abroad, educated in the United States, and working in a profession that defied the local convention.

While in the Arabian Gulf—and working as an American expatriate—I happened to meet the ruler of the country during one of the university's official functions. When it came time to shake his hand, he mentioned casually: "You're Indian, am I right?" I had no way of knowing that this was the frame in which everyone—not only Arabs—would understand my features in my new home. "Yes," I agreed—because, after all, that's what my parents had instilled in me, and Indianness was central to my core identity. "I think you will like it here," he said with a broad smile. Then I moved on because it was someone else's turn to greet him. I thought very little of this interaction, other than of his kindness in thinking of a way to make meaningful chitchat. In the months and years to come, however, these few moments presented a filter from which I could understand the shock, confusion, and sometimes violent reaction people of all ages have to my presence in academic institutions.

The most virulent challenges to my authority were from male students. Their inability to accept authority from a young-looking minority-status woman suggests that even in the absence of White students in a classroom, American institutions perpetuate a notion of Eurocentrism that cannot be evaded by foreign-born professors, even when teaching abroad. My authenticity, power, and legitimacy were challenged in classes with outspoken males, even in cases where female students outnumbered them. The ability of a student to challenge a professor's authority has been documented in Shirley Hune's (2011) study in a process she calls "rebuking." This term is useful in defining the challenges issued to my deadlines, course policies, or other pedagogical strategies. Over the course of a semester, it was not unusual for one particular male student to emerge as the challenger. My assignments were termed to be "high school-ish," answers to quizzes were contested, and explanations for assignment deadlines questioned. These types of challenges were rarely reported by other female colleagues and never from White European or American male colleagues. The hostility expressed toward my asserting authority in class revealed the stereotypes male students had, not only about the discipline of the literature but also about my role as an instructor.

"This is English class," one of the most vocal students said during a business writing course. "There are no right or wrong answers; we get to have dialogue." I explained that dialogue did not include interrupting me, the instructor, while I was talking. In this particular course, the male's extroverted and aggressive challenging of my course policies—that after fifteen minutes from the start of class, a student was considered absent—effectively silenced the female students in the room who were, in fact, the majority. ("My notebook was here at the start of class, so I was here" was his reply.) The conflict between this particular student and me intimidated all the other learners, more introverted males included, to the extent that they sat back and watched, waiting to see who would be the victor. Only when the departmental chair was brought in for mediation, and this student eventually restrained, did the other students begin to participate. Ultimately, *my* ground rules were reinforced by an external agent: a White, male, and North American authority figure. Because he was a representative of the institution, his support gave me back my credibility and authority for the rest of the course.

The other dramatic example of the outspoken male dynamic occurred when I was teaching two sections of the same course, ten minutes apart, in two adjacent rooms. The situation was ripe for a social experiment, although I could not appreciate it at the time. In the first class was an outspoken male who often came to the wrong conclusions during class discussions about assigned texts, yet he persisted in raising his hand and volunteering. Everything in class was seen as a negotiation. Deadlines were fluid. He would often raise his hand and say, "Why?" when I explained an assignment. The next class, occurring immediately after this one, was full of vibrant and high-achieving female students. Teaching the exact same material lent a slight déjà vu air to the section, except for one remarkable difference—the two men in this class were largely silent. When they did contribute, it was often with a diffidence to clarify a particular point or expand on a part of the conversation. At the time, I remember being only grateful for having the "good" class second. In hindsight, I can see the gendered responses at play and understand how to defuse such situations for the future.

While dealing with difficult or combative students is not pleasant, as I can attest to, the presence of female faculty members is essential to the development of female students, whether in American institutions at home

My American Academia  231

or abroad. The semesters in which I had combative male students directly challenge my authority within the classroom are among the most intense periods of my personal development as an academic. My ability to persevere, correct behavior, and garner the support of the institution was essential to supporting such students in their own learning and development.

## Lessons Learned: The Need for Institutional Recruitment and Support

There is much academic institutions can do to support their foreign-born faculty, including their recruitment efforts. Institutions wishing to support foreign-born faculty in their pedagogy as well as research should offer opportunities to discuss the ways in which both instructors and learners approach their understanding of identity from a specific standpoint and location. Facilitating such discussion amongst faculty members in monthly meetings is a good start. Sharing experiences about how the dominant group and foreign-born professors' experiences are differentiated and how that intersects with various identity markers can help colleagues be more supportive of international faculty. Having such conversations inside the classroom, across many different types of courses, can help students to become more aware of their implicit biases and thereby equip them with the skills to understand plural or hybrid identities.

The most challenging aspect of being foreign-born faculty, one's diversity, can also be a considerable strength in the classroom. This potential can be unlocked by a mentoring system or an international faculty club, which could be interdisciplinary across departments or colleges.

## Professional and Personal Networks

Establishing informal networking opportunities is also critical for foreign-born faculty, because it can alleviate professional and personal isolation. Lee and Janda (2006) explain that representation alone is not the entire solution for foreign-born faculty: "the increased numbers of minority professors alone does not ensure a fair and equitable learning environment" (p. 27). Institutions must also provide formal and informal means through which faculty can mingle to alleviate feelings of discomfort, tension, or conflict. In my third year at an American institution abroad, I was fortunate enough to have an office next to the faculty kitchen. Consequently, several times a day, as I prepared cups of tea, I was able to engage in short conversations with a variety of faculty and staff. These seemingly superficial conversations helped establish relationships with other members of the university and presented problem solving opportunities for nonacademic issues, including school applications for children and invitations for social events, which rarely presented themselves when I was in an office at the opposite end of the hall the previous two years. While the distance between these two offices was not

# 232 *Mohanalakshmi Rajakumar*

even 100 meters, I rarely made the trek to the kitchen or had meaningful conversations when in the office at the end of the hallway. Only in my third year at the university did I feel more a part of the community and have opportunities to see familiar faces on a regular basis, outside the bimonthly department meetings.

Foreign-born faculty tend to be more productive than their U.S.-born counterparts (Corley & Sabharwal, 2007), which underlines the value of their work to their academic institutions. Foreign-born faculty are also generally more adaptable and suited to a diverse teaching style because they often have two or more cultures from which to draw. The flexibility and adaptation skills they have developed over time serve them well in the classroom when dealing with a variety of students' abilities or subject matter. One can interpret the mission of education to include teaching students the possibilities for personal and social transformation across the race, culture, gender, class, and location. Instead of existing in binaries or oppositions, learners and teachers create a pluralistic third space, which is more representative of a growing heterogeneous population in the society. Thus, personal and professional development for students, as well as their faculty, is connected.

The makeup of the global population is in flux, as people who may not have interacted before are increasingly integrated through migration and technology. As more American universities sign agreements to offer their degrees—or perhaps, more important, their training—to new populations of students abroad, the diversity of the American academy will become a tangible way through which traditional assumptions about gender, race, and ethnicity are challenged for a new generation of students and faculty.

## REFERENCES

Asher, N. (2005). Brown in black and white: On being a South Asian woman academic. In G. Li & G. H. Beckett (Eds.), *Strangers of the academy: Asian women scholars in higher education* (pp. 163–168). Sterling, VA: Stylus.

Corley, E. A., & Sabharwal, M. (2007). Foreign-born academic scientists and engineers: Producing more and getting less than their U.S.-born peers? *Research in Higher Education, 48*(8), 909–940.

Johnsrud, L. K., & Sadao, K. C. (1998). The common experience of "Otherness": Ethnic and racial minority faculty. *The Review of Higher Education, 21*(4), 315–342.

Hune, S. (2011). Asian American women faculty and the contested space of the classroom: Navigating student resistance and (re)claiming authority and their rightful place. *Diversity in Higher Education, 9*, 307–335.

Hutchison, C. B., Quach, L., & Wiggan, G. (2006, Fall). The interface of global migrations, ESL teaching and learning, and academic cosmopolitan identity development. *Forum on Public Policy Online*, 2006 Edition. Retrieved October 27, 2014, 2011 from http://www.forumonpublicpolicy.com/archive06/hutchison.pdf

Hutchison, C. B., & Wiggan, G. (2009). The intersections of globalization, education, and the minority experience. In G. Wiggan & C. B. Hutchison (Eds.),

*Global issues in education: Pedagogy, policy, practice, and the minority experience* (pp. 1–20). Lanham, MD: Rowman and Littlefield.

Lee, G., & Janda, L. (2006). Successful multicultural campus: Free from prejudices toward minority professors. *Multicultural Education, 14*, 27–30.

Lin, Z., Pearce, R., & Weirong, W. (2009). Imported talents: Demographic characteristics, achievement and job satisfaction of foreign born full time faculty in four year American colleges. *Higher Education, 57*(6), 703–721.

Mayuzumi, K. (2011). *Seeking possibilities in a transnational context: Asian women faculty in the Canadian academy* (Unpublished doctoral dissertation). University of Toronto, Ontario, Canada.

Skachkova, P. (2000). *The ethnic teaches back: Identity formation and academic status of foreign–born women academics in the U.S.* (Unpublished doctoral dissertation). University of New York, Buffalo, NY.

Skachkova, P. (2007). Academic careers of immigrant professors in the U.S. *Higher Education, 53*(6), 697–738.

# 20 Musings of a Foreign-Born Philosopher in the American Academy

## Come è duro calle / lo scendere e 'l salir per l'altrui scale[1]

### Lucio Angelo Privitello

**PRELUDE**

In *The Divine Comedy* (Paradise, Canto XVII, lines 58–60), Dante Alighieri mused as follows: "*Come è duro calle / lo scendere e 'l salir per l'altrui scale*" ("You will come to learn how bitter as salt is the bread of others, and how callous and hard is going up and down stairs that were never your own" [my translation]). In this statement, Dante presciently addressed the future lives of many a foreign-educated professor.

I speak and write as a hybrid: born to immigrant parents and grandparents and raised, educated, and apprenticed in Sicily and Italy, while completing my university studies in the United States. Therefore, I am not foreign-born through and through, although in every sense, I was raised and educated in my most formative years in Italy. To find myself in the States was a dramatic detour and a self-imposed exile. Speaking from the truest sense of a *forma mentis*, I have experienced the "pedagogical shock" (Hutchison, 2005) that immigrants live through as educators: to this day, I strive to share, and somehow translate, very peculiar foreign-born familial, linguistic, pedagogical, and apprenticeship experiences. These sociocultural threads color my work as an educator, and the history and memory of these threads form the struggle and, when pedagogically successful, the graceful balance between forgetting and remembering. This is my voice, my cultural slant, and my attitude.

As far as challenges to professional success go, my hybrid nature takes on what Bruno Latour sees as a "preliminary purification, a divided separation, and a progressive reblending" (Latour, 1993, p. 78). In the classroom, this hybrid nature is presented to students as a distinct style, from the cultural to the sartorial. I use my language skills to access and quote from various foreign texts, and at appropriate moments in class discussions I use sayings from the Sicilian dialect. Because of my areas of specialty in philosophy and literature, I can work from the texts in their language of origin and compare my translations with the translations we are using in the class. Along with

## Musings of a Foreign-Born Philosopher in the American Academy 235

sharing stories from my years as a student and the richness of the bonds with extraordinary cultural conditions in Italy, I comfortably dress in Italian high fashion. My appearance pulls the students into the greater reality behind the tailored silks; it compels students into the appreciation of great workmanship and style behind the culture I project.

This condensed overview sets the tone and raises a few issues at stake in the experiences of foreign-born, or, in my specific case, a foreign-educated scholar. The themes and concepts I mention within this chapter are forgetting and remembering, boundary conditions of memory and hope, reception of host institutions and reception ability, apprenticeships and community, and the wholeness of learning and living; commuter culture; the figure of the storyteller and their imaginarium; *terribilità* and *sprezzatura*; the cultural industry; cultural tourists versus cultural intoxication; apprenticeships in creativity; the union of learning, working, and living; pedagogy of the nuance; regained foreignness; location of fantasy; and autobiography and imagined biography. These are lived issues I have processed and work from as a foreign-educated scholar. I must say that I have found success both pedagogically and professionally in my 23 years of teaching in the American classroom.

### Of the Past—Luggage

If the ties that bind one to the history, ongoing relations, and memories of a life remain active (as I deeply feel them), then the foreign born and foreign educated carry two substantial pieces of luggage: that of forgetting and that of remembering. I have struggled with this since I left Italy. Because both are delicately important, care must be taken not to exchange the contents of one for the other. Yet, as the immigrant carries this mental luggage around, both arms will always be sore from feeling its weight through airports, train stations, and structures of the academe. The craft of teaching, as I have experienced it, involves the handling of these weights through the spaces of autobiography and imagined biography.[2] Often, much of this luggage could remain unpacked, depending on the abilities of the host institution and students (some being more international than others); hence, even if remembered, some of the luggage might as well have been forgotten.

Nonreceptivity and loss are major hurdles I have experienced when sharing through the craft of teaching. I am always interested in sharing, and asking for those moments from the students where the gain of, and from, experiences marks a custody of what is now past. If properly used, this custody of our losses can serve as another key to enlivening and inspiring the classroom. The loss of a way of life and culture is difficult to share in full. I can begin to create a bond with a class if I recount moments when issues or texts call for the wider aura of cultural placement. I must always ask myself, "How much do I allow for my baroque, expansive, and parabolic

## 236  *Lucio Angelo Privitello*

flavor to invade the host language? How far can I mold a syntax from a voice that desires to speak out without overcomposing the space of meaning? Where is the balance to avoid alienating or marginalizing students, or reader?" This very chapter, which deals with encounters with host institutions, reveals examples of this type of problem. It is about the delicate conditions of possibility that the life-worlds of old have bestowed, along with the cultural opportunity that the new grants. It is important not to betray one's becoming.

## A Brief History of a Great Beauty and Its Deep Impact

Being raised within a family of Italian immigrants, along with being educated and living in Sicily and Italy through the formative years of my education, has caused deep impressions—so much so that the lifeworld of those years act as a continuous guiding track of my current life. These impressions remain strong for me even after the majority of my years have now been spent away from my roots. These impressions are present through moments of quiet reflection, within the struggle and practice of creating a vibrant pedagogical venue, in advising, in writing, and through my time as chair of my program. I can feel how the wheels of my foreign education tend to, or even crave to, slip back into the tracks of that deeper, richer, and, perhaps, more romantic cultural experience in which living, learning, and creating was one long and simultaneous apprenticeship. It was also seen as such by the community. The community is a crucial ingredient of wholeness and a living continuity. By this, I do not mean the isolated community of academics; I mean the everyday urban community that lived, worked, and were connected to each other in town. There was a natural type of respect and understanding, something I miss in the present situation. As compared to this, therefore, institutions in my host country appear to be their own oases: The rest is desert. Some of my painful moments of remembrance are because of the impossibility to reproduce this type of history. The impossibility is because of distances, unshared histories, and the rush of a commuter culture. The remains of a counterculture that I dreamed would cross the thresholds of my classrooms have sadly become the rush of a commuter culture.

## Telling Their/There Stories—As a Foreign-Born Instructor

The figure of the storyteller is a clear and real way that, from my particular experience, I best relate to students. Of course, there is the daily work of scholarship, close readings, papers, projects, corrections, drafts, and examples, but all of this is greater when surrounded by life lessons that were handed down from cultural details and splendid goals and hopes. I have done this both with my art background (with visual examples) and with my philosophy background. Of course, the difficulty is always that in the arts and humanities, when very recognizable names for those within the Italian

# Musings of a Foreign-Born Philosopher in the American Academy 237

system, such as Guido Calogero, Luigi Russo, Benedetto Croce, and Achille Funi, to mention a few, fall flat, until a thumbnail information session is given. Fortunately, what remains vital is that we, foreign-trained professors, are the ones with exotic and alluring stories and that we are the ones that can bend language and life to the edge of expressive collapse. This can be used in a positive sense to support the particular lessons or issues that are presented in a course, especially when used from the joy of a non-arrogant memory.

The foreign-born or foreign-educated professor steps back into the tradition of the bard, replete with an imaginarium full of possibilities. In fact, we sometimes have no option but continue to travel with an imaginarium, because that engenders possible success. Once these small legends or lifestories are performed, known and circulate, students look forward to the exotic quality of the course; through the grapevine, they anticipate the telling (descriptions) and the toll (appreciation and values) that follow our legends. This is a most galvanizing example that I experience; this is where the magic of the imaginarium takes students by surprise and becomes a lifegiving offer. At its best, as I have experienced it, students come to class already knowing some of the details and stories and hope to hear more. Word of mouth works wonders in creating a collective arena. This is the re-creating of the aura of intimacy and simplicity. Description and appreciation serve as a way to measure forgetting and remembering, hope and memory. In a busy student world, these connections are often lost to the hurried and unhistorical. It is, as I see it, my vocation to slow things down for this type of growth. One cannot reproduce the experience in words alone, so a particular pedagogical experience that I work from is the need (and ability) to support issues, examples, and problems with a host of sources in the arts, humanities, media, and film, thus rendering the imaginarium replete in a baroque atmosphere. In this rendering, the teacher becomes part of the picture and takes a hold of the chance for creativity and engagement. What I firmly feel is that the pedagogical process for the foreign born and foreign educated are similar to skills required for operatic scenography.

## Acculturation Experiences

A foreign education, along with the lifestyle and the deep familial roots that are a product of a foreign country, can make the reception ability fascinating for students. But this must be seen as integral to the style of teaching. My field (philosophy) lends itself to this integration more easily. I also throw in my visual arts background for good measure. Most get this wholeness. What is most frustrating for me is the ready-made attitudes of detachment of those who hide from foreign cultures and texts, no matter how the host institution pushes a global perspective and cross-cultural savviness. This holding back seems to be a product of the fear of getting too close to the life lessons and ways of life that emerge from the love of culture. Some of those lessons can be

238 *Lucio Angelo Privitello*

devastating, radical, and difficult to master; others call for a change in outlook that then calls for a change in life plans. This is very dramatic and, for many, too dangerous. This protection against culture is due to that major and first foreignness: high culture. Many students have no time, or hope, for higher culture. This holding back acts as a ricochet and returns as an unanswered question for the foreign educated: I am teaching you here, but where does this teaching come from, and what is its aim? I must teach from how I was encultured; I must share a cultural heritage. These three dimensions (past, present, and future) are difficult to focus as one, when the loss of remembrance and the actual will to forget (refusing to sense actual loss) are at play. The sense of time, based on the race into futurity, has pulled the present out from under the past. The time signature lento has become prestissimo. A goal of mine in each class is to wed the dimensions of cultural time. Working toward this is difficult. To experience this recoiling from high culture remains a disappointment that could be called, but is mostly felt as, a "regained foreignness." But I use this as a perspective into the dimensions. This is because of how my particular learning experiences were a long and simultaneous apprenticeship, which was part and parcel of a connection within the community.

The acculturation experience is a particular kind of formation. It is where various dimensions and layers of cultures lend richness to the socioeconomic life, even if that life remains surrounded by simple living. The rich dimensions and layers of culture, along with the natural tendency to share and impart a given ideal life, or what Dilthey (2002, p. 290) would call *habitus*, is lost in the labyrinth of a racing immanence. In such an environment, the educator's art or *apprenticeships in creativity* is only fragmentarily realized. This is because the sense of time is not there because lento has become prestissimo. This creates the loss of the "nexus of lived experience, expression, and understanding," for the very simple fact that "we cannot understand objective spirit through reason, but must go back to the structural nexus of life-units that extends itself into communities" (Dilthey, 2002, pp. 109, 172).

In my particular experience while in Italy, for example, the life of the creative artist, while simple and perhaps romantic, was still seen as emblematic of single-mindedness, discipline, and courage. Racy immanence, or information-driven commodity, could not compete, and was impossible to register against the transcendent evening strolls in piazza after a long day in the studio. Time itself seemed to have been suspended, and I lived in those exacting moments as if in an eternal now. What such a *bottega* (studio) is for the artistic process and apprenticeships, Bottega Veneta is for fashion: inherited swagger. It is the swagger from within culture and creativity. I believe this is the most important thing that I show my students: the deeper accent or style of foreignness. Whether the humanities are fading or not, apprenticeships make for a shared form of life, with particular emphasis in an "essential philosophy," as Karl Jaspers would call it. These formed the bookends to my enculturation. Learning, working, and living functioned as "coexistence and fulfillment" (Todorov, 2001, pp. 139–142). In retrospect,

## Musings of a Foreign-Born Philosopher in the American Academy  239

and now cut from those shores, and that form of life, these experiences and memories make up the beveled edges of *terribilità* and *sprezzatura*.[3] They are a tool and *credo* of my pedagogical approach, and a cross between a Nietzschean unhistorical and superhistorical. Such are the pleasures and hopes of what I work from: the pedagogy of the nuance.

### Pedagogy of the Nuance

To artistically depict the shading a cloud (*nuance nuée*) is relatively simple, compared to unraveling the nuances of a theory, a storyline of a course, the singularity of a student's talents, or the uniqueness of a pedagogue. How can the split between making and observing, reading and writing, reflecting and creating, and forgetting and remembering become twilled, allowing the work of a course to be fully experienced?

I struggle when trying to unfold a text, issues, or problems in a class. The goal is to have students experience the necessary foreignness of the text (of the Other) without assuming the position of hurried cultural tourists. My foreign education allows for a way to live with a text, and not forget about its nuance, its seductive creative engagement, its foreignness. This is possible because I can feel the text in its cultural atmosphere. This atmosphere is mostly imported in a host classroom, but it needs to be slowly shaded, nuanced, and made to come to life. This is not the quick cruise in the hurried tempo of managing information. But how does one teach such nuances? How does one teach from and as an "apprenticeship in creativity"? The main problem one encounters is the lack of similar paths, or shared stories of those paths that lead into the learning arena. My approach is guided by the desire to create the magic that was once lived. This does happen, and it takes a sustained performance, a complete scenography.

A course is a weave of lives: That is exactly how it was framed in my experiences. This is what I mean by a scenography. It is difficult to experience this weave without a common loom. Building the loom is therefore a first priority. It is crucial that in an encounter with a course experience, an intervention with the process of creativity reconstructs the steps of the encounter as creativity itself. This counts as reflexivity in learning, and reflexivity in teaching.

I believe that, sometimes, a kind of intimidating experience is important to set up for students in a way that helps captures the vibrant pedagogy of the foreign educated and the foreign born. Such an experience can be striven for by engaging in the conditions under which discoveries can be reported. This is what I mean by the pedagogy of the nuance. Pedagogy as art and practice of the nuance turns an individual toward the relationship of the lived encounter:

> For any sort of aesthetic activity of perception to exist, a certain physiological precondition is indispensable: *intoxication*. Intoxication must

240  *Lucio Angelo Privitello*

first have heightened the excitability of the entire machine: no art results before that happens. All kinds of intoxication . . . have the power to do this: . . . sexual excitement, feasting, contest, of the brave deed, of victory, of extreme agitation, cruelty, destruction, the intoxication of spring, . . . finally the intoxication of the will . . . of an overloaded and distended will.

From out of this feeling one gives to things, one *compels* them to take, [a] procedure [called] *idealizing*. (Nietzsche, 1968, §8, p. 71)

This *idealizing* is the greatest and most important aspect to reproduce. A cultural intoxication (one may add this to the Nietzschean list of intoxications) is what the training and memory of my foreign education and pedagogical creed brings. Only by setting up this engaging condition for the possibility of a "prose of contact" can a text, lesson, or course surface as a pedagogical vision. *Pedagogical vision is sight/site of the yet un-scene'd.* Once again, it is scenography. It is the drive to train and direct students to create the scenography of their own cultural life. Indeed, it is a sight, and a site of what is not yet a complete scene, but a planning of one. Here is exactly where pedagogy approaches scenography. This captures and retains my foreign-educated experience most fully. The style of teaching that emerges from this is one that imparts lessons, but more importantly, one that shares approaches to a life lived with the texts and cultural lessons. One must teach students to become scenographers of their cultural lives. This aspect of what it is to teach and learn is most interesting and most rewarding for me.

Although our individual lives are less entwined in the work of teacher and student, examples must be given of how these relations could be. This is one of the most exhausting aspects of sharing a foreign education and a life experience that supported that kind of education. Here is where the art of storytelling, and telling of the enchantment of cultural maturation and lived experience, is paramount. Above and beyond any theory of teaching, what I continue to share is this sensitivity. This sensitivity feels the outcome of a changing individual resource that sets itself in motion qua encounter with texts of pleasure.

Text[s] of pleasure [is] the text that contents, fills, grants euphoria: the text that comes from culture and does not break with it, is linked to a comfortable practice of reading. Text of bliss: the text that imposes a state of loss, the text that discomforts . . . unsettles the reader's historical, cultural, psychological assumptions, the consistency of [their] tastes, values, memories, brings to a crisis [their] relation with language. (Barthes, 1975, p. 14)

My task then, in practice, and in theory, is to make-the-foreign. I allow the state of loss, unsettlement, and in the end, disciplined scenographic re-creation. This is what I have happen on a good day. It is something

## Musings of a Foreign-Born Philosopher in the American Academy 241

that is remembered and shared. It is a movement from "what comes from culture and does not break with it" and matures into what "unsettles the reader's historical, cultural . . . assumptions" (Barthes, 1975, p. 14). Students who remember these moments are quick to say how they are missed when they have completed the course. It is a lesson from personal recollections that I now raise as a backdrop when I seek to make-the-foreign. When planned properly, a course in an academic program addresses part of a life and is carried into other courses and into a plan for a life within a culture. This is when living with the texts and issues does not split into making versus observing but forms an apprenticeship in creativity. In total agreement with Roland Barthes, and from his theoretical stance, the "nuance becomes a principle of allover organization (which covers the totality of the surface) and is not about mere intellectual sophistication" (Barthes, 2005).

What I seek to unfold as a pedagogue that is foreign educated-educated is what Barthes (2005) said he was looking for during the preparation of his courses: "an introduction to living, a guide to life" (p. 11). This process is doubled in the foreign educated or foreign born, for as I have experienced, when planning our courses, we seek that guide first in ourselves, and the find a way to introduce it to our students. The "wish for a great pedagogy of nuance" (as Barthes dreamed) is my wish as well. Barthes (2005, p. 130) asserted that, as educators, we must recognize "the price of the 'bit' . . . [never] denying difference, [but always residing] between being and 'bit.'"

The most positive aspects of being foreign born or educated are the natural tendency to outplay and sidestep old, binary pedagogical management and introduce the novel—the pedagogy of the nuance, a way to baffle paradigms. Within this baffling emerges compelling instruction. The pedagogy of the nuance (or the sensitivity of the many shades within cultural creations and their appreciation) allows the Other to embrace the pitch of their creativity. This is to show them a foreignness within themselves, even as they encounter the foreign one. To do this, one must "preserve the discourse from [the all-too-easy] affirmation, in order to nuance it (towards negation, doubt, interrogation, suspension)" (Barthes, 2005, p. 43). This is the notion of "making-foreign."

The struggle of the foreign-educated can be seen as the detachment between the "life-unit [that] takes pleasure in certain attributes to which its feeling of self adheres" and the "meaning-nexus . . . recognized as reality" (Dilthey, 2002, p. 277). The individual, and the place of the individual in the host community, is loosened to the point of being threadbare—a point where institutions and their histories are born from young experiences. This is felt as detachment, social isolation, and a lack from others' recognition of one's sense of loss. This produces a fissure partly because commonality cannot be grasped in an intellectualized way; it cannot be grasped as an ideal construction or an easy crossing of cultures outside people's life-nexus.

242   *Lucio Angelo Privitello*

## Beyond Forgetting and Remembering

There is danger in remembering as "arrogant memory," and this is where "the whole immense and complicated palimpsest of memory unrolls in a single swoop," as Baudelaire envisioned it and as Barthes (2005, p. 168) explained. I have fought against this pull.

Remembering is only symptomatic when employed as a comparison. There it judges and values by devaluing and comparing enculturations. This is what I have found most stressful when exchanging within a host culture and institutions. The only way that the foreign educated may overcome the arrogance of memory of its history is by "serv[ing] life, [and thus] serv[ing] an unhistorical power" (Nietzsche, 1980, §1, p. 14). I took this lesson of Nietzsche very seriously. This type of overcoming of the arrogance of memory can also be seen as the switch from what Proust called "voluntary memory" to "involuntary memory." Involuntary memory is one of evocation, where habit is suspended, pushed back, and not engaged as a compromise or formula. This is a boon for teaching; it allows for fresh encounters, spontaneity, and creativity. Voluntary memory, as explained by Beckett (1994, p. 4), is "the application of a concordance of the Old Testament of the individual." I found this to be a perfect description of what I was experiencing in my cultural and life nexus experiences. This layer of comparison and infra-textual tracking stands in the way of socialization, because it takes on the measure of success in comparison to previous enculturation, and raises a barrier against the utopian dream of an ideal pedagogical arena. It also slights relations with students and how students (projected outside of the concordance) should interact with the work of educational ideals. This is how one throws the book at them; nothing but frustration piles up in this manner. Yet, old habits are difficult to overcome. Habit is nothing but passive forgetting.

Perhaps no one better than Barthes has understood the need to "make peace with this contradiction" of memory and forgetting; in his series of lectures delivered in 1978 at the Collège de France, he projected how, without arrogant memory (and arrogant forgetting), one might also "suspend the arrogance of discourse" (Barthes, 2005, p. 157). This is a tall order, but one that is life-giving, in the pedagogical sense: I have found that the suspension of the discourse of arrogance was key to the success I experienced in a host institution.


## LESSONS LEARNED

Deep within the latent craft of composing and recomposing the contents of the hybrid nature because of one's foreign training or birth, one must internalize the lesson that Nietzsche left us, that is, to have history serve life. The foreign education of the foreign-educated professor is a nuanced

## Musings of a Foreign-Born Philosopher in the American Academy 243

tool that serves students and creates novel intellectual intersections. As an integral part of one's past, foreign-educated professors cannot act from, or serve the memory of, a lost paradise. Thus, with Nietzsche, we require a touch of the unhistorical—of what he called the "enveloping atmosphere," that "divine animal" that roams happily and refrains from overextending horizons (Nietzsche, 1980, §1, p. 11, § 7, p. 38, § 9, p. 57, and § 5, p. 29). We must forget. What must be shaped from the heritage and from a foreign-born education is an *apprenticeship in creativity*. These are segments of life lessons that would retrofit the current sociocultural nexus and its history.

Detachment and comparisons would only harm and alienate the much-needed intimacy and simplicity of contact. Detachment would distill, or rarefy, the warmth of a prose of contact that enhances the storytelling. When the foreign-educated professor becomes well versed in storytelling and is adept at incorporating pop-culture references and lingo, success comes easier. It is a joy to find a vast storehouse of examples and lessons in the everyday unfolding of pop culture—the contrast to my old-world history works for galvanizing the class atmosphere. The magic of an imaginarium is a scenography that is brought to the classroom if, and only if, foreignness by birth or education or its loss becomes a regained foreignness. The making-foreign is a creation of another time and of new spaces (proliferations).

Were Nietzsche asked to admonish the foreign-educated professor, he would assert that he or she must "have the strength to recast the well known into something never heard before and to proclaim the general so simply and profoundly that one overlooks its simplicity because of its profundity and its profundity because of its simplicity" (Nietzsche, 1980, p. 37).[4]

## A Few Key Points

Through my experiences, and as mentioned so far in this chapter, I can see nine key points that speak to my positive pedagogical moments:

- Locate your fantasy of and for culture and share it.
- Overcome your voluntary, "arrogant memories" and allow for "involuntary memory" and evocation to evolve.
- Create wholeness in your learning and living, in such a way that is seen as a style of the life of the scholar/educator.
- Engage your students in experiences of loss (i.e., make-the-foreign) and work slowly on what emerges.
- Seize the chance for creativity (*apprenticeships in creativity*).
- Maintain simplicity in dialogue to create an encounter of cultural context and content.
- Create y/our story (meaning yours and the collective "our" class story) and become the storyteller of the working-out of the course and its fiction.

244  *Lucio Angelo Privitello*

- Baffle paradigms with humor, and search for the symptoms of your love of culture.
- Paint your exile (if it is felt as one) with forgiveness and re-creation.

In summary, I have learned that we must paint our exiles with forgiveness and re-creation. As with novelistic characters, we must reexperience the joy and radiance of fiction in our endless rereadings, and reexperience the magic of the pedagogical imaginarium, as we become poised between the spaces of autobiography and imagined biography.

## NOTES

1. Alighieri, D. (1932). *The Divine Comedy*, Paradise, Canto XVII, *La Divina Commedia*, Testo Critico della Società Dantesca Italiana. Lines 58–59. Milano: Ulrico Hoepli.
2. The mention of autobiography and imagined biography was a surprising lesson I gained from these reflections. My chapter leads to it as a conclusion. When not torn from stoic forgetting, or, on the other hand, from a grinning remembrance, an autobiography may hold within it the inspired, simple, and hopeful moments of an imagined biography. This is an extremely crucial issue for a pedagogy of the immigrant scholar who lives on one path of life, but can envision the other. One must not live in a half-world. This is a great tool to set loose when engaged in class discussions that handle various clashing perspectives.
3. *Terribilità* is best understood as a fearfulness, awesomeness or dread that is part of an arduous creative undertaking. *Sprezzatura* is, as intended by Baldesar Castiglione's idea of an accomplished courtier, a mastery of overabundance, or a nonchalance in what is difficult, but made to seem effortlessly executed.
4. F. Nietzsche, (1980). *On the Advantages and Disadvantages of History for Life*. Translated by Peter Preuss. Indianapolis: Hackett Publishing Company. Section 6, p. 37.

## REFERENCES

Alighieri, D. (1932). *The Divine Comedy*, Paradise, Canto XVII, *La Divina Commedia*, Testo Critico della Società Dantesca Italiana. Lines 58–60. Milano: Ulrico Hoepli.
Barthes, R. (1975). *The pleasure of the text* (R. Miller, Trans.). New York: Hill and Wang.
Barthes, R. (2005). *The neutral, lecture course at the Collège de France (1977–1978)* (R. E. Krauss & D. Hollier, Trans.). New York: Columbia University Press.
Beckett, S. (1994). *Proust*. New York: Grove Press.
Dilthey, W. (2002). *The formation of the historical world in the human science*. (Selected Works, Vol. III, R. A. Makkreel & J. Scanlon). Princeton: Princeton University Press.
Hutchison, C. (2005). *Teaching in America: A cross-cultural guide for international teachers and their employers*. Dordrecht, The Netherlands: Springer.

## Musings of a Foreign-Born Philosopher in the American Academy 245

Latour, B. (1993). *We have never Been modern* (C. Porter, Trans.). Cambridge: Harvard University Press.

Nietzsche, F. (1968). *Twilight of the idols* (R. J. Hollingdale, Trans.). New York: Penguin Books.

Nietzsche, F. (1980). *On the advantages and disadvantages of history for life* (Peter Preuss, Trans.). Indianapolis: Hackett Publishing Company.

Todorov, T. (2001). *Life in common: An essay in general anthropology* (K. Golsan & L. Golsan). Lincoln: University of Nebraska Press.

# 21 The Unified Voices of Immigrant Professors and Their Cross-Cultural Teaching Lives
## Lessons Learned

*Charles B. Hutchison*

If the reader has traversed this book from the beginning, a few points may be clear: International or immigrant professors (IPs) form a constituency of specialized migrant workers who are confronted with peculiar issues that are distinguishable from other international workers (e.g., Collins, 2008; Thomas & Johnson, 2004). Although they face the expected culture shock as other migrants, they also experience a pedagogical shock once in the classroom (Hutchison, 2005). Such pedagogical shocks often come as a surprise to many, because there is a tacit assumption of the transferability of pedagogical skills across national and cultural borders. International migration, however, involves complex interactions of many cultural, social, economic, institutional, and political factors in ways that are not predictable nor amenable to rational planning (Oliver-Smith & de Sherbinin, 2014); hence, a systematic research on such processes is vital.

In Chapter 1 of this book, broad theoretical issues that shape the world of IPs were discussed. The rest of the book focused on the specific experiences of IPs, mostly by way of theorized narratives. The main purpose of this chapter is to systematically and comparatively illustrate the world of IPs. In reaching this goal, in this chapter the experiences across the narratives are analyzed to thematically demonstrate their issues. In addition, this chapter aims to extend our understanding, and therefore the alleviation of, the initial induction issues immigrant faculty are likely to encounter and how to support them.

If one is not starving for time in the consumption of this chapter, a palatable advice would be to read this chapter in concert with Chapter 1, because the said chapters are brewed in the same crucible.

## THEORETICAL FRAMEWORK

In addressing the issues facing IPs, the lenses of worldview and migration theories are instructive. In addition, phenomenology (as a theory) and third space theory are used to explain the composite experiences of the IPs.

Although more fully addressed in the introductory chapter, the crystallized essences of the noted theories include the following:

- Migrations occur because of needs or personal aspirations but are mitigated by physical barriers or policy issues (Lee, 1966; Ratha & Shaw, 2007).
- Teaching is a cultural activity; therefore, how teachers teach is vital for student achievement (Stigler and Hiebert, 1999).
- People's cultural backgrounds and worldviews influence how they view the world and, consequently, how they learn (Cobern, 1996; Shumba, 1999).
- Cultural paradigms dictate how the world works, what questions should or can be asked, procedures for answering questions (i.e., research methods), what constitutes acceptable hypotheses, and what constitutes acceptable answers (Spector & Lederman, 1990).
- Because knowledge is contextualized within cultural traditions or paradigms, but IPs are not fully familiar with their host culture, they can fall prey to cultural processes (Kuhn, 1962).
- Gender, age, class, and ethnicity are key markers of vulnerability for immigrants (Oliver-Smith & de Sherbinin, 2014).
- Objective truth can only be captured when one is conscious of a phenomenon; therefore, perception is reality, since what is experienced by people is more reliable in predicting human interactions than external reality itself (Husserl, 1907/2010).
- Whenever an individual enters a different context to which they need to adapt, they are compelled to create a new (third) space that is different from one's original (first) knowledge world and the new (second) knowledge world (Bhabha, 1994).

The forces resulting from the interplay of these theories create new realities and redefine new pedagogical and sociocultural worlds for IPs.

Given the detailed discussion in Chapter 1 of how the elements of the theoretical frameworks influence the experiences of IPs, this chapter will focus more heavily on the emergent themes from the analysis of IPs' experiences, with parsimonious treatment of theoretical issues as needed.

## METHOD

As a study, the phenomenological approach was employed to examine the experiential narratives of a selected group of eight IPs. This approach was selected because phenomenology studies the ontological essences of human experiences (Heidegger, 1927/1996) and is concerned with how people perceive the world they live in (Merleau-Ponty, 1946/2013). It was therefore useful in explaining the sociocultural processes that either created challenges

248  *Charles B. Hutchison*

for IPs or helped them to navigate their challenges and become successful in their host countries. Using phenomenology, the pedagogical shocks and successes of IPs were captured and explained as dialogical processes and products.

## Selection of Narratives for Analysis

Regarding the delimitation of the contents of this chapter, two important points are noteworthy: First, the chapters in this book represent a diversity of authorship and scholarship: whereas Chapters 2 and 3 are collective studies of IPs with their own internal analyses and categorizations, Chapters 4 and 5 are the collective voices of multiple authors. Besides, Chapter 6 is one that captures the voices of K–12 immigrant instructors for a wider scoped discussion of the issues on hand. For such reasons, such chapters were not used as a part of the analysis in this chapter. To maintain a sense of balance in the analysis, single-authored chapters that appeared specialized were also excluded from the analysis. For this reason, Chapters 16 and 17 were excluded because they were more concerned with immigration matters, Chapter 18 because of its heavy focus on linguistic issues, and Chapters 19 and 20 because the authors were born elsewhere, partly raised or educated in the United States, but focused their writing on their significant foreign influences which affected their lives as professors. Ultimately, therefore, the narratives that were not specialized on specific issues but addressed broad, cross-sectional issues were used.

Another significant point of delimitation is that this chapter has the potential to be very long. To avoid this problem, although each of the selected chapters has ample quotes to merit inclusion in the discussed themes, only quotes that more directly and concisely captured the thematic issues were selected.

## THEMATIC, COMPOSITE VOICES OF IMMIGRANT PROFESSORS

As a prefatory note, the reader should be warned that the tone of this chapter can easily be misconstrued as pessimistic, and if it is so construed, then the larger scope of the immigrant professor's life would have been misconceived. In addressing the themes in this chapter, it must be borne in mind that the IPs discussed in this section have all managed to become successful in their work, and there is some satisfaction that attends such success. Their decisions to immigrate and live the life of an immigrant are partly determined by several factors that ultimately goad their life decisions, notwithstanding any perceived challenges (e.g., see the introductory section of Chapter 1). The tone and emergent themes discussed in this chapter, however, are to be expected because they are natural challenges they encountered because of their immigrant status.

The Unified Voices of Immigrant Professors 249

In harmony with the literature (e.g., Collins, 2008; Hutchison, 2005; Thomas & Johnson, 2004; Washington-Miller, 2009), the data indicate that the major issues confronted by IPs can be placed under two broad categories: sociocultural issues and pedagogical issues—the latter of which is the focus of this chapter. Across these two broad themes are several subthemes. Under sociocultural issues, (a) culture shock and readjustment in a new society; (b) positionality, collegial relationships, and power dynamics; and (c) identity issues were identified. Under pedagogical issues, the subthemes included (a) linguistic differences, (b) systemic barriers, (c) grading expectations, and (d) instructor–student relationships. These observations align with Hutchison's (2005) research on international teachers in America, which were corroborated by Waite's (2009) studies in the United States, Biggs's (2010) New Zealand studies, and independently align with Washington-Miller's (2009) studies in the United Kingdom.

Waite surveyed 152 international teachers for her study and found, among other things, that even while respondents believed that had adjusted relatively well to the U.S. culture, approximately 70% of them thought that they needed support from their colleagues and administrators in their adjustment to the U.S. school culture. In addition, 75% thought they needed support with instructional strategies for diverse students, and 44% needed help adjusting to language and communication patterns. Furthermore, 58% indicated that assessment practices in the United States were much different from those in their native countries. Of interest is Waite's reflection of the other side of the equation—that local students needed to adapt to their international teachers as well.

Biggs's (2010) study involved 25 participants from five South Auckland, New Zealand, secondary schools. Her findings indicated that foreign-trained teachers, despite their previous teaching experience in their native countries, have peculiar needs that are distinct from those of beginning, local teachers. She confirmed the differentiated pedagogical practices across national borders, and the need for adaption, local support, and retraining for immigrant instructors.

Washington-Miller's (2009) research illuminated intersectionalities and power relations between teachers and students. She pointed out that migrant Caribbean teachers in London, as racial minorities, experienced significant challenges, including shock, loss of confidence, impairment of self-esteem, lack of support, financial constraints, and perceptions of abuse by their own students.

It must be noted that these studies were conducted in the K–12 school context and not at the university level. That notwithstanding, the results of the findings are in consonance with the general research findings across higher education (e.g., Collins, 2008; Thomas & Johnson, 2004). Hutchison's (2005) initial research findings included the following (which may also be deemed categories of concern for international K–12 instructors):

- *Sociocultural shock.* Differences in sociocultural practices are likely to result in unexpected experiences and the need for reacculturation.

250  *Charles B. Hutchison*

- *Teacher–student relations.* In less traditionalist societies, teacher–student relations are likely to be smoother for instructors who embrace free speech and open exchange of ideas than those from more traditionalist environments and vice versa.
- *Communication issues.* Even when instructors speak a recognized national language, differences in accents and expressions are likely to pose as instructional barriers.
- *Systemic barriers.* Because of different historical influences, different school systems operate differently. These translate into different national standards, different required credentials, and different administrative setups.
- *Pedagogical approaches.* Partly reflected in their teacher–student relationships, the teaching cultures of traditionalist societies are more lecture based and follow the sage-on-stage approach. On the other hand, egalitarian societies are more likely to maintain conversational classrooms. This kind of difference creates teaching-based culture shock—a pedagogical shock that needs to be negotiated by immigrant instructors who derive from opposing teaching cultures.
- *Assessment issues.* Different countries have different assessment philosophies and grading rigor. Instructors who grade with rigor are more likely to face challenges in a less rigorous grading environment.

As noted earlier, the data indicate that there are there are two broad categories: sociocultural issues and pedagogical issues. The sociocultural issues serve as the external influences that, although are not directly instruction related, determine the mental frame of mind for content delivery once in the classroom. In fact, the more successful one is in managing the sociocultural issues, the more successful one is likely to be in the classroom. In the following section, pedagogical issues, as a general theme, are discussed.

## PEDAGOGICAL ISSUES

The job of the professor it to profess knowledge in the company of others (mostly his or her students); therefore, beyond one's own personal issues and broad, life goals to resolve, professional success is definable in the classroom. Classroom dynamics involve several primary and secondary corollaries; however, the focus of this section is on the primary issues that the IPs noted as having an impact on their classroom and professional lives.

"I felt that I have been well trained to teach in such a program, and the 'fit' could hardly have seemed better—until I met the students," noted Emilie Roy. She spent a lot of space addressing the fact that she, as a Western-trained instructor, had an episteme that was different from that of her students, for which reason there was the need to take the time to learn each other's episteme. On her part, she noted that "as a social scientist teaching in Islamic

## The Unified Voices of Immigrant Professors 251

studies, it was my task to make my students familiar with this *episteme*, this academic tradition"; on the other hand, "it required me to delve into my students' [episteme and, hence,] understanding of *salât* in order to attempt a reconciliation with my own understanding." Ultimately, "the slow transition between two heterogeneous *epistemai* [was] the goal of the program" in which she taught.

Odhiambo also discovered that a pedagogical differentiation was necessary with her new students as she noted that "pedagogically, my shock was based on the style of teaching [in the United States]. Their teaching was very casual." Ndemanu, in retrospection of pedagogical practices back home, noted that

> classrooms in Cameroon are arranged in a way that sets a stage for a professor to stand facing the students with a chalkboard behind him or her while all the students sit in unmovable chairs or benches facing the professor and the chalkboard. This class arrangement does not give much room for any other pedagogy apart from the teacher-centered.

He realized that even after having learned the need to relinquish the lecture method in favor of the teacher as a facilitator of learning, he needed to make a willful-but-compelled change:

> Given that old habits die hard, I became attached to the lecture method, owing to prolonged pedagogic immersion I had been acculturated with. Therefore, transitioning from teacher-centered to student-centered pedagogy was daunting, but quick and necessary.

Besides the broad pedagogical issues noted above, subthemes including linguistic differences, systemic barriers, institutional or cultural differences and expectations, instructor–student relationships, and grading differences were observed.

### Linguistic Differences

As may be expected, linguistic issues emerged as significant factors in the professional and social lives of IPs. They were mentioned in varying degrees by the contributing authors, depending on their fluency of the host language and accent. In the context of international teaching, Hutchison (2005) recognizes two types of communication competence groups: internally proficient and externally proficient. Internally proficient individuals possess the necessary communication tools to successfully teach in the host language without external help. Although they may speak with an accent, they still possess a natural fluency (because of long-term exposure) and the capabilities to employ the flexibilities of the host language, even if they are not necessarily fluent in the local idioms and expressions. Individuals in this

# 252   Charles B. Hutchison

group can become successful communicators with comparatively less effort. On the other hand, externally proficient users of the host language include those who have a limited exposure to the host language and are therefore not adept at using it flexibly or with the needed sophistication in the intellectual environment. In the academic context, such individuals can function at the shallow intellectual level in the host language. Consequently, they would need external help or significant practice to be successful academics in the host culture—unless they are teaching technical skills or academic disciplines that require relatively low language demands. As may be expected, IPs fall on a continuum between these two extremes.

The experiences of the IPs were quite intuitive, and it is instructive to start the thematic discussion with Sakamoto's observation that, in having to function in Japanese (as an externally proficient user of the language—because she was very dependent on the mercies of the locals to even moderately function),

> the realization that the language skills I had possessed all my life were no longer available to me to express my worldview may have very well been the catalyst that forced me to leave the Honeymoon Stage and embrace the challenges of culture shock.

On the issue of accent and other linguistic differences, Odhiambo's comment spoke for all: "I thought I knew English until I got to the U.S., where people spoke a different kind of English. I had to find out the American word for items I had learned the British way."

On the pedagogical level, the notable issue was that of accent. Although accent was an issue in the social scene, it did not concern the IPs as much as its pedagogical impact. The following list includes accent-related concerns:

- Odhiambo: Students wrote in my evaluation that my accent was too thick to understand, and questioned why the department employed people who could not speak English.
- Nayenga: My issue was not that I did not have a mastery of the subject matter in my field, but rather I was initially disheartened to read some students' evaluations making remarks such as, "I do not understand his accent," [or] "he speaks too fast."
- Mfum-Mensah: I vividly recall my astonishment when I received my first peer teaching evaluation from a colleague. The evaluation included small comments on my teaching, and a tall list of comments about how I needed to make the effort to make students understand my accent, and my need to improve upon the way I speak (my accent is not terrible by any stretch).

Mfum-Mensah added that it is rather ironic that institutional colleagues "know how we speak when they recommend us for hire. But once we come to the department, some of the same colleagues turn around and become

# The Unified Voices of Immigrant Professors   253

'enablers' of students' complaints of our accents." He therefore developed the suspicion that lazy students (and perhaps other conversationalists) use the accent issue as a proxy to lambaste otherwise proficient professors with whom they have unfounded issues:

> Students who realize that commenting on a professor's accent is politically incorrect hide behind comments such as, "the professor does not explain things well," or "the professor's questions are not clear," to express their disdain for the professor's accent. The intended meaning behind these comments is that because the professor speaks with a different accent, she or he is incoherent, inarticulate, incomprehensible, and incapable.

To mitigate the accent issue, the professors found various solutions. For example, Nayenga "drafted a textbook" for his courses. He explained that "this somewhat lessened the issue of 'I do not understand his accent,' since the students had something they could refer to." Nayenga used other means to resolve the accent issue:

> To deal with the issue of having a "non-American accent," I had, over the years, devoted a segment at the beginning of each semester in which I discussed with students, what I call "misconceptions about Africa." We also discussed issues relating to different accents in the USA. Students learned that even in Britain where English originates, there are various accents. . . . From this discussion students learned that accents ought to be respected because they are the embodiment of peoples' native locations, and that the issue is not that one's accent is different, but rather whether one can understand what the other party is communicating.

In the same vein, Mfum-Mensah intimated that

> about five years ago, I decided to confront the accent issue head on, so I began to make it a routine practice to help students understand the benefits of learning from an African or other foreign-born professors who speak differently. As part of the conversation. . . . I also talked about my own challenges as a young boy learning biology and chemistry from two American Peace Corps instructors. . . . I utilized the opportunity to let students know that they did not offend me by calling my attention to repeat a word or phrase if they did not comprehend what I said.

Mfum-Mensah leveraged his accent issue to address content matters with success:

> This strategy has been an effective way for us to engage in issues on language, power, and status. . . . I promise students, in a more humorous

# 254  *Charles B. Hutchison*

way, that by the end of the semester, they would come to clearly understand my ways and idiosyncrasies of communicating. Interestingly, a lot of students who take my course for the first time take more of my courses afterwards. These students are my "missionaries" who use the "dormitory lore" as a medium to spread the news about the benefits of my classes.

Nayenga, like Mfum-Mensah, also laid the blame of nonunderstanding of the foreigner's accent squarely on the lazy hearer, as opposed to the careful listener befitting a student or the respectful conversationalist:

> In all, students come to realize that their claims that they do not understand someone with a different accent may not necessarily be due to their accents, but rather because of their failure to listen to them carefully.

## Systemic Barriers

Systemic barriers include the differences in the educational setup and practices, as well as philosophical and canonic limits of knowledge across countries and their impact on immigrant instructors. In the subtheme of *defining one's identity* under Identity Issues section in Chapter 1, it was argued that in any given society, there are certain developmental landmarks and learning that only occur at certain points in human development. For this reason, no matter how educated an IP may be, he or she can never catch up on lost learning so to achieve native cultural proficiency. For this reason, in new learning environments, IPs are likely to encounter situations where their contextualized knowledge and skills on specific topics would be different from their students'. For example, what flowers does one dissect in a biology lab and why? What culturally relevant examples can one offer during instruction? What if the IP has moved from a tropical climate to a temperate one, or vice versa, and is therefore limited by climate-dependent knowledge base (see Hutchison's [2006] notion of *cultural constructivism*)? Along such lines, Nayenga discussed his instructional issues and hinted at the limits of the scope of information he could possibly teach, owing to the limits of the canonic knowledge of his students:

> One of the challenges I confronted is how one can meaningfully teach African history to students with a different cultural background, and in a limited time. . . . Thus, while recognizing the existence of different climatic zones, the enormous size of the African continent, and its huge population, I also emphasize that Africa has commonalities expressed in similarities of world view, socio-economic structures, and economic and political problems inherited from European colonial rule. Such an approach calls for a thematic (as opposed to a chronological one) method of teaching.

*The Unified Voices of Immigrant Professors* 255

On a related note, Emilie Roy noted that in Morocco, her Islamic students practiced a form of knowledge economy that did not fit hers:

> When they first enter the program, students are fully participating in an economy of knowledge in which concepts, beliefs, and practices necessarily fit neatly into the dichotomous categories of "true" and "false." . . .
>
> In contrast to my students, I am the product of an academic tradition where knowledge for the sake of knowledge should be pursued, and where ideas of absolute truth or falsity based on faith have mostly been purged in favor of scientifically prove[n] data.

This difference in knowledge economy needed to be mutually understood and respectfully resolved to create a successful teaching and learning environment. Another surprising practice (observed by Odhiambo) is the fact that, in the United States, for example, students have a rather powerful and even personalized voice that can potentially impact the professional success of a professor:

> Student evaluations had a negative impact on my tenure and promotion process during my fifth year. The tenure committee had questioned why my student evaluations were very low. I was therefore advised not to apply for promotion, as it seemed that student evaluations were going to result in a low ranking. Thank God, I proceeded to apply and got promoted to Associate Professor. All I can say is that this was an experience in itself. My student evaluations continue to climb at a snail's pace. As for student comments, I still get some extremely personal comments.

Fonkem, like Odhiambo, also found it surprising that students could assess their professors in the United States, but attributed his acquiescent acceptance to the nature of the American society:

> In the home country, professors were never accountable to students as their promotions depended on a hierarchical relationship in and out of the university, and even with political connections in the ruling regime. In my host society, professor-student relationships are conditioned by the fact that professors exist because there are students to be taught. Students are consequently at the center of everything that happens in the classroom.

The fact that student power is paramount in the United States with respect to their professors was rudely observed by Odhiambo, who noted that such student power is often tied to rudeness to professors, a practice that shocked many IPs from more traditionalist societies:

> Over the years, I have had to deal with defiant, rude, and disrespectful student behavior in my classes. I have had students who will hold

## 256   Charles B. Hutchison

conversations or whisper constantly as I teach, regardless of my efforts to have them stop. Others challenge what I say both directly and indirectly. Some question the validity of my assignments, even after explanations and documentation [are] given. These behaviors have greatly bothered me, and I have often wondered what one can do.

To Odhiambo's point, Hyeyoung also echoed the following, which is reflected across her chapter:

> A lot of aggression and disrespect occurs after taking tests or getting grades for assignments, especially in the latter part of each semester. Although this probably happens to many American (i.e., non-international) professors, the forms of the aggression and disrespect might be more exaggerated toward foreign-born professors.

In Japan, Sakamoto discovered that in-school hiring was routinely practiced. This contradicts the U.S. higher institutions practice of avoiding the notion of "academic incest" (i.e., hiring one's own child—the equivalence of marrying one's own relative) because the hiring of one's own graduates prevents the cross-fertilization of differentiated knowledge or ideas across systems and thus stifles the creation of new knowledge schemes:

> Once accepted into a company, people will devote their entire professional life to that company. For academics, there is a strong tendency to follow one's advisor and work in the same university or acquire a job through that advisor's connections. It is looked upon as an asset to have graduated from the university where you become employed.

Sakamoto also observed another academic practice that was new to her—something akin to the intermixture of internship and apprenticeship but at the undergraduate level—a practice to which she found difficult to adapt:

> In Japan, it is a tradition during the students' junior and senior years that chosen professors have a "zemi" or a group of students selected personally by the professor to work with, as a group. In the West, it might be viewed as an advisor role, but in Japan it takes advising to a more intense level. The students will meet as a class once a week for two years with the professor, will spend a good deal of time in *nomification* activities throughout those two years, and even go on a two- to three-day summer excursion with their zemi professor. In many ways, the professor serves as the first real adult outside the students' parents who influence the students' life.

In sum, differentiated educational practices constituted systemic barriers that IPs needed to negotiate to become successful in their host institutions.

## Grading Expectations

Different countries maintain different philosophies of educational assessment because assessment is used for different functions in different societies (Hutchison & Bailey, 2006; Lewin & Dunne, 2000; Rajbhandari & Wilmut, 2000). Whereas in developing economies (and also in traditionalist societies) assessment is used for selecting stronger students for more competitive societal positions, this is less so in egalitarian societies, where examinations are written with less rigor, and it is relatively easier for many students to earn top grades. Consequently, having top grades in egalitarian societies does not confer a significant advantage in life—especially at the university level. Conversely, however, Lewin and Dunne (2000) noted that the pass rate for gateway examinations can be as low as 15% in a country where assessments are used for selection purposes. In such an assessment environment, the objective of assessment is to stress selection; therefore, the tests are written with a higher level of difficulty and a greater "power to discriminate between candidates" (Lewin & Dunne, 2000, p. 383). More specifically, they noted that "in most African countries only a minority of students proceed to secondary school. Selection examinations are [therefore] critical to life chances and access to employment" (Lewin & Dunne, 2000, p. 380). Rajbhandari and Wilmut (2000) agreed with this observation and wrote that the same applies to students in Nepal, where "successful selection through the education and assessment systems does not simply give access to a better job, it gives access to influence and status" (pp. 266–267).

In consonance with the research, the IPs from relatively traditionalist societies struggled with grading issues. For example, Odhiambo of Kenya was shocked by the relatively high grades given for student work in the United States. She believed that "some professors took advantage of academic grading freedom and rewarded mediocre student performance." Other IPs observed the same challenge, and Fonkem of Cameroon, for example, rationalized this observation in the United States as follows:

> And because students pay a lot of money for their education in the host country, they also almost always expect to earn 'A' grades irrespective of all the time they spend at their jobs, and therefore away from their books.

Even in an environment where students would give professors negative course evaluations for tough grading, Odhiambo was not going to buy into such a philosophy:

> I let my students know that I am there to help them succeed, but that I am not going to hand out the grade of *As*: they have to study for their tests and work on their assignments, because an A-work is superior to C-work.

## 258   Charles B. Hutchison

Maintaining her tough assessment philosophy would not go unpunished by her students, in her course evaluations:

> My expectations have not been well-received by some students. Due to my high expectations and getting students to do the work, I consistently receive complaints about "hard tests" and "expecting too much from assignments."

Odhiambo, however, eventually learned to appreciate and use different pedagogical styles, including new assessment philosophies.

The nature or types of assessment were also discussed by other IPs. First, they were surprised that multiple-choice tests were used in U.S. higher education; besides, grammatical errors often remained in student work. They therefore tried to include more comprehensive, thought-out assessment methods. For example, Nayenga "downplayed the significance of examinations and instead emphasize learning for its own sake." He initially only gave writing-based examinations because he felt that it was the best way for students to learn. He soon learned, however, that

> this was both time-consuming and frustrating. Some of the students were puzzled as to why an instructor with a "foreign accent" should detect English, grammatical mistakes in their papers. Others could not just understand why grammar should be taken into account when one is grading a history essay or paper. To address these challenges, I changed my grading systems from essay writing to piece-meal testing, consisting of true and false, multiple choice, matching, identifications, short answers, long essay, and papers for higher level classes. . . . To my surprise, many students prefer this grading approach since, as some of them noted in their evaluations, this gave them the opportunity to learn and digest the material.

The fact that many U.S. students view grading differently—because they believe that instructors should grade content, not the manner in which content is communicated—was noted by several IPs. Besides Nayenga's observation above, Fonkem also made the same observation:

> Immigrants in general, in my host country culture, are also perceived as people who do not know English, and so American students generally view immigrant professors as not proficient in English or as people with "a thick accent." From this standpoint, my students probably must feel insulted that I would correct their language after I graded their papers.

Brooks also went through the same evolution as Nayenga in changing from largely essay tests to a mixture of evaluation methods:

> The way in which I evaluate student knowledge and performance mirrors the way I was assessed in my formative years in Jamaica. I rarely

*The Unified Voices of Immigrant Professors* 259

give multiple choice exams, preferring instead to use case studies, essay questions, digitally recorded counseling sessions with clients and integrated theoretical, analysis and practice papers to evaluate their knowledge and counseling competence. I still believe that having students provide in-depth, critically thought-out answers to essay or short-answer questions and case studies, is the best way to assess their knowledge and ability to apply what has been learned. I do see the benefit of using multiple choice questions, as part of an overall assessment process, however.

In Japan, Sakamoto learned the humanistic aspect of assessment—that in a traditionalist, hierarchical society, her innocent gestures communicated more than she initially thought. In working with a struggling student, she related the following experience:

> I was going to fail her and requested that she come to my office hours for an appointment. When I very concretely showed her why she was failing my class, comparing her points earned and how they compared to those required on the syllabus, a look of complete bafflement crossed her face. She looked at me and said, "But you always smile at me. I thought you *liked* me!" I had to explain to her that liking her and grading her were very separate issues for me. I was quite taken aback when she said, "You really *are* American, aren't you?"

## INSTRUCTOR–STUDENT RELATIONSHIPS

The reading of this section should be tempered with the phenomenological question, What becomes of a professor who is saddled with negative course evaluations from students in whom he or she has invested so much? What if they either genuinely do not understand each other's mannerisms, accents, examples, or even jokes? As may be expected, the instructor–student relationships the IPs experienced were a reflection of sociological patterns. Fonkem of Cameroon and working in the U.S. was rather shocked at how her students related to her:

> The relationship was very different in the host country with students who would refer to professors by the professor's first name. Coming from a culture where the use of first names was considered disrespectful, students in the new country would not only call me by my first name, but would sit on their seats and beckon to me with a little finger to come to them.

Contrary to all expectations, Sakamoto of the United States noted that her Japanese students—in a ritual-laden, traditionalist Japanese society—threw

260    *Charles B. Hutchison*

traditions to the wind and thought they should treat her based on what they had learned about the United States from the movies:

> Students have learned through movies and their own limited exposure to foreigners that Americans from the U.S. are to be called by their first names. While this may be true for friends or business acquaintances, I feel that as a sign of respect, I should be called in the same way as students call their other professors. I know that I do not look like a Sakamoto, but that indeed is my name and the one I wish to be called in the classroom. Students will come to my class for the first time assuming that I will be a Japanese professor. When they see that I am not, they immediately start to call me by my first name.

To maintain her sense of respect accorded her peers, Sakamoto changed things:

> It is here I offer my first intercultural lesson and request that they call me in the same manner as their other professors. I have found it most difficult to get students to do this, and for some students, it needs to be a weekly reminder. It causes me to wonder how indeed the students view me in comparison to their other professors: Am I viewed as a "friend" or a "real" professor?

The fact that the immigrant professor is psychologically viewed as a "guest" in the host country often colors how they are viewed and treated by their students. Such dynamics are manifested in different ways, and this section briefly illustrates some of them.

In the Identity Transformations section of Chapter 1, it was discussed that the conventional local image of the professor often deviated from their students' assessment of the immigrant professor, a point that was articulated by many authors, and emphasized by Sakamoto, Bang, and Fonkem. To be a deviant from the conventional professor—a position of respect and authority—also implied that one's immigrant status somewhat compromises such positions (of respect and authority), and this point was discussed by Mfum-Mensah:

> I have noticed that many of our freshmen demonstrate initial discomfort when they come to my class or when they are assigned to me as advisees. Freshmen also tend to second-guess my teaching and scholarship, and therefore provide lower teaching evaluations, and comment on my accent, in my course evaluations. It takes a while for these students to adjust to people like me who are different from them. When I started teaching in my current institution, I was not naïve about how my trifold identity would play out in the classroom and students' interactions with me. There is some level of discomfort among our students when the discussions focus on diversity issues relating to race, language, and sexual orientation—as may be expected in an institution like ours.

The struggle for respect was also noted by Bang and Brooks (in the Identity section of Chapter 1) and by Odhiambo, who wrote the following, when discussing assessment, much in the same vein as did Bang:

> Worse still, they argued about how hard they had worked only to lose points. At times I gave points back. Such experiences sent me looking for what my colleagues were doing, and if they were experiencing such challenges. Some looked at me rather confused, while others just smiled as if they knew what was going on. They knew that students treated foreign faculty that way and hoped it would soon stop. They often shared their observations about such behavior with me.

Overall and across the book, it must be noted that the struggle for respect across all issues (with students and colleagues, as well as in society) is tinged with racial and gender complexities, since people of color were more likely to raise it as a challenge, as compared to Whites—unless those classifiable as Whites had significant language accents, in which case their accents raised an issue with their acceptance. Women were also more likely to report respect issues. Possibly because of such reasons, White immigrants were either silent on the issue or noted how their transitions into their host societies were relatively seamless. It is also possible that Whites IPs from similar societies and linguistic origins as their host societies did not experience as many challenges, because when called by their first names, for example (as opposed to being addressed as "Professor X"), they did not take offense. This cultural congruence may have contributed to their seamless transitions (cf. Phelan, Davidson, & Cao, 1991).

Ultimately, for the IPs to be successful in their host countries, a resolution of their issues was needed, and mutual respect needed to be sought. Emilie Roy noted that, given her students' (mis)perception of her as a professor, mutual respect was necessary for success:

> I was a challenge to many of my students' conception of a "real" professor, and the material I was teaching was a challenge to the epistemological tradition in which the students participated. Nevertheless, in the classroom and beyond, we have succeed[ed] in establishing a mutually respectful relationship that allows for the recognition of differences in expertise and therefore for an exchange, because of our difference(s).

Having rationalized that she, herself, was a challenge to her students, in the same manner as they were a challenge to her, she continued that mutual respect and trust was a fair, but necessary expectation:

> In order to establish a relationship with my students based on respect and trust, I needed, like an ethnographer in the field, to acknowledge a position of relative vulnerability. This implied the recognition of my students' particular expertise (which opened lines of communication

## 262    Charles B. Hutchison

between us but also the temporary acceptance of my students' doubt in me and the need to "prove" myself).

The aforementioned experiences are in accord with several others', including Nayenga, who also fully understood his position (of the immigrant) as a person who himself compelled others to understand him, and therefore, the onus rested on him to stretch his worldview to accommodate others. Ultimately then, he summarized his relationship with his students, as well as others, as follows:

> I have been guided by an open-minded philosophy in my dealings with other people. Consequently, I have over the years developed such general philosophical views as, "There is no such a thing as a perfect person or place." For this reason, I regard challenges not as impediments to one's progress, but inspiration to push further. I believe in the view that "You do your best and hope for the best," and rather than be guided by labels which may be misleading, I have instead dealt with individuals, one-on-one.

### A CONCLUSION OF POSSIBILITY

A perusal of this chapter easily reveals that IPs are perennial learners, by their very natures. Being products of immigration, they are necessarily subjected to multiple, complex processes, some of which are clearly beyond their immediate control; however, in time, those who are determined to succeed do succeed. As Nayenga put it, "over the years, [he] gained self-confidence and devised solutions to address some of the issues that repeatedly appeared in [his] evaluations." As in all things, time presents the gift of experience, and experience brings comfort, and phenomenologically speaking, those who appear comfortable present a confident persona that invites others' trust in them. In or out of the classroom, the value of a confident professor cannot be overemphasized, because, after all, who wants to listen to an unconfident person who wants to "profess" knowledge? Ultimately, therefore, time is the great healer for the issues confronted by IPs—but they need to survive long enough for the future to unfold

In concluding this chapter, it is instructive for immigrants to remember that reality is overrated, if perception, indeed, *is* reality. It is also useful to revisit the discussion of the last section, where it was illustrated that IPs experienced some challenges in their relationships with their students. Of noteworthy, however, is their indication of an important fact: It is not that their students and host cultures are negative in themselves, but cross-cultural differences naturally engender challenges that are only resolved through mutual respect and personal commitment to certainly change oneself, and change others, if possible. For example, notwithstanding the challenges he noted in his chapter, Ndemanu noted that "[U.S.] Americans are generally down-to-earth, generous, and like to socialize with people they know and

The Unified Voices of Immigrant Professors   263

don't know during formal and informal gatherings." He therefore observed the following: "Overall, I get along very well with my colleagues here in the Midwest. We invite one another to family dinners, civic, and sports events on a regular basis. We cook African dishes and invite colleagues and friends over." Similarly, Brooks noted the following: "I have benefitted tremendously from the warmth, collegiality, support and research collaborations with my African American faculty counterparts."

Even in situations where one could be in danger of falling "into the trap of being 'a guest' in the majority culture's house to be pushed around and to the edge," Mfum-Mensah's experience teaches that such a journey toward "achieving validation in scholarship and teaching" is possible, if invested with "efforts and skillful negotiations." It is even possible for an IP to make significant changes in the perception of his or her whole local community regarding immigrants. For example, Nayenga wrote that, in tough times, "rather than accuse the school system of racism, [his family] took it upon [them]selves to educate people in the community." Eventually, his children's "strange names appeared in the newspapers and thus became known to the public" through sports participation.

In sum, one is better served by disavowing fatalism and embracing optimism if one is to become successful as an immigrant professor. As Odhiambo instructs, several pathways need to be taken to successfully navigate the world of the IP:

> My daily stress reliever has been my consistent exercise routine. I am very goal-oriented and focused on success. . . . My philosophy in life is to bring a smile to everyone I meet. I always try to think of positive things about the people around me, and in this case, my students. Positive thinking has helped me walk into class with a smile and crack jokes to make my students laugh. In addition to a smile, I laugh a lot, even at myself.

In closing, one must reiterate Sakamoto's bold confession: "Thirty years on, there are still many areas in which I hope to develop as an accepted professional in my chosen field of academia." Sakamoto speaks for all IPs, because to become an immigrant professor is to embark on an interminable journey that is replete with exciting unknowns, and it is a life for those who thrive on Ilya Prigogine's notion that the possible is richer than the real.

## REFERENCES

Bhabha, H. K. (1994). *The location of culture*. London: Routledge.
Biggs, E. K. (2010). *The induction of overseas trained teachers in South Auckland secondary schools*. Master's Thesis, Unitec Institute of Technology, New Zealand. Unitec Research Bank: (Permanent link to Research Bank version: http://hdl.handle.net/10652/1398)
Cobern, W. W. (1996). Worldview theory and conceptual change in science education. *Science Education, 80*(5), 579–610.

## 264 *Charles B. Hutchison*

Collins, J. M. (2008). Coming to America: Challenges for faculty coming to United States' universities. *Journal of Geography in Higher Education, 32*(2), 179–188.

Heidegger, M. (1996). *Being and time* (J. Stambaugh, Trans.). New York: SUNY Press. (Originally published in 1927)

Husserl, E. G. A. (2010). *The idea of phenomenology* (L. Hardy, Trans.). The Netherlands: Kluwer Academic Publishers. (Original work published 1907)

Hutchison, C. B. (2005). *Teaching in America: A cross-cultural guide for international teachers and their employers.* Dordrecht, The Netherlands: Springer.

Hutchison, C. B. (2006). Cultural constructivism: The confluence of multiculturalism, knowledge creation, and teaching. *Intercultural Teaching, 17*(3), 301–310.

Hutchison, C. B., & Bailey, L. (2006). Cross-cultural perceptions of assessment of international teachers in U.S. high schools. *Cultural Studies in Science Education, 1*(4), 657–680.

Kuhn, T. S. (1962). *The structure of scientific revolutions.* Chicago: University of Chicago.

Lee, E. S. (1966). A theory of migration. Demography, *3*(1), 47–57.

Lewin, K., & Dunne, M. (2000). Policy and practice in assessment in Anglophone Africa: Does globalisation explain convergence? *Assessment in Education, 7*(3), 379–399.

Maher, F. A., & Tetrault, M. K. (1993). Frames of positionality: Constructing meaningful dialogues about gender and race. *Anthropological Quarterly, 66*(3), 118–126.

Merleau-Ponty, M. (2013). *Phenomenology of perception* (C. Smith, Trans.). New York: Taylor & Francis. (Original work published 1946)

Oliver-Smith, A., & de Sherbinin, A. (2014). Resettlement in the twenty-first century. Forced Migration Review, 45, 23–25.

Phelan. P., Davidson, A., & Cao, H. (1991). Students from multiple worlds: Negotiating the boundaries of family, peer, and school cultures. *Anthropology and Education Quarterly, 22,* 224–250.

Rajbhandari, P., & Wilmut, J. (2000). Assessment in Nepal. *Assessment in Education, 7*(2), 255–269.

Ratha, D., & Shaw, W. (2007). *South–South migration and remittances* (Working Paper No. 102). Washington, DC: World Bank. Retrieved November 26, 2014, from http://siteresources.worldbank.org/INTPROSPECTS/Resources/334934-1110315015165/SouthSouthMigrationandRemittances.pdf

Shumba, O. (1999). Relationship between secondary science teachers' orientation to traditional culture and beliefs concerning science instructional ideology. *Journal of Research in Science Teaching, 36*(3), 333–355.

Spector, B. S., & Lederman, N. G. (1990). Science and technology as human enterprises. In B. Spector & M. Betkouski (Eds.), *Science teaching in a changing society* (pp. 1–26). Dubuque, IA: Kendall/Hint Publishing Company.

Stigler, J. W., & Hiebert, J. (1999). *The teaching gap: Best ideas from the world's teachers for improving education in the classroom.* New York: The Free Press.

Thomas, J. M., & Johnson, B. J. (2004). Perspectives of international faculty members: Their experiences and stories. *Education & Society, 22*(3), 47–64.

Waite, W. P. F. (2009). *Establishing the validity and reliability of the survey identifying the professional development needs of international teachers.* Doctoral dissertation, College of Notre Dame of Maryland. (ProQuest Dissertations & Theses, No. 3351505)

Washington-Miller, P. (2009). Reconstructing teacher identities: shock, turbulence, resistance and adaptation in Caribbean teacher migration to England. *Education, Knowledge and Economy, 3*(2), 97–105.

# List of Contributors

Fonkem Achankeng, University of Wisconsin–Oshkosh, USA
Bijaya Aryal, University of Minnesota–Rochester, USA
Hyeyoung Bang, Bowling Green State University, USA
Alice Gail Bier, Brooklyn College, USA
Leonie J. Brooks, Towson University, USA
Amy Carattini, University of Maryland, USA
Curtis Cline, Cedarville University, USA
Xavier Coller, Universidad Pablo de Olavide, Spain
Dave Eaton, Grand Valley State University, US
Faith Fitt, Azusa Pacific University, USA
Claire Griffin, Pennsylvania State University, USA
Rebecca Hong, Biola University, USA
Aminul Huq, University of Minnesota–Rochester, USA
Charles B. Hutchison, University of North Carolina–Charlotte, USA
Alexander Jun, Azusa Pacific University, USA
Scott Kissau, University of North Carolina-Charlotte, USA
Louis Lemkow, Autonomous University of Barcelona, Spain
Obed Mfum-Mensah, Messiah College, USA
Peter F. B. Nayenga, St. Cloud State University, USA
Michael Takafor Ndemanu, University of Southern Indiana, USA
Marcia D. Nichols, University of Minnesota-Rochester, USA
Eucabeth Odhiambo, Shippensburg University, USA
Xavier Prat-Resina, University of Minnesota-Rochester, USA
Lucio Angelo Privitello, Richard Stockton College, USA
Mohanalakshmi Rajakumar, Virginia Commonwealth University in Qatar, Qatar
Emilie Roy, Al Akhawayn University in Ifrane, Morocco
Tanita Saenkhum, University of Tennessee-Knoxville, USA
Robin Sakamoto, Kyorin University, USA

# Index

academic challenges 5
academic freedom 51–2
academic standards and expectations 90–1
accent 82–4, 144–5, 148–9, 152, 206;
     stereotyped 16
acculturation, 18, 85; *see also*
     adaptation; adjustment
adaptation 54–5, 57, 104
adaptive strategy 77
adjunct faculty 102, 103, 108
adjustment: challenges to 43–6; cross-
     cultural 38–9, 42; elements of
     36–7, 42–3; expectations 36
advanced parole 198
advising 168
Africa 149–51
African(s) 144–46, 148–51
African American, 166–7
Africanness 144, 149–50
agency (self) 17
aggression (from students) 91
alien 144; *see also* native-alien
anthropological perspective 22–3
anthropology 110, 113, 119
Asian 225–9
assessment: consumerism and its influence
     on 89–90; issues 90, 250; grading
     89–90, 257; performance and goal
     orientation of 89–90; purposes and
     philosophies of 257
assimilation 18, 104, 106
attitudes 92–3, 98; for success 17
auto-ethnography 63–4
avoidance strategy 78
axiology 10

Bangladesh 63, 65–6, 70, 73
biculturalism 18
bidialectal 174

Black 145 148, 158; *see also* race
blackness 144
borders: artificial 2; international 6

Cameroon 167
Canada 144–5, 202–11
career 22, 26, 27, 32; advancement
     189, 193, 195–6
Catalonia 50
catch-22 dilemma 129
citizenship 25, 26, 29
classroom: culture 55; description of
     56; participation and interactions
     in 214
code-switch 174
colleagues: belongingness 94;
     boundaries 94–95;
     collegiality 94; loneliness
     and alienation 94
color-blind 147
communication (challenges): accented
     English 70; code switching 66;
     humor 68, 72; idiomatic English
     67, 69; speaking volume 68;
     intercultural 214
conflict 50,52; diffusion of 56:
     educational values and 44–5
conformity 18
connaissance 115–19
consciousness 10
content area 7
co-workers 80, 84
credentials 195
credit 190, 198
cross-cultural communication: 120;
     context: 113–14, 120; exchanges
     110; understanding: 117
cultural: positions 19;
     (un)consciousness, 19

268  *Index*

cultural capital 9
culture 25, 26, 27, 28, 29–30, 32, 33, 113, 120–21, 145, 150; clash 67, 68, 70, 71–2; shock 123

Department of Public Instruction 195
dialectical processes 8
dialogical self-theory 63, 64, 65, 69, 70
discourse 117
discursive practice 115, 118
diversity 147
documentation 189, 192, 196–9

English: as a second language 213, 214; language learning and teaching 218, 220; world Englishes 175
episteme (epistemai) 114–16, 118–19
epistemological field: 119; frame: 118; gap 115, 119; shift 118; tradition 117
ethnicity issues 15
ethnography 110, 113; ethnographer 119
evolutionary success 13
existential human (the) 4
existentialism 10

faculty 223, 224–8, 230–1; African-born professors 151–3; faculty colleagues 148; foreign born professors 122–3, 148–50; immigrant professors 151; minority faculty 151–2; native-born colleagues 151; professors 145, 148; senior colleagues 148; underrepresented faculty 144
fees 191, 195, 197
financial constraints 249
foreign accent 218
foreignness: as an asset 56–60; on being foreign 51, 54, 59
foreign-born teachers 76–7, 80–1, 86
French education system 76, 78
funding 170

gender issues 15
Genographic Project 3
Ghana 144, 149, 151
globalization 35, 38, 48
grading systems 51
graduate teaching assistant 220; *see also* teaching assistant
Green Card 95, 204–205; *see also* job security

health care 190
higher education 35, 38–9, 46; (in the U.S.) 213–14
hiring process 95–6
housing 190
human: civilizations 4, 5; curiosity / interactions, 3, 5; existence 2; progress 5; rights 5
hyper-feminine 96

identity 78, 80, 81–2, 84–5, 145, 147, 150, 153, 166, 213; construction 220; development 13; native, 17; transformation 8
immigrant 144, 146, 151–2, 223, 224, 225, 233
Immigrant Petition for Alien Worker 191, 200
immigration 189–91, 194, 196–7, 199, 200; from Canada to the US, 202–5
Immigration Services (in the U.S.) 191–4, 198–200
incorporation 23
institutional racism 170
institutions: Christian college(s) 144, 147, 151–2; Christian liberal arts institutions 152; White institutions 152
instructional strategies 249
instructional technology 169
integration 18, 102, 103, 106, 107
integration policies 6
integrity 100, 108
international and global education 92–4
international faculty: contribute to U.S. education and scholarship 93; empowering 97; importance 92–94, 98; isolation 95; professional development 98; well-being and coping 96
international graduate student 213, 214
international identity 26, 30, 33
International Labour Organization (ILO) 2
Internet (the) 5
intersectionalities (of several factors) 17
-isms 173
isolation 18, 59

## Index 269

Japan 100–9
jargon 77, 79
job security: Green Card 95–6; H-1 visa 95–6

knowledge: limits 3; boundaries 11; conflicts 12

labor 202–203
language 148; acquisition 42–3; barrier and communication 88, 93; and communication patterns 249; demands, 252; English 35, 38, 48; and identity construction 213; Khmer 42–3; learning, 18; use 51, 53; *see also* accent
learning styles 54
legitimacy 170–1
liberal arts 110, 114–16
linguistic(s): capital 84; and cross-cultural challenges 213
living conditions 6

majority culture 145–6, 150, 153; *see also* White
marginalization 18
mental health and well-being 96–7
micro-aggressions 124, 126–8, 132
migration theory 6
minorities 145–7, 151, 170
minority 223, 224, 226, 229, 231
multicultural education 167
Muslim 65–6

native: knowledge 5; German-speaking teacher, 81–2; Italian-speaking teacher, 80, speaker 216; speakers of English 217, 218
native-alien 144
nativeness 217, 220
Nepal 63, 66, 71–2
nongovernmental organization (NGO) 38–41
nonnative English 213
nonnative professional 213
nonnativeness 217
nonnative speakers of English 217, 218, 221
North America: 148, 152; *see also* Canada and United States
nostalgia 63, 65, 67, 68

ontology 10
otherness 110–12, 120; other 112, 114, 117, 120

pedagogical content knowledge (PCK) 11
pedagogical: issues 250; practices 249
pedagogical shock 8, 123, 246
perception 111, 119
perceptual worlds 9
perennial questions 3, 4
permanent residency 191–4, 197–9
phenomenology: as a methodological approach 247; signals, 10
philosophies: Confucian and Aristotelian 9
positionality (and power): 110–11; position 111–14, 117, 119–20
possible human (the) 3, 4
power relations 249
prejudices 5
preparation: cross-cultural 38; international travel 40–1; orientation 39–40; teaching 38, 40–1, 47
preparing for tenure and promotion 137
privilege 188, 196
professional integration 76
professional potential 109
psychological impact 128

race 150, 152
racism 150
realities: external 10; multiple 8
relationships 43; teacher-student 36; team 45
relationships (teacher–student) 250, 259
religion 114–18
religious studies 110, 114, 115, 117–19
research 209
resistance to constructive criticism or instruction 90–1
respect versus egalitarianism 89

Sapir-Whorf hypothesis 3
Second language: acquisition 214, 218, 220; educator 215, 220; learner 214; users 82; writing 213, 215
self-confidence (gaining) in teaching 136
self-efficacy 88, 90, 97
self-esteem 14, 15; loss (of confidence) 249

270   *Index*

self-fulfilling prophecies 15
self-preservation 85
separation 102–3
settling down 139
sexual attraction 3
sexual harassment 96
social 26, 28, 30, 32, 33; agency 105; capital 105–6, 108; codes 9
Social Security Number (SSN) 190, 196, 204
socio-cultural differences 88
Spain 63, 66, 70
spatial variables 23
stereotypes, 76, 80–2, 171; stereotyping 16
strangeness, 78
student(s) 147–50, 204, 206–208; experience 57–58; inspiring 58; learning and engagement 51, 60; perceptions 93, 216
support and challenges 135
symbolic interactionism 10
systemic (structural) barriers 254
systemic barriers 250

teaching 203–11; challenges 125–6; license 195–6, 198, 200
teaching assistant 213; *see also* graduate teaching assistant temporal variables
tenure 192–4, 208–9
third space 11, 12
traditionalist: society 5; classroom 12
transactional (pedagogic approach) 170
travel 192–4, 197–8

United Nations Population Division (UNPD) 2
United States 144–5

vehicle 189, 197, 199
visa 190–5, 197, 199, 200
vulnerability 114, 117, 119

White 146–7; *see also* race
women 226, 227, 228, 229, 232
work 24–26, 31, 32
workers (skilled) 7
worldviews 8

xenophobia 6